Hound Dogged

Hound Dogged

Hound Dogs Series, Book 1

Rebecca Hendricks

For my extraordinary husband, Ken,
Who never stopped believing in me.

Dear Reader,
Never be afraid to be yourself,
Never be afraid to stand up for what you believe in,
And
Never stop following your dreams.
You're worth it.

CONTENTS

PART 1

Part 2

PART 3

PART 1

1

THE LARGE HAND CLICKED INTO place as it covered the smaller hand on the watch's cracked face. Patrick fussed with the winding mechanism, but nothing would change the fact that it was noon and John was late ... again.

"Are you sure he knew what time we were startin'?" Stu asked Patrick.

"Yes," Patrick said.

"You know he's always late," Jerry said.

It was true John was always late, but Patrick had hoped this time would be different. This was the group's first opportunity to play in front of a live audience, and he wanted to make a good impression on the crowd. Sure, the venue wasn't glamorous, and they weren't getting paid, but the experience they would gain would be invaluable. If only John would take the band as seriously as Patrick did. If only John cared, maybe the group could get somewhere.

When Patrick first met John, he was intrigued by John's individualist, bold personality, but now it was plain annoying. Patrick tried pushing his discontent aside because he was sure he could change the situation, but now there were only fifteen minutes left until the show started, and John was nowhere to be seen.

Patrick paced, running his fingers through his wavy reddish-brown hair. "He does this on purpose. You know that? I don't know why I even bother to explain things to him. He just ignores me."

Lacing his long fingers behind his head, Stu reclined on the wooden platform. "Maybe he's with Jane."

"Nah, he broke it off last week," Patrick said, finally resting his tall frame against a tree.

"I thought they just got together."

"She wanted to go steady, big mistake."

Jerry was sitting on the platform's edge, swinging his legs over the side. His unmatched socks crept down his legs in a lazy slouch. "Hey, did you guys hear that Eddie Cochran will be playin' at The Beaumont this summer?"

"You got rocks in your head?" Patrick said. "There ain't no way in hell Cochran is gonna play a no-account town like Madison."

"Yeah, who told you that malarkey?" Stu asked, brushing his sandy brown hair off his forehead.

Jerry shrugged his slim shoulders. "Nobody, really."

"You went down to the record store, huh?"

"So? Everyone goes to the record store."

Stu set his foot on top of his knee, exposing the patched hole in the sole of his tennis shoe. "True, but you know better than to listen to Eddie Bruer—he's a goofball."

"He said he read it in the paper."

"In the funny papers, maybe," Stu chuckled.

"I think I better recheck the mic," Jerry said, eager for something to do.

"Don't fuss with it so much that it quits workin'," Patrick warned.

"I'll be careful."

◻◼◻◼◻◼◻◼◻◼◻◼◻◼◻◼◻◼◻

The one pathetic mic the group had was old and hardly ever worked. A friend of Patrick's older brother had given him the mic when he bought a new one. Of course, Patrick's brother quickly lost interest in his once-aspiring music career, so the mic sat out in the garage for years, neglected and collecting dust. Jerry checked to ensure the mic was functioning and the cord wouldn't fall off in the middle of the performance. He decided to wind some extra tape around the base for good measure.

Jerry was a short, slight young man with red hair. He hated the tiny freckles that speckled across the bridge of his nose and onto the tops of his cheeks because they made him look like he was a pubescent boy. Once he had tried to cover them up with his mother's makeup, but it didn't match his skin tone, and all the kids laughed at him, causing him more humiliation.

When Jerry felt confident that the mic was secure, he placed his hands in the back pockets of his blue jeans and surveyed the park.

Spring had come to Madison, and the community gathered for the annual spring social. Small clusters of families sitting on blankets, eating picnic lunches, were scattered across the green grass, and exhilarated children ran, expelling their pent-up energies from the winter. Teenagers played horseshoes, badminton, and volleyball at the park's west end, and the smell of popcorn and hotdogs filled the air, causing Jerry's stomach to remind him that he hadn't eaten all day. Fishing around in his sweater pocket, he wished he could find a nickel to buy some popcorn, but all he found was a hole. Disappointed, he returned to his friends.

❏■❏❏■❏■❏❏■❏■❏■❏❏■❏■❏

John rambled through the park, observing the various activities while munching on peanuts from a greasy paper bag. It was a beautiful day, and for once, something was interesting enough to entertain his restless mind. He planned to meet up with his friends at the southeast corner of the park, where they would entertain the crowd by playing a couple of rock-n-roll songs on their guitars. John thought it was a bad idea that would only cause them embarrassment, but his friend Patrick argued that the only way the group would improve was to start gaining experience. John decided to humor him, and now he was stuck.

Headed toward his destination, John was distracted by a group of teenagers playing horseshoes. He loved to play horseshoes. Patrick would be upset if he was late, but how could he resist a chance to win some beer money? A half-hour later, John continued his path with a smile and a dollar in his pocket.

CRITICAL

When John finally strolled up to the platform, Patrick was about at his wit's end.

"Hey, knuckleheads."

"It's about time you showed up," Patrick snapped. "You know we are going on in five minutes."

"So? I ain't late then, am I?" John said, hopping up on the platform.

John was tall with broad shoulders, and his light brown hair was tussled and uncombed. His unkempt appearance did not conform to society's expectations, but he didn't care what other people thought of him. He was confident in his identity and had no problem voicing his opinion, no matter how unpopular.

"I thought you promised not to wear that jacket today," Patrick said.

John glanced down fondly at the old worn wool jacket. "I never go anywhere without it."

"I know that, but we agreed today would be different. We need to make a good impression on the crowd. You never know who might be watching."

"True. I did see a couple of dogs running around out there."

"I am talking about club owners or someone from the music business."

"I think Eddie Bruer might be here," Stu said

John and Jerry laughed, but Patrick was frowning.

"Look, I promise I will take off my jacket for the performance," John said.

"And you will tuck your shirt in?"

"I bet James Dean's mom never told him to tuck his shirt in."

Patrick grimaced.

"Where's my guitar, Jerry?" John asked Jerry.

"You don't have it?"

"It's over there by that crate," Patrick said.

"And I have to go get it?" Jerry said.

"You're the squirt," Stu said.

Jerry groaned and headed over to the crate.

John sat down across from Stu. "So, where's your friend? He ditch you again?"

"What friend?" Patrick said.

"Stu says he has a friend that plays like Chuck Berry."

Patrick rolled his eyes. "Yeah, right."

Stu sat up. "He said he was comin'."

"He's told you that before," John said.

"He said he might have some trouble gettin' out of the house, count of his old man and all."

"What's up with his old man?" Patrick asked.

"He's sick."

"Again?" John said.

"He's ditchin' you," Patrick said.

"He's my best friend."

"So?" Patrick scoffed.

Stu slumped his shoulders.

"Here's your guitar," Jerry said, handing John his guitar.

"Is there a big crowd, Jerry?" Stu asked.

"I guess if you wanna call a bunch of middle-aged frumpy housewives with stiff shirt husbands and a half a dozen ankle-biters runnin' around a good crowd, then yeah."

"Come on. We're already late," Patrick said.

John took off his jacket and laid it across one of the crates. "Anything happens to my jacket, I'm takin' it out of your hide, Patrick."

"The only thing that would want somethin' to do with your smelly old jacket would be a skunk that thinks it's his girlfriend," Jerry said.

John took a playful swipe at Jerry, but he was wiry and dodged the blow.

The boys walked to the center of the creaking platform made from old boards that city workers nailed together. A group of giggling teenage girls in bobbysocks began forming at the platform's left-hand side.

Patrick turned on the buzzing microphone.

"Good afternoon, Madison. I hope you're enjoyin' the beautiful spring sunshine. We are looking forward to entertaining you this afternoon with a bit of rock-n-roll."

A few people looked around to see where the disturbance was coming from, then, losing interest, they returned to their lunch.

"We are starting the show today with an Eddie Cochran tune some of you might know. It's called 'Summertime Blues.'"

The boys played the song to a disinterested crowd annoyed by the buzzing microphone. Between songs, a group of older ladies approached the platform, a look of judgment on their pinched faces.

The leader of the group shook her finger at them. "You young men should be ashamed of yourselves! Playing the Devil's music at a family gathering!"

"Wait a minute—I don't remember ever playin' any Devil music. Do you boys?" John said, leaning on Jerry's shoulder.

They shook their heads.

"We're all perfect angels," Jerry said with an innocent grin.

"You know, if you want, we could gyrate like Elvis," John said, moving his hips around in a pathetic circle.

The ladies gasped and started whispering among themselves.

"Well, I never!" the leader said, fanning herself.

"I bet you have," Stu said with a wink.

She stuck her chin out. "Come along, ladies!"

A couple of ladies smiled sheepishly at John as they passed. He waved at them, and they hurried away before he could see their blush.

2

THE BOYS TOOK A BREAK after a couple of songs because they wanted to leave the crowd hungry for more, but mostly, the crowd was thankful for the break from the buzzing microphone.

Stu stood in line at the concession stand, wishing there was some way to bypass the line. He was hoping to have a chance to look for James. He refused to believe his best friend was ditching him. Not when he promised to be there.

Stu understood that it was difficult for James to get away from the house since his mother had passed away last fall, but it was important to Stu that James see his success with the band.

James and Stu had been best friends since grade school. Stu admired James because he was intelligent, athletic, and had the perfect family. Stu loved the days when he could play at James's house because he had the best toys, the best room, the best mother, and a ... father. Sometimes James's father would throw the football or baseball with the boys, and he always made Stu feel welcome. On those days, Stu pretended he was James's brother instead of his friend, and for a moment, he could be happy. When Stu was with James, he never felt stupid or awkward because he could be himself, and for James, that was enough.

When Stu spotted James, he was heading back to the platform with two root beers in his hands.

James's brown hair was combed in a neat DA, and his hands were in the pockets of his gray felt trousers. Stu nudged his way through the maze of people to reach him before he lost sight of him again.

"Hey buddy, I didn't think you were gonna make it," Stu said.

"Sorry, I've been lost trying to find the stage."

"Yeah, well, it isn't a stage exactly. It's more like a platform."

"That would explain it," James said, rocking back on his feet. "It was nice of you to bring me a cold drink."

"Oh no, this is for Jerry."

"Oh."

"You could go get one. The line is kinda long, though, and I don't have another dime."

"Never mind."

Stu blew some foam off the top of his mug, and James licked his dry lips.

"How's your dad?" Stu said.

"Better I think. Going back to work has been hard on him, but at least he isn't spending all day moping around the house anymore. How's your mom?"

"The same, you know. Always naggin' at me to do this and that. I have just learned to say yes, ma'am, and then go about my business."

"Does that work?"

"If she's had a few drinks, it does. Come on then, I want you to meet the group. I told um about you."

"You did?"

"Yeah."

"Why?"

"Why wouldn't I? You're my best friend."

During the break, Patrick stretched his legs and leaned back against the tree. Jerry tried to remember where his fingers needed to be to play a G chord, and John was lying on his side, his head resting on his left hand.

"So whadda you think, John, am I getting it?" Jerry said, strumming his guitar.

"Yeah, I noticed you sounded better today."

Jerry smiled widely.

"Where is Stu?" Patrick said.

"I think he went lookin' for his friend," Jerry said.

"Great, he'll never make it back in time now," Patrick said, folding his arms.

"Hey, I think I see him comin'," Jerry said.

Patrick squinted. "Who is that with him?"

"His friend?" Jerry said.

"It can't be," Patrick said.

"Why not?" John said.

"He looks like a prep boy," Jerry said.

"What? A prep boy with Stu? No way," John said.

"Look for yourself," Patrick said.

John sat up. "Well, I'll be. Look at them fine threads."

"His loafers are shined so bright, they reflect the sun," Jerry said.

"Prep boys always got to look perfect," Patrick sneered.

Stu and James walked up to the platform.

"Hey, fellas," Stu said.

"Where have you been?" Patrick asked.

Stu sat his hand on James's shoulder. "I was lookin' for my friend James here. James, meet the guys. This is John, Patrick, and Jerry."

"Hello," James said, giving them a smile that wasn't returned.

"You brought me a root beer, Stu?" John said.

"I got one for Jerry and me."

"Correction, you got one for Jerry and *me*," John said, taking the root beer from Stu. Stu opened his mouth to protest, then decided against it.

"So, you're the genius that Stu's been ravin' about, huh?" John said.

"Who me?" James said.

"I told him how smart you are," Stu said.

11

"He says you play the guitar like Chuck Berry."

"Hardly."

"So, you don't play then?" John asked.

"No...I do...I mean, I can pick out a few tunes," James said.

"He's just being modest," Stu said.

"Stu . . ."

"He's one of the best I've seen."

"Stu is such a kidder," James said, slugging Stu in the arm.

"You know, if he's that good, maybe he could teach us a few things," Patrick said, crouching down next to John. "Maybe he should play us a tune. What do you think, John?"

"Hey, now wait a second. I just came out here to watch you play. I never said I wanted to play."

"Are you afraid?" John said.

"He's afraid he might blister his baby smooth fingers," Patrick scoffed.

"Bet he doesn't know the G cord," Jerry said, puffing his chest out.

"He's not afraid. Are you James?" Stu said.

James's eyes darted from one to the other, words trapped in his throat.

Patrick stood up. "Stu's right, he's not afraid. He's just a chicken."

James narrowed his eyes. "I'm not a chicken."

John jumped off the platform. "Good, let's see what you can do."

"But I don't have my guitar with me."

"You can use mine," John said.

"You seriously expect us to play with this creampuff?" Patrick said to John.

"You're the one that wanted to see him play. Let's see what he's got."

"He will make us look like a bunch of idiots," Patrick protested.

"Give him your guitar then, and I'll play," John said.

"What? You're telling me to sit one out?"

"It's your choice."

"Look, fellas . . ." James said.

Patrick chuckled. "If you're willing to look like an idiot, who am I to stand in your way? But I want Jerry to play my guitar, and he can play Jerry's."

Jerry frowned. "I don't want him to play my guitar."

"Sure you do," Patrick said, placing his arm around Jerry. "It sounds so much better than mine."

"It does?" Stu said.

"Fine, but don't scratch it," Jerry said, reluctantly handing his guitar to James.

"Have fun," Patrick said, walking away.

"Come on you two, times a-wastin'," John said, stepping onto the platform.

"I can't do this," James said to Stu.

"Sure, you can."

"What are you crazy? I haven't played in months."

"Then you just fake it. That's what we do."

"I don't even know what song I'm faking."

"I'm runnin' out of good humor here," John said.

James followed Stu onto the platform.

"All right, Stu, count us in," John said.

"What song are we doin'?" James asked.

"'Walkin' with Baby,'" Jerry said to John with a wink.

Stu stepped up to the mic that let out a high-pitched whine.

"Glad you fixed the mic, Patrick," Stu said.

Jerry stifled a laugh.

"Are you kiddies ready to go for a walk?" Stu said.

A few halfhearted claps came from the people who were paying attention.

Stu counted the beats, and James was lost from the first note. The song sounded nothing like James remembered. He attempted to play along with the rhythm, but it didn't take long before he realized Jerry's guitar was out of tune and a large crack ran down the side. No matter what he did, he couldn't even fake a cord in the right key. John's brows drew together, and James shrugged. It seemed like hours before the song ended, releasing James from his misery. He unstrapped the cursed instrument and looked forward. Patrick was looking straight at him with a taunting smirk. James sat down Jerry's guitar and jumped off the platform.

"Hey, where you goin'?" Stu said.

James turned and walked away, Stu following behind him.

"What happened to the princess?" Patrick said, standing beside John.

"Dunno," John said.

"Come on, Jerry, and help me pack up the gear," Patrick said.

"Isn't it someone else's turn?" Jerry said pointedly.

"Someone else doesn't wrap the cords right."

"But my stomach hurts."

"Your stomach hurts?" Patrick said.

"Yeah, I haven't eaten anything today."

"No food at the house again?"

"I haven't been home in a couple of days," Jerry said, swinging his foot.

Patrick glanced at John.

"Come on, buddy. Let's pack up, and I will buy you lunch," John said.

"You actually have money?" Patrick said.

"I may have had a bit of luck."

Patrick opened his mouth.

"And no, I'm not buying you lunch too."

Patrick rumpled his lip.

3

JAMES'S FAVORITE PLACE TO STUDY after school was the park next to the college. It was secluded and quiet, and he could focus on his studies and relax before returning to his arduous home life.

James had made the mistake of thinking his life would be predictable. He had spent his high school years carefully planning for his future. He hadn't spent time participating in normal adolescent activities like going to the malt shop with friends, going to the drive-in, or dating girls. He focused on studying and making his first year of college a success, and by the spring of 1957, he had met his goal. He spent the summer of that year working at the local department store, and by the fall, he was prepared to start his second year of college. He was excited to move out and live on campus, but his mother passed away. Her passing had devastated the family, but for James's father, it was the end of his world. His very existence revolved around her; now, his once vibrant life had faded, and he had become a recluse.

Instead of moving on campus, James stepped in and took over most of the household responsibilities his mother would have handled. It was hard for him because he hadn't had the chance to deal with his grief. By immersing himself in his studies, he could escape reality and focus on the future.

James was finishing his math assignment at the table under the huge oak tree, when Stu surprised him.

"Hey buddy, I have been looking all over for you. I can't believe I had to hunt you down on campus," Stu said, sitting on the bench across from him.

"I didn't think you even knew where the college was," James said.

"Very funny. How come you haven't called me?"

"I've just been busy with chores and studying."

"Is your brother helping at all?"

"Between school and social activities, he's hardly ever home."

"What about your social calendar?"

James shrugged. "I don't need one."

"You know, you're missin' out on smellin' all the roses."

"What are you talking about?"

"You know, stop and smell the roses? Take those girls, for example. They are sittin' over there laughin' and chatterin'. Why they are just waitin' for someone like me to go talk to um."

James chuckled.

"Don't you want to go smell them roses now?"

"No thanks. I need to get home and make dinner."

"So now you cook too?"

"I don't mind cooking. It's better than having TV dinners every night."

"There's a lot to be said for cardboard food."

James laughed.

Stu watched his finger make circles on the table. "So, I was wonderin', would you want to come with me to practice tonight?"

"You're joking, right?"

"No."

"Why on earth would I want to go to practice with you?"

"Because it would be fun."

"Like Saturday was fun?"

"I thought it was fun."

"Seriously? I made a fool of myself."

"No, you didn't."

"Yeah, I kind of did."

Stu looked up at James. "Look, you know more about music than anyone else I know. That is why I want your opinion."

"I don't know, Stu. I don't think they liked me very much."

"I promise tonight will be different. We can have a few beers, and you can tell me what you think of the group."

James tapped his pencil on the table. "I don't need to see them again to tell you what I think."

"Well, tell me, then."

James observed the look of curiosity on Stu's face. Was he genuinely oblivious that the group looked and sounded terrible? James knew Stu struggled with making friends or having any meaningful purpose in his life. He couldn't bring himself to destroy his illusion that the group would ever amount to anything more than just an adolescent pastime.

"I think the group has potential," James said.

"And?"

"And I'm sure you will sound better once you've all had more time to practice."

"That's what Patrick says."

"Well then?"

"Not everyone agrees with him."

"I kind of guessed that," James said, closing his book.

"This is important to me, you know? I'm not like you. I don't wanna wear a suit and go to a dumb ol' job and sit at a desk for the rest of my days. I wanna get out and live life while I still can. This is my chance to make somethin' of myself, to be somebody."

"There are other groups, you know."

"None that would want me."

"You don't know that."

"Please?"

James sighed. "All right, I'll come, but the moment I feel unwelcome, I am going to leave."

"You won't regret this," Stu said with a pleased grin.

James and Stu left the park together. James could tell he had lifted Stu's spirits, and he wanted Stu to feel supported, even if that meant seeing Patrick again.

4

THE GROUP PRACTICED IN PATRICK's backyard in a lopsided wooden structure that Patrick and his brother constructed. Their mother hated the eyesore and begged them to tear it down because she was afraid of what the neighbors might think, but Patrick's father reminded her that if the boys didn't have a place to play, they would be causing havoc inside the house. She quickly changed her mind and accepted the atrocity.

Initially, the practice sessions were an excuse to spend time together listening to the radio, looking at pictures of girls, and drinking beer instead of playing music. But recently, Patrick's attitude changed, and he implemented a few new rules that made practice feel more like a chore than fun.

John was sitting with his feet propped up on a makeshift table constructed from a couple of boards nailed down to a box. Jerry was sitting on the ground, and Patrick was sitting on a crate when James and Stu arrived.

"Hey, Stewy," Jerry said.

"Hey, little man."

John looked up. "Look at what the cat drug in."

"Hey, John," Stu said. "You want a beer, James?"

"No beer before rehearsal," Jerry said.

"What?"

"New rule."

"Who said?"

"I did," Patrick said with a scowl.

"You tryin' to kill me, Pat? You know I need a beer to limber up my fingers," Stu said, flexing his hand.

"It also makes you sloppy. It's time we start practicing and not goofing around," Patrick said.

Stu frowned and sat on the ground next to Jerry, and James sat next to Stu.

"I thought we agreed on no outsiders at rehearsals," Patrick said.

"James isn't an outsider—he is my friend," Stu said. "Besides, he played with us in the park."

"We're covering official group business tonight for members only."

James looked at Patrick's flat lips and knew he wasn't welcome. "Look, Stu, I am obviously not welcome. I think I will go."

"Ignore Pat. He has the manners of a sewer rat," John said.

"John, can I talk to you for a minute?" Patrick said.

"Sure."

"In private."

"Anything you have to say to me, you can say in front of the group."

Patrick met John's solemn eyes, then chuckled and turned away.

"We could wait outside?" Jerry said.

"Great idea, Jer," Stu said.

"Just forget it," Patrick said.

"So, what is this official group business you want to tell us?" John said.

Patrick picked up his guitar. "Let's just start the practice. Let's play 'Summertime Blues.'"

"Let's play somethin' that James hasn't heard. Like 'Crawlin' Dog,'" Stu said.

"Yeah, that one is easier for me," Jerry said.

"Let's crawl the dog," John said.

Without another word, the four began to play another song James had never heard before, but he could tell it was something they had rehearsed because they all could maintain the rhythm and keep in time. The song had a bluesy feel that was different from anything popular or mainstream, and James didn't even realize his foot was tapping along with the beat.

"You like that song, James?" Stu asked.

"It's good."

"Just good?" John said.

"Yeah, I liked it."

"I think you need to play a song for us now," John said, reclining.

"He can borrow my guitar again, John," Jerry said.

"I would rather not."

"It's only fair we played for you. Now you play for us," John said.

"He doesn't want to play for us. Cause he stinks at it," Patrick said.

"I just don't like playing on a guitar that is out of tune."

"Say what?" Jerry said.

"Your guitar. It's completely out of tune, the strings are loose, and there is a crack in the body."

Jerry held his guitar close.

"It's all he's got," Stu said.

"Ummm ... I'm sorry ... I didn't mean to . . ."

"Be a jerk?" Patrick said.

"Let's play another one, hey, John?" Stu said.

John agreed.

❑■❑■❑■❑■❑■❑■❑■❑■❑■❑

The group played a couple more songs that were made-up versions of another tune with different words because no one knew the real ones. When the band decided to take a break, James approached Jerry, who was fiddling with his guitar.

"Hey, I'm sorry. I didn't mean to hurt your feelings."

Jerry ignored him.

James sat down next to him. "If you want, I can show you how to tune it."

"No sweat. I'm missing a string."

"I know."

"I can't afford to buy a new one yet."

"I got a few spares. I could bring you one if you want."

"Really?"

"Yeah."

"Okay."

James smiled at him.

The boys didn't return to playing. Patrick was in a bad mood, and it seemed like a good idea to spend the rest of the evening drinking beer and critiquing songs on the radio and moving away from conflict.

"Hey, Stu, I need to get going. I have an early class tomorrow," James said.

"You okay walkin' by yourself?" Stu said.

"I think I can handle it."

"I'll see you later?"

"Yeah," James headed toward the door.

"Runnin' away again?" John said.

"I got a class in the morning."

"So do I."

"Oh?"

"Does that surprise you?"

"No."

"What are you studyin'?" John asked.

"Finance."

John smiled and took a drink from his bottle.

"You?" James asked.

"I haven't picked a major yet."

"I thought it would be music composition."

John chuckled, and James left.

5

THE COFFEE GROUNDS WAS A small coffee shop popular for students to study or socialize. The coffee was decent, and the freshly baked muffins were delicious and sold out fast. James headed toward the shop between classes, hoping the caffeine would help him survive the afternoon. Usually, the crowds thinned out by midafternoon, but several male students gathered around the counter because a new waitress was working with Millie. Young women rarely held James's attention for more than a few moments, but something about her had his attention. Maybe it was her pleasant smile or smooth auburn hair tied up with a red bow. Whatever the reason, he understood the attraction.

"You havin' your usual today, Jamie?" Millie asked.

"Yeah," he said, fumbling for his money.

"This is Jamie, Marcy. He's one of the regulars."

"It's James," James said, handing his money to Marcy.

"Here you go, sweetie," Millie said, passing his cup.

"You want your change?" Marcy said.

"No, you can keep the change."

"Thank you."

"You're welcome."

"Come back soon." She smiled at him, her hazel eyes sparkling.

"I will," he said, almost spilling his coffee on the person behind him.

James took his coffee across the street and reclined under a tree. A pleasant breeze was blowing, and he was soaking up the calm. He shut his eyes for a moment when a voice startled him.

"Cuttin' class, huh?"

James looked up to see John.

"I'm on a break," James said.

John sat on the grass next to him.

James had no idea what John wanted, and it made him nervous.

"What are you studyin'?" John said, taking James's book. "*Principals of Accounting*", how exciting."

"What are you reading?" James said, picking up John's notebook. John snatched it roughly out of his hands.

"Don't touch my notebook," he snapped, handing James his book back.

The two sat silent for a while.

"So, you comin' to practice tomorrow night?" John asked.

"I may be busy."

"Doin' what? Readin' about accounting?"

"Studying is important to me."

"All the time?"

"I don't study all the time."

"Great, then you'll be there tomorrow night."

"Wait . . ."

John hesitated.

James sighed. "I truly don't understand why you want me there."

"I thought you were interested in joinin' the group."

"I told Stu I would come and watch him play and give him my opinion."

"And what's your opinion?"

"Well. . . ."

"You don't know your opinion?"

"I know my opinion."

"And?"

James tapped the side of his coffee cup.

"By not answering the question, you are tellin' me what you think, and yet here I am askin' you to come to another practice."

"So, if you know my opinion, why would you want me there?"

"Because I want to learn how to improve."

"What makes you think I can help you improve?"

John leaned back on his hands. "I don't, but you know how to tune a guitar, and from what little bit I saw, you seem to know how to play one."

"You all know how to play the guitar."

"We do, but it's about more than that, isn't it?"

James met his eyes. "It is, and I don't think I can help you with that problem."

John twitched his feet and was silent.

James finished his coffee and wished he had more.

"You're smart, and I think your perspective would be helpful," John said.

James felt the edge of his book.

"I won't ask again."

Before James could answer, two girls walked down the path. They stopped about fifteen feet away and started whispering. They turned around and went in another direction.

"I know you want it, baby," John yelled at them.

Embarrassed, they ran away.

John smiled at James, who couldn't help but laugh.

"Bring your guitar this time," John picked up his books and left, whistling down the path.

6

John was almost always late to English composition class, math class, or any other subject that he took little to no interest in. Why is taking English composition after high school even necessary? Hadn't he suffered enough of the exasperating topic?

He strolled into the room, causing a minor disturbance among the students. He favored sitting at the back of the room next to the window, but to his annoyance, someone was already occupying that desk. He had no choice but to take the desk in the next row.

"Mr. Chandler, you are late," the teacher, Mr. Miller, said. He watched John make his way to his seat through his square wire glasses, always a quarter down his aquiline nose.

"Oh yeah, I forgot my watch," John said.

"You do realize when you come in late, you disrupt the lesson flow."

"By all means, carry on," John said, folding his hands in front of him.

"All right, class, let's resume on page thirty-six. You do have your book with you, Mr. Chandler?"

"It's with my watch."

Mr. Miller sighed and tapped his foot. "I think I might have a spare one."

"Hey," John said to the girl sitting two desks up from him in the next row.

She was busy writing in her notebook and didn't respond.

"Hey," he said a bit louder.

She continued to ignore him.

He threw a piece of paper at her. Annoyed, she turned and looked at him.

"Give me a pencil," he said.

She blinked at him.

"Are you deaf?"

"I don't have a pencil to give you. I could lend you a pencil, but I want it back."

"Okay, sure, fine, whatever."

She pulled a pencil out of her bag and handed it to him. Mr. Miller came over to John's desk.

"I am only loaning you this book. I expect you to have yours when you come back to class next time."

John gave him a lopsided grin.

Mr. Miller returned to the front of the room and resumed the lesson. John opened his book and pretended that he was listening to Mr. Miller jabber on about a topic that was already extremely boring. If he had been sitting at his regular desk, he could have watched the girl's physical education class going on outside the window. John looked at the student occupying his seat. He was paying close attention to the lecture and taking notes.

"Psst," John hissed.

The student ignored the sound.

"Hey, buddy."

Still no recognition of the disturbance.

"Hey, pimple face."

The student turned to look at John.

"Switch places with me."

"What?"

"I said, switch places with me."

"No."

"I'll give you a quarter."

"No."

John was becoming annoyed with the student's obstinance. He fumbled around in his pockets, looking for more money. All he had was a dollar, and there was no way he was parting with his beer money.

"Hey, I'll give you one of my cards."

The student frowned at him. "I don't collect baseball cards."

"It's not that kind of card, dummy."

"What other kind of card is there?" the student said.

John ensured Mr. Miller was busy before holding the card for the student to see. His eyes bugged as he gazed at the image on the card. John stuck it back in his pocket.

"Where did you get that?"

"Does it matter?" John said, checking to make sure Mr. Miller was still busy.

"All right, I'll switch with you."

John was in the process of switching seats with the other student when Mr. Miller turned around to witness the card exchange. Unnoticed, he walked over to them.

"I see my lecture has inspired you to exchange notes."

Startled, they both attempted to come up with a believable answer.

"Not notes, pictures," the student said.

"Pictures of what?"

"Joe Pistachio," John said.

Mr. Miller raised his eyebrow. "Joe Pistachio?"

John noticed that several students were snickering.

"I would like to see this picture, Mr. Brooks," Mr. Miller said.

"Uh... uh . . ." Brooks fumbled, opening and closing his mouth like a grouper.

"He's not feeling well," John said. "He probably needs to go to the nurse."

Brooks frantically nodded.

John jumped up and ran to him. "You better run before you start puking."

Girls sitting nearby jumped up and ran toward the wall, waving their hands in the air and screaming, "Ewwww!"

Brooks grabbed his books and quickly left the room.

Mr. Miller glared at John, knowing he had somehow managed to wiggle out of a sticky situation. Letting his disapproving glare linger a bit longer, he turned on his heel and walked back to the front of the room.

"All right, everyone, take your seats. The excitement is over."

John took advantage of the opportunity to move to the now vacant desk, but sadly, the girl's physical education class was almost over, and he had missed out on watching the girls do jumping jacks.

"Your assignment for next time is to read chapters five and six and complete the exercises in your workbooks. In addition, Mr. Chandler, you will write an essay on how you plan to persuade me not to expel you from my class."

John closed his eyes and felt his temples.

"Thank you, class. That is all for today."

Books closed, and chatter and laughter resounded through the classroom as the students began to depart.

John had returned the book to the shelf when he made eye contact with the girl that had loaned him the pencil. Tucking the pencil behind his ear, he smiled at her and left the classroom.

7

J AMES SAT AT THE DESK in his room, immersed in his accounting
book. His father was listening to an old serial drama on the radio
downstairs. The sound of the garbled dialogue penetrated his
concentration, and he was struggling to stay focused. The phone rang,
adding another brick to James's cracking patience. Occasionally, Stu
would call for James, and a relative might call his father, but most
of the calls were for Mark, his younger, popular brother. His father
hated to answer the phone, and James got tired of being his brother's
answering service, so most of the time, it just rang until whoever was
on the other line realized no one was going to answer and hung up.
Not able to stand the interruption any longer, James walked across the
hall to this brother's room. He found him stretched out on his bed,
reading a book, oblivious to what was happening downstairs.

"Did you not hear the phone ring?" James said.

"Wha?" Mark said, looking around the corner of his book.

"The phone, it's been ringing."

"Oh, do I need to get it?"

"Not now. They hung up."

"They'll call back," Mark said, returning to his reading.

"Do you realize that every time it rings, it breaks my
concentration?"

"Sorry."

"Maybe if you listened for it, we wouldn't have this problem."

"If I leave my door open, I have to listen to that dumb radio show Dad listens to."

"No kidding. I can hear it too, and I'm trying to study."

"When are you not studying? Sometimes I think you study on the toilet."

"Funny."

"Fine. Leave my door open."

"Thanks."

James returned to his room, and his gaze landed on the guitar case propped up in the corner. A thin layer of dust was visible on the black surface. How long had it been since he had opened it? How long had it been since he held it, tuned it, played it? He wished he could open the case, and all the memories stored inside would evaporate. If only he could turn back time to his fourteenth birthday. The exhilaration and excitement he had felt would be reborn, the possibilities endless, and she would be there listening … always listening.

Grabbing his jacket and the guitar, he walked across the hall.

"Hey, Mark, I'm going to meet Stu. You think you can handle things here?"

"Sure."

"I won't be late."

Mark waved at him over the top of his book. James smiled and left the house.

❑■❑■❑▨❑■❑■❑▨❑■❑■❑▨❑

James managed to arrive at practice on time. Stu and Jerry were talking when he walked in.

"James, I knew you'd be back," Stu said with a smile.

"I promised Jerry I would bring him a string," James said, handing the string to Jerry.

"Gee, thanks."

"I see you brought your guitar this time," Stu said.

"I did."

"You even have a case. I've never had a case. Have you, Stu?" Jerry asked.

"No."

"It must be a fancy guitar."

"I wouldn't go that far," James said.

"Let's see it then."

James took his Gibson J-45 out of its case. The smooth surface felt divine in his desolate hands.

"Wow, it's so shiny. Can I hold it?" Jerry asked.

"Um. . . ." James held it tight.

"Are you afraid I might break it?"

"No, it's just that it's tuned exactly as I want it. You understand, right?"

Jerry blinked his eyes.

"James is very fussy about his guitar," Stu said.

"Okay," but James knew Jerry took it personally.

James sat down in the chair.

"I wouldn't sit there, that's John's chair," Jerry said.

"Okay then," James said. Sitting on the ground, he began to tune.

"I thought you said it was tuned?" Jerry said.

"Oh, it is. I am just checking the tone."

"Uh-huh, sure."

"Well, look whose here," John said, stepping into the cramped space. He had to stoop over to clear the deformed doorway. "Are you sad you're not studyin' accounting?"

"It was a hard choice."

"What you got there?" John said, sitting in the chair.

"It's his guitar," Jerry said.

"I was beginnin' to think you didn't have one. Well, let's have a look, then."

"He doesn't let insignificant people touch it," Jerry said.

"What?" John said.

"We might break it or somethin'."

"I just tuned it is all," James said.

"It should sound perfect, then," John said.

"But . . ."

John held out his hand. "Let me see it."

The sneer on Jerry's face dared James to turn John down.

Reluctantly, James handed it to John.

John admired its beauty. "Very nice, clean, polished even. Not a scratch on it?"

"Yeah."

John gently played a few chords. "You tuned it yourself?"

"Yes, doesn't everyone?"

No one answered.

"She sounds like a contented lover, so perfect and clear." John began to play a slow, quiet song. "Every lover likes it slow to start, right?"

Jerry hid a smirk.

"Later on, the tempo picks up," he said, quickening the pace of his strumming. "Now, the important thing to remember is not to go too fast or push too hard because you might lose the perfect rhythm, and if that happens, the climax is ruined."

Stu was struggling not to laugh.

James knew John was trying to embarrass him and make him crack somehow, but there was no way he would give him the satisfaction.

A few moments later, Patrick walked in.

"Hey, Patrick," Jerry said.

"Hey," he said, not even looking at Jerry.

"Rough day?" Stu said.

"Yeah, my boss is hasslin' me again. I need a beer."

"I thought the new rule was no beer before practice," Stu said.

"Yeah, well, I am breakin' it," Patrick said, opening the empty cooler. "Who was responsible for the beer tonight?"

Jerry brought his knees up to his chest and hugged his legs.

"It was my turn," John said.

"Figures," Patrick said under his breath. Crossing to his seat, his eyes fell on James and his body tensed. "What's he doing here?"

"I invited him," John said, passing James his guitar. "He was just about to start class."

"Class?" Patrick and James said together.

"Yeah, I thought it would be a good idea if he demonstrated how he tunes his guitar."

"What is he? Some kind of professor?" Patrick scoffed. "There is only one way to tune a guitar."

"Great. Then you can demonstrate for us," John said, picking up his guitar.

Patrick rumpled his brow. "What?"

"Feel free to start whenever."

"This is ridiculous. Every one of us knows how to tune a guitar."

"Hmmm," John said, thumping his thumb against the guitar's body. "Then why were we out of tune on Saturday?"

Patrick gave him a blank look. "Because...Jerry's guitar is cracked."

"What do you think, Professor?" John said, turning to face James.

James's eyes darted from Patrick, then back to John. "Because you all didn't tune together as a group."

Patrick blinked his eyes, and his mouth was dry.

"You may resume your lesson," John said to James.

"So, is that it? Just like that, he's a member?" Patrick said.

"I'm not a member," James said.

"No, but you want to be."

"Patrick . . ." John warned.

James put his guitar in his case. "I knew this wasn't a good idea."

"James," Stu said.

"If you run after him again, don't come back," Patrick said.

"All right Patrick, that's enough," John said.

"You did this on purpose, didn't you?" Patrick said. "You thought you could just invite this pompous candy ass to rehearsal, and he would show me up with his expensive education and his fancy guitar? Well, you're wrong. As long as this group has inferior members, nothing in the world will change the fact that this group sounds like shit!"

Everyone was silent, afraid to make a sound.

John was glaring at Patrick, and everyone could see the fear in his eyes as John rose slowly to his feet.

"You're lucky I don't bloody your stupid mouth."

"I'm not afraid of you," Patrick said.

"Show me," John said, taking a step toward him, his eyes dark and jaw set.

Patrick hesitated, then took two steps backward.

"That's what I thought." John turned and picked up his guitar.

"John, I didn't mean . . ."

"Oh, yes, you did. You have felt this way for a long time. You just never had the guts to say it."

"John—" Patrick said, stepping toward him.

John held up his hand. "Don't say one more word to me."

Patrick averted his eyes.

John turned and left.

Patrick turned to James. "This is all your fault."

James held tight to the handle of his guitar case.

Jerry stepped between James and Patrick. "Come on, James."

James followed Jerry outside.

Patrick turned to Stu. "You don't have to leave. We can go get some beer. I'll buy."

"Nah, that's okay. I promised my mom I would try to get in early tonight. We'll talk later, eh?" Stu said to Patrick.

"I didn't mean for it to come out that way, honest."

Stu set his hand on Patrick's arm and gave him a small smile before leaving with James and Jerry.

The trio walked along in silence, trying to understand what had happened.

"I guess I am sleepin' in the park tonight," Jerry said.

"Not a good night to go home?" Stu said.

"No night is a good night when he's there."

"He's been there a lot, then?"

Jerry nodded.

"You can sleep on my floor tonight."

"Are you sure your mom won't mind?"

"Nah, she stays out of the basement," Stu said.

"I will talk to you later, then. Hey, Stu?" James said.

"You have to go? It's early yet."

"I have a paper I need to finish."

"You know, James, we really don't do a very good job tuning our guitars. Do you think you could help us out?" Stu said.

"I'm not sure I can even put this string on right," Jerry said.

James sighed. "Okay, yes, I will help you. Maybe we can meet later in the week?"

"That would be great."

"Okay, I'll call you," James said.

"Promise?"

"Yes," James said with a smile as he crossed the street.

Jerry and Stu continued their walk to Stu's house.

"You think the group is through, Stu?" Jerry asked.

"I don't know, Jer."

"I haven't seen John that mad in a long time."

"I thought he was gonna flatten Patrick."

"He's not someone you want to tangle with, believe me."

Stu sat his hand on Jerry's shoulder. "Let's not think about it anymore tonight, heh? We'll go back to my house and heat some fish sticks and French fries. Then we can watch the tube."

"What about your little sister?"

"What about her?"

"You think she will bother us?"

"Nah, it's a school night. Mom makes her go to bed."

"She'll still find a way to bother us, I'm sure."

"Yeah, but if Mom finds out she wasn't behaving, she keeps her allowance."

"That works?"

"Oh yeah. Carly goes nuts if she has no money to buy bubble gum."

"I can see that," Jerry said.

"We got it made in the shade," Stu said, and Jerry laughed.

8

I T WAS EARLY IN THE afternoon when it started to rain. James was unprepared, forcing him to dash for the coffee shop. Fortunately, he found an empty seat at the counter. Reading in the cramped space was hard, but he wanted to keep his mind busy while he waited to head home.

James hadn't seen Stu since the last practice, and he wondered what was happening, but what did he care if the group split up? He had enough to worry about in his life without being a part of that headache.

"Hey, big spender."

James looked up to see Marcy's charming smile.

"Hey," he said, thankful for the distraction.

"You want your usual? Or are you thinking about trying something different?"

"No, I think I will stick with the usual."

"Not much of a risk-taker, huh?"

"I guess not."

"Maybe you should be." He watched her slight form walk away. His concentration was broken, and it would be hard to get it back.

Marcy returned later with a cup. "So, since you're not comfortable trying something new, I decided to spice things up for you. You know, break the mold and add excitement to your life."

"Oh?" he said.

"I think you'll like it—if not, your cup will be free of charge."

James didn't appear apprehensive, but he wondered what she had added to it.

"Come on. It won't bite."

"Okay." James took a sip.

"Oh, come on, you didn't even taste it."

James reluctantly took a drink.

"Well?"

"It's not bad," he said, nodding his head.

"See! I knew it." She grinned.

"What did you add?"

"Nothing much. Just the eye of a newt and a pig wart."

James blinked at her, his face losing its color.

Marcy laughed at him. "I added some cinnamon and a pig wart."

"How did you know that was my favorite?"

"Lucky guess."

James chuckled.

"So, what are you reading?"

"*The Grapes of Wrath.*"

"Wow, that's some heavy reading."

"I have read it before."

"Really?" Marcy said, leaning on the counter.

"Yeah."

"You really do need to spice up your life."

"What do you read?"

"Mickey Spillane," she said, playing with a stray tendril of hair.

"No foolin'?"

"Yep, his detective novels are exciting and fun."

"Hmm, I will have to check one out."

"It beats reading about the Depression any day of the week."

He laughed.

"I'll check back with you later?"

"Okay."

The faint smell of honeysuckle abducted his concentration as he watched her go about her duties. She stopped and chatted or shared a laugh with several customers. What made him think he was so special? It was her job to be friendly with customers. Besides, someone that attractive had to have a boyfriend.

Once more, he returned to his reading when he heard a voice call out his name.

"James!"

He looked down the counter and was surprised to see Stu coming toward him. Water was dripping from his flattened hair.

"Hey, buddy," Stu said.

"Hey, what are you doing here?"

"I stopped by your house, and Mark said you were either studying in the park or here."

"Mark was home, and he answered the door?"

"Sure did."

"Wow, that's a first. So, what did you want to see me about?"

"Honestly, I just needed to get out of the house. Carly invited some girls from her Brownie troop to come over and make cookies."

"Oh."

"Those girls look so sweet and innocent, but get a group of them, and they huddle together like spiteful gremlins contemplating mischief." Stu sat on the stool next to James.

"Hey, I think someone was sitting there," James said.

"Oh, really?"

Marcy spotted Stu when he came inside and walked down to greet him. "Hello."

"Hello," Stu said, smiling widely.

"Can I get you anything?"

"You got a beer behind the counter?"

"No, this is a coffee shop."

"I know—I was just teasing. I could use a glass of water."

"Coming up. Are you doing all right?" she asked James.

"Fine."

Marcy smiled at James and walked away.

"Wow, that's a fine-lookin' skirt there," Stu said.

James shook his head.

"You know what they say about redheads," Stu said, nudging James.

The man that was sitting next to James returned.

"Excuse me," he said to Stu.

"For?"

"You're sitting in my seat," the man said, annoyed.

"I am?"

"Yes."

"Oh, sorry." Stu stood up.

The man wrinkled his nose as he looked at the wet stool and the puddle on the floor. "I'll find another place to sit," he said, walking away.

"Wow, nice guy, heh?" Stu said.

Marcy came back and set the glass of water on the counter.

"So, what's your name?" Stu said.

"Marcy."

"I like that name. I'm Stu," he said, offering his hand.

She shook his hand, and he held onto it longer than necessary.

"Nice to meet you," she said, wiping her wet hand on her apron.

"You been workin' here long?"

"Couple of months."

"Well, a pretty girl like you shouldn't be stuck behind a coffee counter."

She smiled. "I like it here—it pays the rent."

"Oh, so you have your own place?"

"I rent a room at the Morisey Boarding House."

"Oh yeah, I know that place."

"You do?"

"Well, I've seen it."

She laughed. "I'll check on you guys later."

"Promise?" Stu said.

She smiled and walked away.

"She's real pretty, ain't she?" Stu said, setting his arms on the counter.

"She is."

"She reminds me of a strawberry shortcake in that little red and white dress with a red bow on top like a cherry," Stu said dreamily.

James shifted uncomfortably in his seat.

"You think she would go out with me?"

"So, have you talked to John?" James said, wanting to change the subject.

"No. It's best not to bother him if he's in a bad mood," Stu said, messing with the sugar dispenser.

"Stu, are you sure being in this band is what you want?"

"Well, yeah, if there is a band to go back to, that is."

"Maybe the band splitting up isn't a bad thing. There did seem to be a lot of problems."

"Jerry and I were thinking about starting our own band," Stu said, turning to James.

"That might work."

"Maybe you would like to join us?"

"Me?" James said.

"Yeah."

"Thanks, but I'm not looking to join a group."

"Why not? It could be a lot of fun."

"I am sure it would, but finals are coming, and I need to find a summer job."

Stu set his chin on his hand. "So, you're saying no?"

"For now, but I will still help you two learn how to string and tune your guitars if you want."

"Will you come over tomorrow night? Say around six?"

"Okay."

"Cool. I better go before the gremlins tear down the house."

"See you later."

Stu walked down the counter and stopped to talk to Marcy. James wondered if he was asking her out. He watched them chat for a few minutes. She was laughing, making James nervous. Would she really go out with Stu? Stu finally left, making James breathe easier. A while later, the storm ended, and James decided to head home. He picked up his books and went to the register to pay his bill.

"That will be a nickel," Marcy said.

"Keep the change," he said, passing her the money.

"Here, I have something for you," she said, pulling a book out of her pocket and passing it to him.

"*One Lonely Night.*"

"I think you will like it."

James nodded. "Thanks. I will give it a go."

"So, I will see you again soon?" Marcy said with a grin.

"Maybe," he said

"Maybe I could fix you another special cup."

"I would like that."

They exchanged a captive smile.

"Don't let the book keep you awake all night," she said, leaning against the cash register.

"I won't."

James left the coffee shop, gazing at the picture of the terrified girl shaded in green on the book's front cover. It surprised him that Marcy would be reading a detective novel instead of a syrupy romance, but he knew Marcy wasn't like any other girl he had met. She was special. Smiling at the book, he put it in his jacket pocket and headed for home.

9

THE CHAOTIC HUM EMANATING FROM the group a few tables away had dissipated with their departure. At last, John was left alone to absorb the calming quiet he desperately craved. Moments of complete solace were rare for him. His mind was constantly clamored with unwanted aggravation and angst that blocked his inner peace. His notebook was his outlet to release his fractured musings. His pencil coasted along the curves of his thoughts, flowing unhampered by any outside annoyance. The pencil was off the paper and rolling between his fingers as he surveyed the familiar terrain of the outdoor student break area. Sitting at a table across the area near the fence was the young woman who had lent him the pencil.

Her head rested on her left hand while writing lazily with her right. A light warm breeze teased her long blonde hair, causing it to rustle from her shoulders. She wore the same uninteresting A-line dress that every other girl in the school wore, but her pink polka-dotted hairband stood out like a rose in a desolate field of the ordinary.

Had she walked past him in the hallways, her image would have blended within the forgotten featureless crowd, but now he saw her without any other distraction to divert his attention. He watched her run her fingers through her hair, separating the tangled ends. The unintentional actions motivated him to sketch the moment. Every contour, every faint nuance flowed effortlessly onto the lifeless, bleached paper. He imagined walking over to her, pulling her attention away from whatever she was writing. She would glance up at him with her dark brown eyes, and her lips would part slightly to speak. Her voice would be light and sweet, her laughter would brush against his aching ears ... and then ... like an unwanted fly, he appeared, bringing the whole dream to a screeching halt.

A young man walked up to her table and began talking to her. Who was this? Who dares interrupt this tender moment? He was a cookie-cutter image of the perfect, clean, wholesome young man that every parent envisioned for their daughter. He looked like he had stepped out of an advertisement for some Macy's department store. Maybe they were just friends; it wasn't like he had joined her. He could tell they were laughing, but then he bent over and kissed her.

Reality always finds a way to pay an ugly visit. The unwanted ache in his brain was growing, and the pencil. . . broke.

10

J AMES RARELY WENT TO STU'S house because there was always a sense of discord and unrest. If Stu wasn't arguing with his mother, he was dealing with his little sister's obnoxious, disruptive behavior that caused Stu to be an anxious, nervous wreck.

Stu answered the door, which indicated that his mother wasn't home, and the night would pass without incident.

Jerry was downstairs when James and Stu joined him. James sat by Jerry on the floor and showed him how to put on the new guitar string correctly, and Stu was playing some records that his friend Len had lent him.

"Tell me these guys aren't the best!" Stu raved. "Can you imagine bein' able to play like that?"

"Can you be quiet? I am tryin' to watch the Professor string my guitar," Jerry said.

Stu walked over to them and sat on the edge of the crooked coffee table.

"When was the last time your guitar was strung, Jerry?" James said.

"Whadda, you mean?"

"When was the last time you replaced the strings?"

Jerry scratched his head.

"They are loose and out of order."

"Really?"

"Placement is important—only the new one is where it should be."

"That would explain why you sound so crummy," Stu said.

Jerry's shoulders fell.

"As soon as I get a job, I will buy you a new set of strings, Jer," Stu said.

"When are you gettin' a job?"

"Soon."

"What kinda job you gonna get?"

"I dunno yet."

"I think they're hiring at the gas station," James said.

"You're talkin' about fillin' tanks for a bunch of opinionated middle-aged men who scrutinize every move you make. Then they tell your boss you don't know what the hell you're doin' so they can cheat you out of a tip? Forget it."

"Let me see if I can make this work, Jerry," James said.

"Gee, thanks, James."

A loud thumping sound startled the trio. Stu's little sister came jumping down the stairs two at a time. Her crouched landing sounded like an elephant was coming down the stairs instead of a ten-year-old girl.

"Carly, didn't I tell you not to come down here when we're practicin'?" Stu grumbled.

Carly jumped over to them, chewing on a large wad of bubble gum. Traces of the sticky pink goo was on her face. "That weird guy is at the door for you."

"What weird guy?"

"The one with the messy hair and strange clothes."

"The name, Carly."

"I don't wanna know the names of your weirdo friends." She twirled her finger around her ginger-curled pigtail.

Stu sighed and went upstairs.

Carly sat on the floor close to James. "Whatcha doin'?"

"None of your beeswax," Jerry said.

"Are you tryin' to fix that old piece of shit again?"

"Why don't you scram?"

"I don't gotta—this is my house."

"You would be in trouble if your mom heard you saying dirty words," Jerry said.

"Neh," she said, sticking out her pink gum tongue.

Stu came back downstairs with John behind him.

"So, this is where you keep the girls, hey Stu?"

"Told you he was weird," Carly whispered to James.

John set his guitar down and sat on the faded tan couch. Its springs were broken, and he sunk almost to the floor. "What are you listenin' to?"

Stu handed him the album cover. "It's the new Martin album. Ain't it kickin'?"

"Sounds pretty canned to me," John said, looking at the back cover.

"I like um. I think we could do some of his tunes. Whadda, you think?"

"I think you're cracked. You got anythin' to drink around here?"

"Just Mom's vodka," Carly said.

"Carly, go play with your dolls," Stu said.

"I don't play with dolls—that's for babies."

"Well, go upstairs, then."

"Why? Are you wantin' to show them the nudie pictures you have?"

"I don't have any of those."

"Yes, you do. You keep um under your mattress."

"If you don't go upstairs, I'll carry you up by your ankles!"

"If you lay a hand on me, I'll scream!"

"I'll give you a dollar if you get lost."

"Five."

"I ain't got five."

"Then I ain't movin'," she said, folding her arms.

"You're a brat," Jerry said.

"You're a goober."

"Hey, Carly, there is a new show on the television tonight," James said. "I am going to miss it. Would you mind watching and telling me what happens?"

"Sure, I will," she said, leaping to her feet. "What channel?"

"Not sure, but you're a smart girl. You will figure it out."

Her smile twinkled like gumdrops at him. Sticking her tongue out at Stu, she ran up the stairs.

"So, what brings you by, John?" Stu asked.

"Do I need a reason?"

"What? No. You've just never dropped by before."

"Well, Jerry told me that there was a class tonight. So, I thought I would come and check it out."

"Cool. We weren't sure if you wanted to, you know, hang out with us after what happened the other night."

Confusion crossed John's face. "Why? What happened the other night?"

Stu looked at Jerry, who shrugged his shoulders.

"Well, you know . . ." Stu said, running his hand up and down his arm.

John gave him a blank look.

"We thought maybe you wanted to dump us," Jerry said.

John frowned at him. "What does that mean?"

"What Patrick said is true, John. The group would do better if you had talented members," Stu said.

"We know we're draggin' you down," Jerry said.

John looked at Stu and then at Jerry. "Did I ever say you were draggin' me down?"

"Well . . . no," Stu said.

"Jerry?" John said.

"No."

"You know, I am not some genius guitar player with nothing left to learn. My skills are limited at best. I am not playing guitar so I can be better than everyone else. I am playing guitar because I want to make music with my friends."

John leaned back and put his feet on the coffee table, lowering the couch cushion.

"Let the teaching begin, Professor."

"All right, Stu, I assume your guitar is strung correctly?" James said.

"Yeah."

"Pluck your D string for me."

Stu scrunched up his face.

"Okay, the G string then."

Stu's face remained scrunched up, but he was blinking as if it would make the answer clear in his mind.

"How about you, Jerry?" James said.

"Can't you tell us by the number?"

"Number?"

"Yeah, like number one, two, three, four, five, or six."

"That would be a lot easier," Stu said.

James looked at John, who had a serious look on his face.

"Are you considering this top string to be number one?" James said.

"Yup," Stu said, and Jerry nodded his agreement.

"Okay, so this is your low E."

"Wha? Why would it be low if it is the closest to the top?" Stu said.

"Yeah, seems like the one on the bottom should be the low one," Jerry said.

James closed his eyes.

"Look, it's really easy," John said, picking up his guitar. "It's all about sound, really. Slowly strum your guitar, Professor."

James complied.

"Now you, Stu."

Stu strummed his guitar.

"Now, it doesn't take a genius to tell that two very different sounds are coming from both instruments. Agreed?"

They all nodded.

"Did you check Jerry's guitar to make sure the strings are on correctly?" John asked James.

"I managed to create a workaround until he can get new strings."

Jerry gave a small smile.

"Check mine," John said, passing his guitar to James.

"I don't need to. . . ."

"Check it."

James checked the placement. "It's good," he said, passing the guitar back to John.

"Okay, here's what we're gonna do. We're gonna tune to the Professor's guitar. It will be a challenge, but we should all be close in the end. Pluck your first string," he said to James.

"But. . . ." James said.

"Humor me," John said.

James plucked his first string.

"It isn't as easy just to pluck the string. You see where his fingers are?"

Stu and Jerry nodded.

"Good. Now I pluck mine." John plucked his first string. "I am off. So, I will tighten this plug and continue until my string sounds like the Professor's. Once that is done for everyone, we move on to the next string. All right?"

"Yeah," they concurred.

What should have been a simple exercise was a trying test of patience and resolve. They went around the circle, one by one, plucking and tightening until everyone's guitar was tuned in the same pitch as James's.

"We need to play somethin'," Stu said.

"Let's do 'Walkin' with Baby,'" Jerry said.

"I don't know that song," James said.

"Tell us what song you do know," John said.

"I can play 'Hound Dog.'"

"Don't move your hips," Jerry said. "I don't think Stu's sister could survive it."

They all laughed.

"I think we can all manage to play that tune," John said.

"Let's give it a go," Stu said.

"Count us in, Professor."

James counted down the beats, and the tiny group began to fumble through a melody imprisoned between the mind and the hand. Boundaries of familiarity were pushed, and notes were fractured as fingers found different paths along a fretted board. Humming when words were forgotten and moving along with Jerry's bobbing head, the music they created penetrated the small space between them and bonded a common thread.

"Not bad, hey Professor?" John said.

"Not at all," he said.

The session ended, and James walked out into the brisk night air with John. They walked silently for a couple of blocks before James stopped to cross the street.

"I got to cross the street here."

"All right," John said.

A hesitant beat passed between them, neither knowing how to put what they were thinking into words.

"I guess I'll see you around," James said.

"Yup," John said, continuing his path.

James watched him walk away into the darkness before crossing the street, humming "Hound Dog's" tune.

11

EING HOME ALONE ON A Saturday afternoon without his father or brother was a rare occurrence for James. The time to study without interruption or petty annoyances would be invaluable to him. After he had completed all his chores, he went up to his room with a bounce in his step. He sat down at his writing desk and pulled out his books and notes—quick, easy, organized, perfect. Fully awake and attentive, he began to read chapter eight. Halfway down the third page, his thoughts got bored, and he decided to time-travel back to the last practice at Stu's house.

Sitting on the floor next to Jerry, the events of that invigorating moment of reuniting with his abandoned companion filled the empty chasm of his fretful spirit. The freedom of imperfect artistic expression without judgment or expectation with friends had been incredible, and for that one trapped moment, he had forgotten how empty his life was.

James opened his eyes, not even realizing he had closed them. He looked at the clock on his nightstand; a half-hour had passed. Shaking his head, he went downstairs to drink a glass of cold water. Refreshed and determined, he took his pencil in hand, but it didn't take long before thoughts of the other night teased his mind again. He rubbed his temples; he had to find something to distract him from daydreams or ideas of such foolishness.

He turned on the radio, and a Fats Domino tune was playing. James's foot started tapping. His fatigued mind and the page before him began to clear. When the song ended, the boisterous voice of the DJ assailed the airways.

"Hey guys and dolls, it's Roarin' Digsby here spinnin' the platters on KTWB, your home for the hottest rockin' tunes! I know you're all enjoyin' this sunny afternoon away from the classroom and all that boring studying!"

James frowned.

"Tonight is Saturday night, and you know what that means—it's time to wrap your mittens around your kittens and take her out for a night on the town. It's a double dose of horror night at the Madison Cinema followed by a soda and fries at Be-Bops-Malt Shop, or if you're a hip cat with cash to spare, you can catch The Dice at the Beaumont. I have to tell you, kiddies, that is one smokin' hot show! I wouldn't be surprised if I am spinnin' their platter here soon! It's the top of the hour, and let's start it off right with some howlin' from the King!"

"Hound Dog" came over the speaker, causing James to glare at the green Bakelite box. He turned it off and stared up at the ceiling. What was wrong with him? Why couldn't he focus?

Grabbing his jacket, James decided to go for a walk to clear his mind and get back on the right track.

12

THE FRESH AIR AND BRISK exercise revived James as he walked with his hands in his jacket pockets. He wasn't thinking of any set destination, but somehow, his feet headed toward Stu's house.

Carly was in the front yard, jumping rope with the same obscene amount of gum in her mouth. She smiled when she saw James.

"Afternoon, Carly."

"Hi."

"Is your brother here?"

"No."

"Do you know where he is?"

"I don't keep track of that booger."

"Was he with his friends?"

"I dunno."

James sighed. "If you see him, can you tell him I stopped by, please?"

She nodded as she blew a sizeable pink bubble.

James knew the chances of Carly telling her brother anything was very slim.

James could hear the music of Buddy Holly as he approached The Beat record store. It was a warm day, so the front door to the small shop was wide open. James stepped through the door onto the black-and-white tiles that covered the uneven floor. A couple of girls were standing by the magazine rack, swooning over the latest issue of *Teen* magazine. Eddie was at the counter, bopping around to the beat. His latest attempt at styling his short black hair in a pompadour had failed, leaving a spikey mess stuck at odd angles.

"Hello, Eddie," James said.

"Hey," he said, nodding his head.

"What's going on?"

"Not much. Just doin' inventory."

James lifted his eyebrow. "It doesn't look like it."

"There are customers in the shop, James. I have to make sure I am available to cater to their every need."

James glanced over at the giggling girls in the corner. "Have you seen Stu?"

"No, not lately."

"How about Len?"

Eddie placed a crate full of records on the counter. "Nah, Len got a job."

"He did?"

"Yup, he's a delivery boy over at the market. Guess he doesn't mind it. He takes care of the little old ladies. They tip him well."

James sat on the stool next to the counter. "Maybe Stu could do something like that."

"He said he doesn't need to work."

"He did?"

"Said the new group he joined will make him famous."

James wrinkled his brow. "I wouldn't count on that."

"You never know what may happen, James. Fame and fortune could be out there waitin' for all of us. Take me, for example: someday, I will be big in the *biz*."

"The biz?"

"The music biz."

"You play guitar?"

"No, I want to work with the talent, James. I have the background, and customers come here all the time to see me."

James wasn't going to remind him that The Beat was the only record shop for fifteen miles.

"I want to be a promoter or a manager. Who knows, maybe someday I will be working with Buddy."

"Buddy?"

Eddie frowned. "Holly."

"Oh."

"I already got chicks on my tail, count of we look so much alike," Eddie said, throwing his shoulders back.

Eddie's only resemblance to his idol was his black-horned-rimmed glasses. He was skinny and short and with wide brown eyes. Eddie was smart and managed the store that his father owned. He was personable and anxious to make friends, but he talked too much, giving people the impression that he was obnoxious.

James noticed an old guitar hanging on the wall. "What's the story with the guitar?"

"That old thing?"

"Yeah."

Eddie shrugged. "Pop found it and brought it in. He said it might be worth a few bucks."

"Mind if I look at it?"

"You lookin' to buy a guitar, James??

"No, not really. I just wanted to check it out."

Eddie took it down and handed it to him. "I didn't know you played."

"I know a few tunes." James played a few chords and played along with the record.

The girls came closer and watched him play with flirty smiles.

"Hi, girls," he said, stopping.

"Are you in a band?"

James shook his head. "No."

"You're really good."

"I am very rusty." He set the guitar down on the counter.

"I play guitar too," Eddie said.

They ignored him.

"I'm MeLinda, and this is Patty. What's your name?"

"James."

"We're goin' to the Beaumont," MeLinda said.

"Yeah, The Dice are playing there," Patty said.

"The Dice?" James said.

"Yeah, they are so dreamy." They giggled, swaying their hips, causing the poodles on their skirts to swing.

"I am getting two comp tickets to the show. Maybe one of you would like to accompany me?" Eddie said, winking at them.

They flounced their Aqua Net sprayed hair.

"Are you going to the show?" MeLinda asked James.

"No."

"You should. Their sound is tight, and they're going to be the next big thing around here," Eddie said.

"I am so going to meet Joey," MeLinda said.

"How are you gonna do that?" Eddie said.

"We got a plan," Patty said, giggling more.

Eddie rolled his eyes.

"We're goin' to Be-Bops. Want to come?" MeLinda said, batting her eyes at James.

"I would, but I have to get back to my studies."

"Who studies on the weekend?" Patty said.

"My final exams are coming up."

"Maybe you can give me a call sometime when you're not studying," MeLinda said, taking a pen out of her purse. She wrote her number on a flyer lying on the counter, kissed it, and handed it to James.

"Thanks," he said, smiling.

"Maybe we could double date," Eddie said.

"Talk to you soon," MeLinda said, winking at James.

MeLinda and Patty left the store, whispering and giggling.

The flyer had MeLinda's number and a big red lip print.

"You lucky dog! I would give anything to have her number," Eddie said.

James handed him the flyer. "It's your lucky day."

Eddie's eyes got wide. "You don't want to call her?"

"That girl looks like she might be a little too fast for me. I'll talk to you later, Eddie."

James left the store and continued down the street. He knew he should go home, but he was close to the coffee shop. Maybe if he stopped in and had a cup of coffee, it would help distract his mind for a while. He walked in and had a seat at the counter.

Carol came down with a cup in her hand. "Hey, Jamie."

"Hello."

"I figured you would want your usual."

He nodded.

"So, what brings you in here on the weekend?"

"I was in the neighborhood and thought I would stop in."

"Um, hmm," she said.

"What?"

"You thought maybe you would see Marcy?"

"Oh, no."

"You have been coming into this shop for a long time, and I've never seen you light up like you do when she's around."

James hid a blush.

"You should ask her out."

"What? Me? No," James said, shaking his head.

"Why not?"

"Because I am sure she already has someone."

"No, she doesn't."

"I am too busy with school and home and . . ."

"She likes you too," Carol said.

"She does?"

"You seem so surprised."

"I always figured she would never go for a guy like me."

"Don't sell yourself so short."

"You really think she would go out with me?"

Carol nodded and walked away.

James smiled and drank his coffee.

13

THE SMELL OF FRESHLY CUT grass wafted through the humid air. James was relaxing in a chair on the front porch with his feet propped up on the railing, drinking a glass of cool lemonade. He had spent the morning raking and mowing the sleepy spring yard. Picking pieces of dead foliage out of his shoes and jeans, he heard someone mumbling unsavory words. The cantankerous gate latch wasn't letting Stu enter the yard, so he jumped over it, barely landing on his feet.

"I thought your dad fixed that dumb ol' gate," Stu grumbled.

"He wanted to keep you out," James said.

"Real funny."

"So, what's been going on?"

"Not much."

"I called a couple of times and even went by your house. I am assuming Carly didn't tell you?"

"I don't talk to her unless I absolutely have to."

Stu flopped on the porch. He wore thick dark sunglasses, his hair was a matted mess, and his clothes were wrinkled. Leaning his back on one of the porch posts, he stretched out and propped his feet against the opposite post.

"What happened to you? You look like you've been in a dogfight."

Stu crossed his arms. "I went out last night."

"Where?"

"I dunno. Just out."

"You're hungover."

"Can I have some of that?"

"Lemonade?"

"You're drinking that on purpose?"

"It tastes good after you've sweated all morning doing yard work."

"You should make your brother do it."

"He does some of it," James said, taking a satisfying drink.

"Uh-huh. Does your dad at least give you an allowance?"

"We have an arrangement."

"It's called James does everything around here, so no one else has to."

"You know, I missed your company, and now I wonder why."

"I just hate seeing you being taken advantage of. If you don't start layin' down the law around here, you'll be an old man before your time."

James took another drink of his lemonade that was getting warm, and the tart taste was making his mouth shrink. He set the glass down and put his hands across his stomach. He couldn't tell if Stu had fallen asleep behind his glasses or if he had just decided to be quiet.

Two high school girls riding bicycles passed by in front of the house. Their vibrant hair and shapely legs made James smile.

"Hey, James," they said, waving.

He waved back.

"Damn," Stu said. "You know those girls?"

"Yeah," James said, closing his eyes.

"How well?"

James shrugged.

"I don't understand how someone can know so many beauties and still be a virgin."

James threw a lump of mud off his shoe at Stu, hitting him upside the head.

"What was that for?"

"You know what for."

"Am I wrong?"

"You know you are."

"First base doesn't count."

"You know I could throw you in the big mud puddle on the north side of the house."

Stu folded his fingers behind his head. "You know I am just kiddin' you."

"So ... uh, you have any new band news?"

"No, not really."

"You guys haven't practiced since the other night?"

Stu shook his head.

"Oh."

"I think John wants us to get together sometime this week. He might have talked to Patrick. He doesn't tell me much of anything."

James crossed his leg. "I don't think he tells anybody much of anything. Most of the time, he talks in riddles."

"He's complicated."

"What is his story, anyway?"

"Whadda ya mean?"

"How did you meet him?" James asked.

"Patrick."

"Patrick? You knew Patrick first?"

"Yup," Stu said.

James sighed, realizing that Stu wouldn't tell him anything useful.

"What's wrong?" Stu said.

"Nothing."

"You're lying."

"I am not."

"I have known you long enough to know when somethin' is botherin' you."

"I just got a big test next week."

"I think bein' locked up here all the time is making you stir crazy. You need to get outta here. Why don't you come over tonight? It could be like old times. We could play some tunes together."

"Not tonight."

"You could come over on practice night."

"I don't think I should do that anymore."

"Why not? I know you had a good time the other night."

"Maybe John doesn't want me there."

"If he didn't want you there, you would know it."

James rubbed his neck. "Has he … you know. . . ."

Stu looked clueless.

"Has he said anything about me?" James said, refusing to meet Stu's eyes.

Stu started to smile. "Oh, I get it. You want to join the group."

"No, I don't. I just was curious if he had said anything."

"You want me to ask him?"

"No. Just forget it," James said, sitting up straight.

"You got it bad, hey James?"

"Forget I said anything."

"I can give you his address. His stepmom is kind of mean, but. . . ."

"I'm not going to his house."

"It felt good, didn't it? Playin' again."

"What is wrong with me, Stu? I don't have time to play in a band. I need to forget about it."

"I can tell him you want to meet with him."

"No, don't tell him I said anything."

"He takes a break between his second and third class on the east side of the campus."

James didn't say anything.

"I know he can be a little hard to talk to, but he really ain't that bad. Hell, he puts up with Jerry."

James smiled.

"I guess I better get goin'," Stu said, standing. "You know you haven't done anything for yourself since she died. You deserve some happiness."

"I'll talk to you later, Stu."

"Yeah." And he left, jumping the fence.

14

THE SCHOOL LIBRARY WAS ON the opposite side of the campus from the student break area. The doors were marked with large red-lettered *Keep Quiet* signs. The old spinster librarian, who wore small reading glasses on her long nose, enforced the rules.

James didn't like studying in the school library, but he was annoyed at himself for having passed by the student break area twice looking for John. Studying in the library would remove him from the situation and force him to focus. James was slumped over his book, making notes, when he sensed someone standing next to him. He looked up to see John.

"Are you stalking me?" John asked.

James's mouth hung open.

"Don't try and deny it 'cause I've seen you. Twice."

James was dumbfounded.

"I am used to the chicks watchin' me, but this is somethin' new, kinda disturbin'."

The librarian spotted John and walked over to him, slapping her ruler against the palm of her hand. "You are disturbing the silence, young man."

"What?" John said.

"You are disturbing the silence," she repeated.

"What? I can't hear you?"

Everyone turned and looked at them.

She had a stern look on her prune face as she looked him over. "I know you. You're the ruffian whose picture is posted on the front desk with instructions that strictly forbid your admittance into this library."

"Who me? Obviously, there must be some kind of waffle. Why I'll have you know that I am a condemnable stooped pupil who is in the pursuit of justice and the American way."

She raised her eyebrow at him and pointed at the door with her ruler.

"Don't think that this shameful bereavement will not be a scrub on your apartment record. I will be reporting you to the minorities forth thee wit," John said, waving his finger at her.

Several of the students were laughing.

She turned to them.

"We are meeting at Stu's tonight. Don't be late," John said to James. He slipped out of the library before the librarian knew he was gone.

15

WHEN JAMES ARRIVED AT PRACTICE, Carly and a couple of her girlfriends played hopscotch in the driveway.

"Hey, Carly," James said.

"They're inside," she said, ignoring James.

"Thanks," he said, walking up to the porch.

"Who is that?" one of her friends said.

"That's James."

"Oooh, he is cute," the little girl said, twisting her bubble gum around her finger.

"Yeah, he isn't creepy like the rest of your brother's friends," a girl with yellow chalk smudged on her face said.

"Yeah, I think the one with the messy hair has cooties," Carly said.

"Grody!" the girls chimed. Then giggling, they returned to their game.

James trotted down the steps.

John was lounging on the couch looking at a comic book, Stu was relaxing, and Jerry was tuning.

"Hey, James, I think I got this tuning thing," Jerry said. "It doesn't sound half bad for a beat-up, old guitar."

James sat next to him and opened his case up. "That's great news, Jerry."

"Did you bring the beer?" John said.

"No, I didn't know I was supposed to."

John didn't look up from his comic. "You're the newest member, so it's your responsibility."

James looked at Stu, who still had his eyes closed.

"We rotate," Jerry said.

"Oh. I thought the rule was no beer before practice."

"Still doesn't excuse you from providing the suds," John said.

"I talked to Len, John. He wants us to play at his birthday party," Stu said.

Silence.

"Whadda, you think?"

"You know what I think."

"We know we are rough, but now we got James," Stu said.

"What?" James said.

"Congrats!" Jerry said, setting his hand on James's shoulder.

"Wait a second—what's going on?"

"You're a member of the group," Stu said.

"I am?"

"Isn't that what you wanted?" John said.

"Well. . . ."

John set the comic aside. "Or did you want to ask me in private?"

"No."

"So, what's the problem?" John said.

"I want to know what happened to Patrick?"

"What do you mean?" John said.

"Is he still a member of the group?"

John set his hand on his knee. "No."

"Why not?"

"You saw what happened."

"I did, but I thought you two might be able to work it out."

"That time has passed," John said.

"So, are you in?" Stu said.

"I just don't know if I can make that kind of commitment. I have a lot of responsibilities," James said.

"You know what I think?" John said, standing. "I think you need to lighten up and stop overthinking everything, or you will have an ulcer before you're twenty-one."

John offered James his hand and helped him to his feet. "Once you graduate college, you are going to have the rest of your life to dress in a grey flannel suit with a stiffly starched collar sitting next to some other schlub who looks just like you on the commuter bus, and when you look back on these days what do you want to remember? How you studied so hard that you let your college years pass without any fun? Or do you want to remember how you took a chance, joined a rock-n-roll band, chased some girls, and drank beer with your friends?"

James blinked his eyes.

"Are you in?"

"I am," James said with a wide smile.

"The Professor is buyin' us beer, boys!" John said.

Stu and Jerry cheered.

"Just don't let Carly know where we are headed," Stu said, following James and John up the stairs.

"Will she tell your mom?" Jerry said.

"No, worse. She'll blackmail me."

"Good point," Jerry said.

16

THE 2 SHOT WAS A dive bar located between the reputable part of town and the rough part. The small building that had been a grocery store was now a neglected shadow of what it once was. A painting of a Coke bottlecap and the word refreshing in seven-foot-high letters spanned the south wall. Most of the paint had worn off, exposing the crumbling bricks to the harsh elements. The community petitioned the city to condemn the building as a safety hazard because adventurous children, believing the rumors that the building was haunted, loved to explore the creepy property. The current owner dismissed the rumor as rubbish and reopened it as a place for young adults to buy cheap drinks and mingle. Much to the dismay of the senior community, the rumors of the haunting didn't divert the unscrupulous from patronizing the establishment.

Wednesday night was quiet compared to the weekend, so the place wasn't completely packed. The doors were opened, allowing some fresh air to relieve the unpleasant odor of cigarettes and cheap beer. The dim lighting revealed faded tan paint and uninspired pictures of abstract art. John was welcomed by several serene beatniks when he came through the door. He slipped his arm around a black-haired beauty in tight pedal pushers and joined them at the bar. James had never seen him more engaged.

"Let's get a table," Stu said to James.

"Can we sit up front, closer to the door?"

"Why so you can make a quick escape if you see a ghost?"

"No. It's just that the stench in here is nauseating."

"John likes to sit toward the back."

"Do you always do what he says?"

"Do you want to tell him that we are sitting upfront?"

"Never mind."

Jerry, Stu, and James found at a table toward the back of the bar.

"Are you sure he will join us?" James said. "He looks busy."

"It takes him a while, but he eventually makes his way back here," Stu said.

James shook his head.

"Why don't you go get us some beers?" Stu said to Jerry.

"Why don't you make James do it? He's the new member."

"Cause I asked you."

"You can't just boss me around."

"Fine, we'll just sit here holdin' our peckers. You do that a lot anyway, don't you, Jerry?"

"You're a real ass, Stu."

"I tell you what—I'll flip you for it."

"That's probably one of your trick coins."

"Then I will flip your coin."

"I ain't got none."

"Here," James said, rummaging around in his pant pocket for a quarter. He finally pulled one out and handed it to Stu.

"Thanks, pal. Call it," Stu said, flipping the coin.

"Heads," Jerry said.

They all watched as the coin hit the table and spun until it finally fell over, revealing its favored side.

"Tails!" Stu exclaimed victoriously, sticking the coin in his pocket.

Jerry frowned, got up, and walked to the bar.

"So, what do you think?" Stu asked James.

"Think about what?"

"Your first night as a member. It's pretty cool, huh?"

"I guess."

"Do you remember the first time we came here?"

"Oh, Stu . . ."

"Well, do you?"

James rubbed his temple. "That was a long time ago."

"Not so long, by my way of thinkin'."

"That's 'cause you're still twelve."

"You were so sure your mom would smell the alcohol on your breath that you ate almost ten Altoids that made you sick."

"It was the cheap beer that made me sick."

"We had fun, though, didn't we?"

James smiled. "We did."

Jerry returned to the table. "You'll never guess who's here?"

"Your mom?" Stu said.

"No. Eddie."

"Has John seen him?" Stu said.

"I don't know. He is still talking to those clod heads."

"I can't believe they let that goober in here," Stu said.

"What's wrong with Eddie?" James said.

"You have to ask?" Jerry said.

"So, he's a little different."

"A little? He's downright annoying."

"Hey, where are the drinks, Jer?" Stu said.

"They're comin'. Ruthie wants the cash upfront because she doesn't believe we have the money."

"Hey, check it out," Stu said, nodding toward the bar. "Johnnie is at it again."

They looked toward the bar where John was flirting with the black-haired girl.

"He has all the luck," Jerry said.

"Whadda, you bet she goes in the back with him?" Stu says.

"That's a fool's bet," Jerry said.

"I give him an hour. What do you say, Jer?"

"He more than likely will piss her off before then. You know he can't keep his mouth shut."

"He's bein' real sweet too."

"It always starts that way. I bet she slaps him before he gets her in the back."

"How much?"

"All I got is a nickel."

"You're on," Stu said, spitting in his hand and shaking hands with Jerry.

James rolled his eyes.

The waitress came over. Her hair was piled on top of her head with a pink bow. Her thick makeup failed at covering up her age.

"You better have the money for this, or I am throwin' you out!" she snarled.

"Customer service with a smile, hey, Ruthie?" Stu said.

Ruthie sat the tray down. "You don't deserve no smiles, Stu."

"Aw, come on, honey, I thought I was your favorite customer," Stu said, winking at her.

She began to laugh. "You're dreamin'. Hurry up. I ain't got all night."

"How much do I owe you?" James said.

She wrinkled her nose. "Who is this guy?"

"He's my best friend," Stu said.

"What's a nice-lookin' kid like you doin' with these chowder heads?"

Stu placed his arm around James. "I'll have you know that Jamie has been my friend since the second grade."

"And he still talks to you?"

Stu sneered at her.

"That'll be a buck," she said to James.

James handed her the money.

"I'll bring back the change."

"Keep it," James said.

"Now that is a man who knows how to get what he wants. You could take a lesson from him."

"Hands off him," Stu said.

"Piss off, Stu," Ruthie said, leaving.

"Hey, fellas!"

"Oh no," Jerry said as Eddie approached their table.

"What's shakin'?" Eddie sat down before Jerry could tell him not to.

"What are you doin' here, Eddie?" Stu asked.

"You know, just checkin' out the scene."

"What scene? You mean the old broads?" Stu said.

"That's the only way he can get a date," Jerry said.

"Ha, ha, you two are a couple of real jokers. Hey, James."

"Hey."

"What are you doin' here with these losers?"

"Hey, watch it, squirt," Stu said.

"Just having a beer," James said, taking a drink of the foul-tasting liquid.

"So, where's Patrick?" Eddie asked.

"I dunno," Jerry said.

"I heard he got cut from the group."

No one said anything.

"Is it true?"

"Why don't you ask John?" Stu said.

"Is he here?" Eddie asked.

"He is."

"Where?"

"Behind you," Jerry said.

Eddie turned to see John standing behind him.

"Hey," Eddie said with a nervous smile.

"You're in my chair."

Eddie jumped up. "Oh, yeah, sorry about that."

John looked sideways at him and sat down. "Where's my beer?"

Stu passed it to him.

Eddie grabbed an empty chair and wedged himself in between Stu and Jerry.

"Did we invite you to join us?" Stu said.

"Well, no, but . . ."

"You're scarin' away the chicks," Jerry said.

"Hey, girls are drawn to me," Eddie said.

"Don't you mean the flies?" Stu said.

They all laughed, and Eddie rumpled his brow.

"You know, Eddie, if you're gonna sit here, you're buyin' the next round," Stu said.

"I ain't got that kinda money."

"Then you need to buzz off."

"I just want to know if what I heard is true."

"What?" Stu said.

"I heard you guys are playin' at Len's party."

John about choked on his drink.

"Who told you that?" Jerry said.

"Len."

"It wasn't confirmed," Stu said.

John was glaring at Stu.

"You gotta do it, man. It's all anyone is talking about."

"He told a lot of people?" Jerry said.

"Well, hell yeah. It's gonna be the biggest bash of the year! There will be all kinds of liquor, and the chicks will be smokin'," Eddie said, moving his eyebrows up and down.

Stu felt sweat beading on the back of his neck.

"I didn't know your official band name yet, so I just put Johnny and His Hound Dogs on the flyer. Catchy, huh?"

"Flyer? What flyer?" John said.

"The one I posted in the store. Oh, and Len took some too!"

John was drumming his fingers on the table.

"Eddie, I think your mother is callin' you," Jerry said.

"All right, all right, I can take the hint. I'll make sure that Len fills you in on the rest of the details."

"You do that," Jerry said.

Eddie got up and left, bobbing his head.

Stu couldn't bring himself to look at John, who was fuming.

"I think I need to hit the head," Stu said, standing.

"Sit down," John growled.

Stu sat down like a condemned man.

"Did you tell Len that we would play the party?"

"I ... uh ... well ... uh ... not exactly."

"What did you tell him *exactly*?"

Stu scratched his head. "I might have said something about us maybe doin' it."

"Did you not think to consult me first?"

"I didn't think I had to. How was I supposed to know that Patrick wasn't with us anymore?"

John's eyes narrowed.

"We really thought it would be a good move for the band," Jerry said quietly.

"You're in on this too?"

"Now wait a second, everyone, just calm down," James said. "Let's just talk this through. We don't have to do this, you know."

"If we back out of this, we will look like dummies," John said.

"Look, we go on later when most people are drunk. They probably won't even be paying attention to what we play. I think we can pull something together to fake our way through this," James said.

"We can hardly play one song," John said, leaning back in his chair.

"Well, we just have to practice. How much time have we got?" James said.

"Ten days," Stu said.

James sighed, and John looked up at the ceiling.

The girl John had been flirting with came over to the table.

"Hey, Reginald, are you comin'?" she said, giving John a flirty smile.

Stu smiled at Jerry, who was frowning.

John stood. "Practice tomorrow night at Stu's."

He took the girl's hand and thumped Stu upside the head as he left with her.

"Ow," Stu said, rubbing his head.

17

THE NEW SITUATION WEIGHED HEAVILY on James as he walked to Stu's house. It had become painfully apparent that Patrick had been the group's backbone. He did most of the singing, played lead guitar, managed the band, and made up for the group's other shortcomings. Now that he was gone, the situation began to unravel, and the difficulties he had maneuvered could no longer be ignored.

James was surprised when Stu's mother answered the door. She appeared to be serene and kind, but underneath all the makeup and peroxide, beat the broken heart of a bitter, lonely woman that lived a mundane life.

"Hello, James," she said, opening the door.

James managed to smile as he walked into the house. "Hello, Mrs. Williams."

"How are you this evening?"

"Good."

"And how is your father doing?"

"Well, thank you."

"I am surprised you're not home with him. Stu told me about how miserable your life has become now that you are responsible for caring for your father and brother."

"Miserable?"

She rested her hand on his arm. "That is quite a responsibility for such a young man."

An unsettling shiver went up James's arm. "I am doing my best."

"Of course you are," she cooed. "Can I get you something to eat?"

"That won't be necessary."

She led James into the kitchen. "I want to."

"I should join the group."

"They can wait. It will only take a moment."

Defeated, James sat down at the table while she busied herself making the sandwich.

Stu came upstairs. "There you are. We've been waitin' on you."

James opened his mouth, but Stu's mother cut him off.

"Now, don't you go upsetting, James. Poor dear is tired and stressed," she said, bringing the turkey sandwich to James.

Stu frowned. "How come you never dote on me like this?"

"Because you're lazy." Walking to the refrigerator, she got a soda for James. "James has important responsibilities. He cares for his ailing father and little brother." She set the soda on the table in front of James. "You sit around and do nothing all day."

"That's not true. I do stuff."

She folded her arms.

"Someone has to look after Carly when you're not here."

"Your little sister keeps you in line, and she does most of the chores. I told you to go to the market the other day, and you didn't bring home half the things on the list. You're a drain on my pocketbook."

"Thanks for the sandwich, Mrs. Williams," James said.

"When are you going to call me Helen?"

"Let's practice, heh, Stu?"

James stood and went downstairs, Stu right behind him.

"Where the hell have you two been?" John snapped.

"James was eatin' a sandwich my mother made him."

"She never makes me any sandwiches," Jerry said.

"Me neither," Stu said.

"I didn't ask her to make me a sandwich. She just insisted."

"And you just had to eat it," Stu snarled.

"Are you two done?" John snapped.

"Yeah," James said.

"We don't have a lotta time, you know."

Stu walked over to his guitar. "Have you decided what songs we're playin'?"

"No. I'm having a hard time comin' up with somethin' you all can play," John said

"What about 'Hound Dog'?" James said. "We seemed to do okay on that tune the other night."

"Too fast," John said.

"But . . ." James said.

"I said no," John snapped.

"Does anyone else have a suggestion?" James said.

Stu was pouting, and Jerry was playing with his shoelace.

"What about 'Summertime Blues'? You all know that song, right?"

"That was Patrick's song," Stu said.

"Yeah, we just kind of faked our way through it," Jerry said.

James sat down slowly on a chair and stared into space.

"We were workin' on 'That'll Be The Day.' It's slow, John," Jerry said.

"It's slower," John said.

"I think I can handle that one," James said.

"Oh well, if you can handle it, we're all set," Stu scoffed.

"Well, someone has to take the lead," James said.

"What?" John said.

"Isn't that what Patrick did?"

John's face hardened.

"Isn't that what you want? Someone one to fill the hole that he left?"

"I didn't ask you to fill the hole." John said.

"But if I don't, we are doomed for failure." A sharp pain filled James's stomach, and he closed his eyes.

John nodded his head, stood up, picked up his guitar, and walked toward the stairs.

"Are you leavin' us?" Jerry said.

John didn't answer as he disappeared up the stairs.

"Wonderful, now see what you did?" Stu said.

"Me?" James said.

"You're the one that brought up Patrick."

"I did not! You guys were the ones talking about how he played, and you just stood around behind him and . . ."

"We're losers?" Stu said.

"Now you're putting words in my mouth."

"We really did fake it," Jerry said.

"That's right," James said. "That day in the park, that is what you said to me. 'Just fake it. That's what we do.'"

Stu's cheeks puffed in and out.

"Stu," James said.

"Just leave me alone!" Stu went into his room and slammed the door.

Jerry glanced at the closed door. "I should have known this wasn't gonna work."

"Jerry, this isn't my fault. I was only doing what I thought was expected of me."

"I know." Jerry stood up. "I guess I have to go home tonight."

"You have a hard home life, don't you?"

"You could say that."

James followed Jerry up the stairs. Helen was sitting on the couch reading a magazine while Carly watched the TV.

"You boys are already finished?" Helen said.

"Apparently," James said.

"That kooky guy left a while ago," Carly said.

"Carly, you shouldn't speak poorly of people less fortunate than you. It isn't his fault that he dresses like a homeless person. His parents obviously can't afford to buy him suitable clothing," Helen said.

"He could get a haircut and take a bath," Carly said. "We had a class in school about proper hygiene. He probably failed that class with Jerry."

James pulled Jerry toward the door before he could respond to Carly's comment. "Goodnight, ladies."

"Goodnight, James," Helen said, waving at him.

It was a relief to leave the suffocating house and be in the fresh, cool air. James and Jerry walked together, listening to the sound of their footsteps.

"I am going to fix this, Jerry," James said.

"Oh, and how are you going to do that?"

"I will talk to him."

"John or Stu?"

"John, Stu will get over it … I think," James chuckled.

"Stu shouldn't have told Len we would play his party," Jerry said.

"Sometimes Stu says things before he thinks about what he is saying. I am sure he was so excited by the thought of the opportunity that he jumped at the chance. He really wants the group to be a success."

"I do too. I just don't know if it can be with us."

"I know you practice hard, Jerry. Stu likes to think he does, but let's be honest."

Jerry laughed. "You really are pretty cool for a prep boy."

"Gee thanks, Jerry."

Jerry stopped. "This is my street."

"Wish me luck, huh?" James said.

"Just talk to him. He has a hard head, but he will listen."

"Thanks, Jerry."

"I hope to see you tomorrow night," Jerry said, turning up the street.

James looked up at the sky. How had he ever gotten himself involved in such a mess? The last thing he wanted was to confront the ogre. Surely, he would be reasonable. He did want things to work out, didn't he? Shaking his head, James resumed his path toward home.

18

J AMES WAS SEATED AT JOHN'S favorite break area table, watching
students surging through the doors. Their conversation splintered
the quiet like harried buzzing bees. He was hoping John would
be by himself, but to his disappointment, he was accompanied by a
small group of friends. James's knee began to bob up and down on its
own, and his clammy hands brushed against the corduroy textured
pants.

John's friends were shocked that someone had dared to invade
their space. John glanced over at James, who waved at him. John did a
double-take, and James wanted to flee, but he was tired of letting his
fear dictate his actions, so he remained in his seat.

John talked to his clique from a distance. James was about to
give up and leave when John parted from the rest and walked over to
the table.

James smiled at him. "Hey."

"Hey."

"Nice day, isn't it?"

"Sure," John said.

James nodded, then was silent.

"Did you need somthin' or did you just want to talk about the
weather?"

"I wanted to talk to you."

"About?"

"Last night."

John watched James rubbing his hands together. "What about it?"

"I wanted to apologize."

"For?"

"What I said last night. I didn't mean to imply that Patrick was better or the leader or that I wanted to take his place."

"I know it."

"You do?"

John sat down. "I do."

James blinked his mouth slightly open.

John tilted his head. "Is there a reason you look like a frog?"

"You just surprised me, is all."

"How so?"

"I just thought this conversation was going to be, I don't know, difficult."

John rested his arms on the table. "Am I that unreasonable?"

"Everyone seems to think you are."

"Well, everyone gets pissed off because I am blunt and honest."

"I think people have difficulty talking to you because they think they piss *you* off."

"True."

"I mean, frankly, I was scared to talk to you," James said.

"Yet here you are," John said, spreading out his hands.

"Because I realize, if this is going to work, we need to find a way to communicate with each other. Dancing around subjects and feelings isn't going to work anymore."

"Agreed."

James took a deep breath. "So, what do you want to do about our current situation?"

John leaned back and put his feet on the bench next to him.

"I know you don't want to talk about it."

"I'm just frustrated," John said.

"We all are. Ever since the decision was made to play Len's party, practice has turned into a nightmare. We're tense and snapping at each other because we have no idea what to do. If playing the party isn't going to be fun and cause nothing but heartache, let's just forget about it."

"What does that mean?"

"It means we don't play the party. We thank Len for the opportunity, but we thought it over and decided against it," James said.

"Because it would be too hard for us?"

"Well, yeah. Surely, he would understand that the band is in transition."

John rested his elbow on the table and ran his hand through his hair.

"Can you please tell me what happened between you and Patrick?"

"Is it important?"

"I think it is."

John rubbed his thumb against his index finger. "He changed."

"How?"

"It was like you said, Professor, it wasn't fun anymore. What started as something casual and creative started to sour because he wanted more. We started to argue about dumb stuff, and he didn't think that I should be making any decisions because he was contributing more than I was."

"And was he?"

John shrugged. "He had the money and the place to practice. So yeah, he was."

"So, you were happy just hanging around strumming out what you could, and Patrick wanted to be taken seriously?" James said.

"Seriously?"

"You know, playing gigs, writing songs, pursuing a record contract, and becoming the next big thing."

"I guess," John said, tapping his foot.

"And you don't want that."

"Do you have any idea what it would take for us to be taken seriously?"

"It would take a lot of hard work."

"Right."

"I can understand if you don't want to work hard. Playing music for you is more of a hobby. That makes sense."

John's face still held no humor.

"Did I say something wrong?"

"So, say we put in all of the work. Do you think someone would take a group like us seriously?"

"Why not?"

"Because we aren't like them," John said, folding his arms.

"Like who?"

"Like the empty-headed, executive conformists that decide if you are good enough or not. Decide if you get to succeed or fail. They turn you into a perfect little mindless twit so they can dictate your life. The next thing you know, you got a fake smile to match your fake life. Why would I put in all that hard work so that I can be some corporate asshole's puppet? I won't let them control me."

"But they already are."

John glared at him.

"Don't you see? Because you think they feel that way about you, you won't even try. You have more power than you realize. What happens with your future is up to you, not them."

John's gaze was turned away from James, and he wondered if he had upset him again.

"I need to get going," James said, gathering his books. "If you decide that you want to play the party, I will do everything in my power to help us get through it and if you don't, it is your decision. After all, you are the leader."

John watched James walk away, and he knew James was right. Things couldn't go on like they were. He had been avoiding the subject of Patrick's absence because he didn't want to deal with it. He needed to decide what he thought his future should be, but right now, he had to deal with the upcoming party.

He closed his eyes, hoping his head's dull and ever-present ache would go away. He concentrated on the sun's warmth, which appeased the clamor for the moment. When he opened his eyes, he saw her sitting at the table by the tree. She was reading a book, her leg swaying and her finger twisting the strands of her lustrous hair. It had been a few days since she had come outside to sit, and he missed seeing her. He drummed his fingers on the table. How long was he going just to sit there and watch her? He was tired of merely daydreaming, so he rose to his feet and walked over to her.

"Hello, Miss Prim."

She turned her head; the sight of him startled her.

He smiled at her and sat down across from her. Her body tensed, and her pupils enlarged.

"What are you readin'?"

"None of your business," she said, hiding the book from his view.

He placed his elbow on the table and rested his chin in his hand. "I bet it's one of those romance novels, heh? I bet it's one of those cheap raunchy ones. The kind that comes wrapped in brown paper. The kind that women only whisper about and hide under their panties in the dresser drawer. I bet you sit alone in bed at night under the covers with a flashlight, thinkin' no one will know what you're readin,' or what you're thinkin'."

Shock held her face captive.

"Oh, I'm sorry, forgive me. I forgot you were a proper girl, very respectable. A girl like you doesn't have any naughty thoughts, do you?"

"What do you want?" she squeaked.

"Nothin'."

He could tell she was flustered and wasn't sure how to react.

"I'm busy."

He leaned in. "Am I makin' you uncomfortable?"

His eyes locked on hers, and she swallowed the lump in her throat. One quick move, and she would have probably screamed.

"Actually," he said, sitting back, "I have somethin' for you."

She watched him apprehensively as he reached into his pocket.

"You know that pencil you lent me? It's defective," he said, laying the broken pencil on the table.

She looked at it, then back at him.

"I need another one, and be quick about it because I have to get to class."

"I am not giving you another pencil."

"Come on, hand it over."

"No," she stood up and gathered her things.

"You aren't very friendly, are you?"

She ran away from him, but in her haste, she dropped one of her books. He casually walked over to where the little pink book had fallen. He picked it up. *My Diary* was on the cover in gold letters. He smiled to himself as he put it in his pocket.

19

JERRY KICKED A SMALL ROCK along the mundane road he took
to Stu's house. He had spent his afternoon sitting among the
ragweed and sun-parched crabgrass, practicing the songs the
group would be rehearsing. He had played guitar for a long time,
but for some reason, it never came naturally to him. Instead, it was a
constant struggle to keep up. He hated letting the group down and,
most of all, John. Something hard hit him on the head, causing him
to whirl around.

"What the hell?" he said.

John was following behind him with a large grin on his face.

"Why can't you be like normal people and say hello or something
like that?"

"I could have given you a knuckle rub."

"No thanks."

The two walked down the road while Jerry was still rubbing his
head.

"Oh, come on, it was only a small rock."

"What if I hit you in the head with a rock?"

"I would hang you upside down from that tree over there."

Jerry frowned at him.

"So ... how are things?"

Jerry wrinkled his nose.

"What?"

"You never ask me how I am."

"That's not true."

"Is too."

John sighed. "All right, I am asking you now."

"Okay, I guess."

"What is it? Your mom's old man again?"

Jerry shrugged.

"You need to deck him, Jerry. Just lay him out once, and he'll leave you alone."

"That's easy for you to say."

"You want me to come over there and take care of him?"

"No."

John kicked a rock. "I would, you know."

"Then you would be in jail. I really just need to move out for good."

"Where you been stayin'?"

"Wherever I can," Jerry said, looking off into the distance.

"If I had my own place, you could stay with me."

"I know that. Maybe I could get a decent job if I wasn't so dumb."

"You're not dumb, Jerry."

"Yes, I am. For example, I have been practicin' every chance I get, but my fingers are always a beat behind."

"You'll get there."

"I know what a disappointment I am to you."

"Jerry, you're not a disappointment to me. You're my best friend," John said, ruffling Jerry's hair.

"I thought Patrick was your best friend."

"You're joking, right?"

"You two were inseparable for a while."

John picked up a rock. "That was before he thought he was Fabian."

"I know it hasn't been easy without him."

"It wasn't easy with him."

"Have you seen him?"

"Nope, and I ain't lookin'," John said, throwing the rock.

"So, how is school?"

"Frustrating."

"Your grades gone up?"

"I may be sleepin' out on the ground with you very soon, Jerry."

"I don't know if there's enough room under the porch."

"You sleep under the porch?"

Jerry kicked a rock. "Sometimes."

"Don't you worry about the creepy crawlies?"

"Nah, they know better than to mess with me."

John laughed.

"You're in a good mood. Did you see that girl again?"

"What girl?"

"The one you left with the other night."

John rumpled his brow. "Are you kiddin'?"

"You didn't like her?"

"Like has nothin' to do with it."

"You know, you should give one of these girls a chance."

John shook his head. "Nope, no way, not gonna happen."

"Why not?"

"Come on Jerry, you know me. I am not gonna get tangled up with some female. They're nothing but trouble. They get inside your head and drive you mad. I'm fine on my own."

"I wish I had a girl."

"You could."

"Nah," Jerry said.

"You're just shy, is all. You just need to build up your confidence."

"That's not all I need."

"You ... a ... still got your problem, then?"

Jerry didn't answer.

"I could talk to one of the girls."

Jerry shook his head. "I already told you no."

"Okay, just checkin'. If you change your mind . . ."

"Yeah, yeah."

John smiled as they walked the last block to Stu's house.

"You know, I don't think Stu's little sister likes me," John said.

"You scare her."

"I do?" John said, his eyes lighting up.

"Now, don't go gettin' any ideas."

"Ah Jerry, don't spoil my fun."

"The last thing we need is for you to get us in trouble with Stu's mom. She already doesn't like us comin' over here to practice all the time."

The two passed through the gate, and Jerry knocked on the door. John cackled.

"Stop it," Jerry said.

Carly answered the door, a look of disgust on her face.

"Evenin', Carly," Jerry said.

"Mom said for you to wipe your feet—you're tracking in mud."

Jerry forced a smile as he wiped his feet on the mat. Carly reluctantly opened the door and let Jerry inside. "You too," she said to John.

He gave her an evil grin as he slowly stuck his hand in his coat pocket. "Did you know I have a spider in my pocket?"

"Stu!"

Jerry looked at John and shook his head as Carly ran down the stairs screaming.

20

CONVINCING CARLY THAT JOHN DIDN'T have a spider was difficult. She refused to stop ranting and threatening to tell their mother. They all had to chip in some money to send her to Be-Bops for ice cream to appease her.

"I told him not to tease her, Stu," Jerry said.

"I thought she would never stop screamin'," Stu said.

"The upside is she probably won't bother us anymore tonight," Jerry said.

"I'm sure she'll hold this incident over my head for weeks to come."

Jerry observed the room. James was sitting on the ground, fiddling with his guitar, and John was lazily strumming his, while Stu fretted about Carly. Finally, he cleared his throat and asked the question that was on everyone's mind.

"So, are we still a group?"

They all looked at John. "Whadda you lookin' at me for?"

"You were pretty upset last night," Jerry said.

"Yeah, sorry about that. The Professor and I had a talk about our communication problems, and I have agreed to be more—approachable."

"Everyone needs to feel like they can express their opinions and concerns without judgment," James said. "That means no more storming out or slamming doors."

Stu folded his arms.

"Can we all agree on that?"

"Yes," Jerry said without hesitation.

"Yes," John said.

"Yes," Stu muttered.

"Perfect. Then I think we can approach the next subject which is the party," James said.

"I think we will be fine playing, 'That Will Be The Day' if you sing. James and I will take the lead. Fair enough?" John said.

James nodded. "Yes."

"All right, we don't have much time left, so we best get busy, boys," John said.

◻◼◻◼◻◼◻◼◻◼◻◼◻◼◻◼◻

After practice, James stayed behind to talk to Stu.

"Do you mind if I hang out for a while?" James said.

"Are you sure you don't have more important things to do?" Stu said.

"Stu, I never said those things. Your mother did."

Stu frowned.

"Sometimes you can be such a pain in the ass, you know that? I have never once thought I was better than you."

"She does," Stu said, mindlessly kicking the coffee table.

James sat on the couch arm and faced Stu. "Your mom just wants you to get a job."

"And that magically is going to make things better?"

"It's a start. At least that way you could work on getting your own place."

"You mean, move out?"

"Yeah."

Stu stretched out and sunk down on the couch cushion. "By myself?"

"You could find a roommate."

"Maybe I could go live with Len."

"Maybe, but I think you should think about finding a place of your own."

Stu knocked the toes of his shoes together. "What am I gonna do? I'm not good at anythin'."

"Have you talked to Len? I heard he's got a job at the market."

"I don't want to stack boxes, stock shelves, and deal with fussy old ladies."

"Okay, then you do something else."

"Like what?"

"There's always work at the mill."

"Yeah, I bust my ass, sweat, and ruin my back? No thanks."

"You could bus tables or wash dishes at Be-Bops."

"My fingers would shrivel up like prunes from bein' in the dishwasher. Then I couldn't play the guitar."

James put his hands up. "You're impossible."

Stu laid his arm over his eyes. "That's what my mom says."

James picked up the flattened throw pillow that sat on the edge of the couch to cover up the hole and threw it at Stu, hitting him in the head.

Without even thinking, Stu picked up his hand ball and threw it at James. James ducked, and the ball ricocheted off the wall and flew across the room and hit a ceramic pink poodle on the other side of the room. For one slow motion moment, the boys watched the doomed poodle fall to the floor and break into a hundred pieces. A few moments later, Stu's mom came down the stairs, her backless shoes slapping against her heels.

"What the hell is going on down here?"

Before Stu could answer, his mother saw the smashed pink pieces on the floor. She walked over to it and picked up poodle's head. Its red chipped tongue sticking out at her.

"You killed Muffy!"

"I...I..." Stu stuttered.

James stood up. "It was my fault, Mrs. Williams. I killed Muffy."

Helen blinked at him, then looked at Stu, then back at James.

"If you want, I can bury her in the backyard," James said as he folded his hands in front of him.

Stu's eyes began to water as he pulled in his cheeks tight and swallowed a laugh.

Helen put her hand on her hip. "You think this is funny?"

"No, Mom. I am just trying to hold back my grief. I know how much she meant to you."

Helen set the dog's head on the shelf it had fallen from; its fake plastic eye fell off onto the floor, bounced, and rolled under the couch.

"Clean up this mess," Helen said. She gave them one last glare before disappearing up the stairs.

Stu looked at the one-eyed poodle head staring at him. "We need to have a funeral, I guess."

James slapped his hand over his mouth.

"I will give the eulogy," Stu said.

James ran as fast as he could into Stu's room, closed the door, and broke into hysterics.

Stu smiled and grabbed a broom.

21

THE BOYS DIDN'T TALK MUCH as they walked the half-mile to Len's party. Their guitars weighed heavy in their sweaty hands as foreboding thoughts of the upcoming event splintered their fretful thoughts.

"My shoes are killing me," Stu said.

"At least your pants don't look like they would fit a ten-year-old," Jerry said.

"You think I like wearing this jacket that is tight on my shoulders?" John said.

They all looked with envy at James, who looked sharp in his fine-pressed clothes.

"What?" James said.

Rounding the corner, they could see the bright lights of the community center chasing away the gloom. Laughter, exclamation, and music surged through the air as cars full of enthusiastic young people flooded the parking lot.

"The place is totally antsville," Stu said.

"Let's go in through the back door," John suggested.

Holding their guitar cases out in front of them like shields, they nudged their way through the crowd. Clusters of guests huddled outside the back door to share a cigarette or a nip from a bottle hidden in a brown paper bag. The girls giggled and leered at them as they stepped inside. The excitement from the energized room knocked them back with an overwhelming punch. Fast dance music was playing, and couples were whirling around the floor. Those who weren't dancing were hunting for tables or socializing in the middle of the aisles, making it difficult to pass them.

"What do we do now?" James asked John.

"Find Len."

"Easier said than done."

"Just stay close."

Halfway across the room, Jerry realized Stu wasn't behind him.

"Where did Stu go?" Jerry said to James.

"I don't know. I thought he was behind you."

"So did I."

"What's wrong?" John said, annoyed.

Jerry scratched his head.

"Apparently, Stu wandered off," James said.

John narrowed his eyes. "He better not be drinkin' beer."

"There's Eddie," James said. "Maybe he knows where Len is."

Eddie was submerged entirely in his element. His flashy black jacket with silver musical notes danced along the light, and his attempt to style his hair resulted in a funky spikey mess.

"Hey, Eddie," James said.

He was oblivious to their presence as his head bobbed, and his snapping fingers didn't miss a beat.

"Hey, banana head," Jerry said.

Eddie whirled around to see them. "Hey, fellas!"

"Hey, Eddie, any idea where Len is?" James said.

"He's around here somewhere."

"Where, somewhere?" John said.

"Huh?"

"Never mind."

"Any idea when we are going on?" James said.

"A little later, after everyone has had a chance to coast in," Eddie said, doing a suave sidestep.

Jerry rolled his eyes.

"Where's the stage?" John said.

"Stage?"

"That's what I said."

"I wouldn't call it a stage, exactly. It's more like a platform."

John shook his head. "Great."

"It's over there," Eddie said, pointing to what looked to be several risers pushed together.

"What are you thinking?" James said to John.

"You don't wanna know."

□■□■□■□■□■□■□■□■□■□■□

Stu was easily distracted and when he laid eyes on all the lovely, glorious girls, his desire to flirt overtook him. It didn't matter if the girl was short, tall, blonde, brunette, brown eyes, or blue, Stu couldn't resist wooing them and making them laugh. He was standing by the refreshment table, drinking a beer and chatting with three girls who looked like Easter eggs in pastel chiffon dresses.

"Hey, Stewy!"

Stu turned to see Len waving at him. Len was unusually tall and bulky with a boisterous deep voice. His thick face was trimmed with a well-groomed beard, and his green eyes always had an irresistible gleam that quickly charmed people.

"Hey, buddy, happy birthday," Stu said, raising his mug.

Len smiled. "Thanks. I see you found the suds."

"And the girls!"

"Oh yeah, there are a lot of lovelies here tonight."

"Yes indeed. I have been conversing with several already."

"So, uh, where is the rest of the group?" Len said.

Stu's eyes widened. "Uhh . . . ."

"What's wrong? Did you forget about them?"

"I didn't forget … exactly."

"Uh-huh," Len said.

"Well, it's not my fault they left me behind. I was right there behind Jerry, and then I wasn't."

"You just couldn't resist the countless temptations that surrounded you."

"Exactly."

"You better hurry up and finish that beer before John finds you."

"Good point."

"I'll catch you later."

"Hey, Len, if you happen to run into him, you won't say anything, right?"

Len shook his head and walked away.

22

THE PARTY WAS IN FULL swing, and it was only a matter of minutes until the live entertainment would be expected to start.

A young man was casually strolling through the crowd toward the makeshift stage. His black hair was combed in a sleek ducktail, and a guitar was slung over the back of his leather jacket. He stood next to James silently for a few moments with his thumbs hooked through the belt loops of his blue jeans.

"Small stage, huh?" he said.

James became aware of the young man standing next to him. "Yes, it is."

"Good thing we don't have an orchestra tryin' to set up here."

James smiled.

"I am guessin' those are risers pushed together?"

"Yeah, I think so."

The young man crouched down to look at them. "I hope they're sturdy enough."

"Me too."

"You know, I've played on some pretty rickety old stages before, but this one looks like if Len stepped on it, it would collapse."

James laughed.

"Nice guitar," the young man said to John. "You guys playing tonight too?"

John ignored him.

"Yeah," James answered.

"Oh, so you must be John."

"No, I'm James."

"I've heard so much about John."

"Really?"

"Yeah, my cousin has told me all about him."

"Who's your cousin?"

"Eddie Bruer."

John started to cough.

"You all right?" the young man asked, sitting next to John.

"Fine."

"So, what songs you guys playin'?"

James put his hands behind his back. "Good question."

"Oh, you're not wantin' to spoil the surprise."

"So, are you here with a band?" James asked.

"Heck no. Right now, I'm solo," he said, swinging his guitar around.

"Ahh, and you are?"

"Name's Daniel. And you are?" he said to John.

"Barnabus."

James pursed his lips.

"Mind if I tune with you?" Daniel said.

John looked at the eager face next to him. "Sure."

"Is this your first time in front of a crowd?" James said.

"Nah, I play around as much as possible, just for fun."

"There you are," Eddie said to Daniel. "I was wondering where you got off to."

"I'm just hangin' out here with James and Barnaby."

"Barnaby?"

"Hey, Eddie, have you seen Stu?" James said.

"No. So, you about ready to start the show, Danny?"

"I was born ready," Danny said, playing a few chords. "What about you guys?"

"As soon as Stu and Jerry come back," James said.

"Which better be soon," John said, his patience running thin.

"Give us a few minutes, hey Eds?" James said.

"Yup," Eddie walked away with the usual bounce in his step.

❑■❑■❑◼❑■❑■◼❑■❑■❑◼❑

Stu knew he needed to reunite with the rest of the group, but he was talking to a cute redhead when he heard his name.

"Hey, Stu."

Stu turned, and when he saw him, the euphoria he was feeling evaporated into thin air.

"Hey, Patrick," Stu said.

Patrick tapped Stu on the arm playfully. "How you been, pal?"

"Good, how about you?"

"I'm doing great."

A forced smile raised the corners of Stu's mouth. "Great."

"Is this your date?" Patrick said.

"Uh, no, we just met."

"Aren't you going to introduce us?"

"Uh . . ." Stu wrinkled his brow because he couldn't remember her name.

She turned up her nose at him.

Patrick extended his hand. "I'm Patrick."

"Bernadette," she said, twisting a strand of hair around her finger.

"Nice to meet you. Maybe we could dance later?"

"Maybe." She turned and walked away, swinging her hips.

"Cute girl," Patrick said.

"Yeah," Stu sighed.

"I was hoping I would see you tonight."

"Really?"

"Yeah. When I saw the flyer, I just knew I had to come to check it out."

"Cool."

Patrick leaned back on the table behind him. "So, I guess the band is doing all right without me?"

"It's definitely been different."

"I thought maybe when I left, the band may fold, but I see I was wrong. Did you guys find a replacement?"

Stu rubbed the back of his neck. "You could say that."

"That's good. I figured it would only be a matter of time."

"So, what are you doin' now?" Stu said, wanting to change the subject.

"Actually, I have an audition next week."

"Oh?"

"Yeah, it's with an established group. They even have a drummer." Stu chuckled.

"They're popular around here and have a strong following. It won't be long before they cut a record."

"Wow, that's great. Look, I should probably find the others, but I wish you the best of luck."

"Stu, I want to apologize for what happened."

"Hey, it's no problem."

"I was a real jerk."

"Nah, forget it."

"I don't want to forget it. We were friends once. It was my idea for you to join the band."

"I don't remember ever saying we couldn't be friends. Whatever happened between you and John doesn't change our friendship."

"Did he tell you what happened?"

"You know he doesn't like to talk about that kind of stuff."

Patrick folded his arms. "I tried to talk to him, you know. Smooth things over, but he wouldn't listen."

"People change."

"So, how is he?"

"Oh, you know, the same."

"Obstinate?"

"Sure," Stu agreed, without a clue what the word even meant.

"Hey, Stu!"

Stu turned to see Jerry.

"Hey Jerry, I wondered where you wandered off to."

"Me? I've been looking all over for you. We better get back, or John is gonna kill us."

"Hey, hold on a minute—look who I found out in the crowd," Stu said, resting his hand on Jerry's shoulder.

"Hey, Jerry," Patrick said.

"Patrick?" Jerry said.

"How are you, brother?"

"Fine, I guess."

"Things getting any better for you at home?"

"Not really."

"You know, sometimes I miss you sleeping on my floor."

"You mean when I slept in the leaky cold clubhouse?"

Patrick didn't respond.

"Patrick tells me he has an audition next week with another group," Stu said.

"Oh, really?"

"Isn't that great?"

"Yeah."

"He says they got a drummer," Stu said.

"Neat," Jerry said.

"If I make it in, you both will have to come to check us out."

"For sure," Stu said.

"We really better get back," Jerry said.

"I'll see you soon, Stu?" Patrick said.

"Yeah, I'll be around."

Jerry pulled on Stu's arm, forcing him to follow.

"Good luck tonight," Patrick said.

"Thanks," Stu said.

23

JERRY AND STU FINALLY JOINED John and James.

"Found him," Jerry said triumphantly.

"Where have you been?" John snapped at Stu.

"Checkin' out the ladies," Stu said.

John stepped closer to Stu. "Were you drinkin'?"

Stu took a step backward. "I may have had one small one to calm my nerves. You should try it."

John's eyes narrowed.

"Hey, why don't you stand by me while Danny plays?" James said, grabbing Stu and pulling him off to the side. "Are you crazy? Drinking before the performance?"

"I only had one small one. Besides, whatever pleasure it gave me is long since gone. I don't think I have ever felt so sober," Stu said.

"What happened?"

"Patrick is what happened."

"He's here?" James said.

"Yep."

James felt his temples. "That's all we need."

"I don't think he is looking for trouble."

"I hope you're right."

"Me too," Stu said.

Len stepped up on the stage and took the mic in his hand. "Good evening, everyone.

I want to thank you all for comin' out tonight to help me celebrate my birthday."

A happy birthday cheer came from the crowd.

"We promised you some live entertainment tonight, and I think we put together a rockin' little show."

More cheers of approval.

"Our first guest comes to us all the way from Ramer. Yes, he is related to Eddie Bruer, but we promise not to hold it against him. Let's give a big warm welcome to Danny Bruer!" Len set the microphone on the stand and stepped off the creaking platform.

Danny stepped up onto the platform, waving at the crowd. "Thanks for the intro, Len! It is a thrill to be here with all you crazy cats and kittens tonight! I say we rock the roof off this joint!"

The crowd cheered loudly as Danny started to play "Blue Suede Shoes." He may have only been a one-man show, but his charisma and exuberance intoxicated the crowd. His voice was strong, and his playing was flawless as his frolicking fingers struck every chord with profound accuracy. His head swung from side to side, causing his hair to fall in curls on his moistened brow. The crowd was on their feet, cheering and dancing.

The boys' spirits deflated as Danny stirred the crowd into a frenzy. It felt like a noose was tightening around their necks. The crowd cheered and clapped when Danny finished the song.

"You're all too kind to me. Thank you so much for making me feel so welcome," Danny said, jumping off the platform.

He walked over to the boys and took off his jacket. He ran his hand over his brow. "Wowee, it's hot."

The crowd's cheers grew louder.

"I think they want you to play another one," James said.

"Really?"

"Danny, Danny, Danny," the crowd started to chant.

"Imagine that," Danny said.

Len came over to them.

"Hey Danny, you mind doing another one?"

"Do you fellas mind?" Danny asked the boys.

"Not at all," James answered for them.

"All right, then."

Danny stepped back onto the platform and played "Be Bop a Lula," driving another spike into the boys' already failing confidence. There was no doubt that Danny would be an impossible act to follow.

Danny finished the song and walked over to the somber group. A huge smile was on his flushed face.

"You guys ready?" Len said to John.

"As ready as we'll ever be."

"Good luck, fellas," Danny said, sitting on the table and resting his feet on the chair.

The boys followed Len onto the platform like mourners going to a funeral.

"Boy, that kid got the crowd fired up for you," Len said.

"We changed the name, Len," James said. "Just call us The Hound Dogs"

"Anything you say. You guys are gonna do great!"

James gave him a half-smile.

Len turned and grabbed the mic. "Wow, that was some performance. That kid is going places!"

Another loud cheer punctuated the point.

"Our next group is local, and they have recently taken on a new member. So please put your hands together for The Hound Dogs!"

James stepped up to the mic. "Thank you, Len. Evening, everyone. Danny's performance got everyone's blood pumping and left us with some amazing energy. Thank you, Danny. We would like to play a number that is a bit more mellow but still snappy. 'That'll Be the Day.'"

The song was a slower tune than the ones Danny played, causing the noise from the crowd to evaporate. Anxiety and nerves threw the tempo off, but James adjusted his singing to make it work. The end of the song couldn't come soon enough, and the claps from the crowd were uninspired.

"Well, we appreciate your listening and hope we can play again for you sometime," James said, wanting to get them off stage as fast as he could, but a few audience members expressed their displeasure.

"Play something fast!"

"Yeah, play some rock-n-roll!"

"Rock-n-roll, rock-n-roll," the audience began to chant.

Fear gripped James as he looked at John. "What do we do now?"

"We give them what they want," John said.

John walked up to the microphone. "Listen to all of you out there. You sound like a pack of hound dogs!"

The crowd cheered.

"You think you want some rock-n-roll, do you?"

Louder enthusiastic cheers came from the crowd.

"How do I know you can handle it?"

They cheered.

"I can't hear you."

A loud, rowdy cheer responded.

Stu smiled at Jerry.

"All right, kiddies, if you want it hard, I'll give it to you!"

"Yay!" the crowd screamed.

"But you all can't sit around and be lazy hound dogs. I expect you to be makin' a whole bunch of noise out there. Can you do that?"

"Yes."

"What?"

"*Yes!*"

"Now, you all know the song 'Hound Dog,' so I expect you to clap, stomp your feet, or bang on anything you can get your grubby hands on! Are you with me?"

"*Yes!*"

"Count us in."

"One-two-three-four!" the crowd yelled in unison.

John howled at the end of the count, and the crowd joined him. The audience had so much fun making random noises that they practically drowned out the band. Then, without warning, as the guitar solo approached, Danny jumped up on the stage next to John and took over the lead. The group was dumbstruck, as Danny impressed the crowd with his playing and improvised dance steps. Even John's stoic expression faded when Danny gave him a playful nudge. His performance was just what the group needed to lift their confidence and the roof.

The rowdy crowd was jumping up and down when the song concluded with a strong confident finish. John smiled at Danny, who applauded him.

"More! More! More!" the crowd cheered.

"Let's do 'Crawlin' Dog,'" Stu said.

"Yeah, come on, John," Jerry said.

"Well . . ."

"You gotta do it, Johnny," Stu said.

"Professor?" John said.

James nodded.

John turned to Danny, who smiled at him.

"All right, you animals," John said. "Let's crawl the dog!"

John started the song, and the rest joined in. Danny added his own unique riff, which changed the entire song's dynamic. John stepped back and let Danny take over the spotlight. He truly was an amazing talent. When the song came to a close, John applauded Danny. Danny bowed to him, and the noise was deafening as the boys left the platform.

Len was there to meet them, shaking his head and clapping. "You guys rocked it!"

"It wouldn't have happened without Danny here," James said.

"Ah, heck, I just wanted to be a part of the fun!"

"It was amazing," John said to him.

"I kept a table over there open for you guys," Len said.

Eddie came over to them, smiling. "Oh, Dan, you are the man!"

"I was only havin' fun."

"You are gonna kill 'em on Thursday, man!"

"What's Thursday?" John said.

"He has an audition with the hottest new group," Eddie said, beaming.

Stu exchanged a glance with Jerry.

"I don't know if I am even gonna go, Eddie," Danny said.

"What? Are you crazy? Tell him, Len," Eddie pleaded.

"It's up to him, Eddie," Len said.

"He's got a shot at the big time!"

"What band are you talkin' about?" Stu said.

"The Dice, bud!" Eddie said.

"Are they that big, Len?" Stu said.

He nodded. "They are pretty smokin'. Word is they might get a record contract."

"See what I mean?" Eddie said.

"I said I would think about it," Danny said, ending the subject.

"Why don't you, gentlemen have a seat, and I will get you some beers?" Len said.

"Thanks, Len," Stu said.

"I am going to help Eddie secure the gear. I will be over soon," James said.

"You mind if I join you?" Danny said to John.

"Not at all."

Danny and John headed toward the table, but Stu set his hand on Jerry's arm.

"Hey, I think I am going to walk around and check out the scenery. You want to come with me?" Stu asked.

"Nah, I'm gonna go ahead and sit with John."

Stu smiled at Jerry, but the minute he was out of sight, his smile faded. True, Danny had saved them from a disaster, but did John have to be nice to him so fast? Stu realized he had nothing to worry about, after all, it was not like it was going to last. Tomorrow things would go back to normal. With that thought in mind, he headed toward the refreshment table.

24

J AMES WAS PUTTING HIS GUITAR in its case when he felt a gentle
tap on his shoulder.

"Hey, pop star."

James turned to see Marcy. Her hair was pulled away from her
face with a colorful headband that complimented her red polka dot
dress.

"Marcy," he said with a big smile. "I didn't expect to see you
here."

"I didn't know accountants moonlighted as pop stars."

"I don't know if I would go that far."

"You guys were great."

"Danny was great," James said.

"He does have something special, that's for sure."

"So, are you here with someone?"

"No, just some girlfriends."

"Oh," he said.

"Want to get something to drink? I am sure you're thirsty."

"I am, actually. Let me finish up here first."

"I got it," Eddie said.

"You sure?"

"Yeah."

"Well, come on, then," Marcy said.

The two walked over to the refreshment table and got some punch.

"Are you disappointed it isn't coffee?" Marcy asked.

He laughed. "No, I like the change."

"So, how have you been? I haven't seen you at the shop lately," she said, sipping her punch.

"I've been busy with school and the band. I hardly have a moment to myself anymore. However, I did finish the book you lent me."

"And?"

James nodded. "I liked it."

"I knew you would," she said, moving her hips so that her taffeta made a swishing noise. "I like this song."

"Me too," he said, watching the couples on the floor.

Marcy stood closer to him, and he gave her a clueless smile.

"So, are you gonna ask me to dance or what?" she said.

James shifted his weight. "I'm not very good at it."

"I don't believe you."

"You will when I step on your toes."

"If you step on my toes, you might have to carry me home."

She gently took James's hand and led him onto the crowded dance floor.

She turned to him. "Now, don't think about it too much. Just move with the music."

"That's easy for you to say."

"Don't look at your feet. Look at me."

He looked at her delicate features that were complimented by a faint touch of makeup, and her hair fell in lovely waves under her ears.

She started with a two-step, then adding some sway to the step, she turned into his arm before twirling back out. When she was sure he was comfortable, she let go of his left hand, spun out to the side, and came back. It was so easy to be with her that any anxiety or inadequacy he felt had left him.

"Wow," she said. "Not only can accountants play guitars, but they can dance too!"

He laughed. "I was only following you."

She took his hands. "I didn't wear you out, did I?"

"Not yet."

"Umm, I will have to try harder."

A slow song came on, and their hands were still intertwined.

"This song is more my speed," he said.

"Does that mean you don't need me to lead?"

"Yeah, I think I got this one," he said, placing his arm around her middle.

Her smile shrunk, and a hint of pink filled her cheeks. She rested her hand on his shoulder as he took the other one firmly in his hand. His movements were smooth, and her feet floated as they danced around the crowded floor. When the song finished, another fast one started, and James pulled his arms away.

"My, it's warm, isn't it?" Marcy said, fanning her face with her hand.

"Are you saying I wore you out?" James said.

"Never, but I think we should take a break. Would you mind if we sat down with my friends?"

"I don't mind."

She took his hand, and they walked toward her table.

"Well, there you are, James."

James turned to see Stu. "We thought you left us."

"I confess, I kind of abducted him," Marcy said, holding onto James's arm. "He has been whirling me across the dance floor."

"I have had a hard time keeping up with her."

"I bet you did," Stu said.

"We were just taking a break. Why don't you join us?" Marcy said.

"I wouldn't want to impose."

"Oh no, not at all. I think my friends would love to meet you."

"I would love to meet your friends," Stu said.

Stu walked with Marcy and James over to the table where her friends were engaged in lighthearted conversation and drinking punch.

"Hey girls, do you mind if these gentlemen join us?" Marcy said.

"No," they agreed.

"This is James, and this is Stu."

Each girl politely said hello, but the fair-haired, slender young woman with striking blue eyes and a flirty smile was what caught Stu's attention.

"This is Mollie." Marcy pointed to a reserved, thin young woman with brunette hair pulled away from her face by a plain white headband. Her high cheekbones accented her slim nose, and her round brown eyes were like shiny buttons. She wore hardly any makeup and a plain yellow dress.

"Mae," Marcy said, sensing Stu's attraction to her, but most men were attracted to Mae because she resembled a fashion model. Her hair was always perfectly styled, and her makeup was thicker than the others. Her dresses were always a couple of inches shorter than was fashionable because she wanted to draw attention away from her small breast size.

"And Doris." Doris was a pleasant young woman who struggled with a few extra pounds. Her petite nose was set between her plump cheeks, and her brown hair was teased into a stiff bouffant.

The girls moved over so that James could sit between Marcy and Mollie, and Stu sat between Doris and Mae.

"Thanks for making room for me, ladies," Stu said.

Mae smiled. "No problem."

"Hey, weren't you both playing in the band?" Mollie said.

"Why yes, we were," Stu said.

Doris giggled. "Can you believe it, girls? We are sitting with celebrities."

Stu smiled at James.

"You girls liked the show?" Stu asked.

"Oh yeah, Danny is very handsome," Mollie said, a light blush on her cheeks.

"Well, he isn't exactly a member of our band," Stu said.

"Well, he should be!" Doris said.

"Hey, Stu, do you think you could introduce us?" Mollie said.

"Oh, that would be a dream," Doris said.

"Sure, I could. Come over, and I will introduce you to the rest of the group."

"You guys are coming?" Mollie asked Marcy.

"Do you want to, James?" Marcy asked James.

"Yeah, sure."

Mollie latched herself onto James's left arm while Marcy held on to his right.

Danny, John, and Jerry sat at the table Len had set aside for them. Jerry was bored because Danny was occupying John's attention.

"Hey guys," Stu said. "Look at what I brought, lovely ladies who are dying to meet you. You don't mind if we join you?"

"Of course not. Let me pull out a chair for you," Danny said, pulling out a chair that Mollie slipped in before Doris could.

Mae sat on the other side of Mollie, and Stu made sure he was beside her.

James sat down next to Jerry. "How's it going, Jer?"

"Okay."

"Not having a good time?"

He shrugged.

"Why don't you ask a girl to dance?"

"Oh, no, I couldn't do that."

"Why not?"

"He's too shy," John said. "I have been tryin' to get him to dance, but he won't hear of it."

"Since there are so many of us here," Stu said, "we should all go around the table and introduce ourselves. Fair enough?"

Everyone agreed and went around the table, sharing their names, until they reached John, who seemed hesitant.

"His name is Barnaby," Danny said. "He is a bit shy with the ladies."

John hung his head down and pulled his shoulders up.

"Of course, you all know who I am, and if you don't, you weren't paying attention."

"When we told Stu that we wanted to meet you, he invited us over straight away," Mollie said.

"Yeah, you were dynamite up there," Doris said. "You should be making records."

"Maybe someday."

"Would you like to dance with me?" Mollie asked Danny.

"Sure, why not?"

Doris crossed her arms tightly across her chest, and her pinched expression made her cheeks puff out.

"Why don't you go get me another beer?" John said to Jerry.

"Because he is going to dance with me," Marcy said, standing. "That is if you want to?"

Jerry looked at John.

"Don't look at me."

"Okay."

James smiled at Marcy as she went to the floor with Jerry.

"Why don't you ask Doris to dance?" Mae whispered to Stu.

"Who me?"

"I think she's jealous because Mollie is dancing with Danny."

Stu didn't want to leave Mae alone at the table with John. She was so beautiful, and John could be very charming if he put his mind to it. At the moment, John seemed contented talking to James, but Stu was afraid once his back was turned, John's interest would shift, and Mae would be under his spell in a matter of moments.

"Please, for me?" Mae said, resting her hand on Stu's. Her big blue eyes vexed him.

"Okay, but you must promise to dance with me next."

"Of course, I will."

"Doris, I know I ain't Danny, but would you like to dance with me?" Stu said.

"Sure," she said with an eager smile.

Stu smiled, reluctantly pulled himself to his feet, and went to the dance floor with Doris.

"I need a mug, Professor," John said.

"Okay," James said, not moving.

John stared at James.

"I am not the barmaid," James said. "You are more than capable of getting one yourself."

John continued to stare at him.

"You're insufferable, you know that?" James said.

"I can go get you one," Mae said.

John looked at her. He hadn't noticed her until now. Her delicate, soft features were appealing, but her dense makeup obscured his vision.

He smiled. "I would be oh so grateful."

She took the mug from him, her fingers gently trailing over his. He watched her walk away, her lovely form swaying.

"You look like you're about to start drooling," James said.

"Is it a crime to look at a beautiful girl?"

"I think you have more on your mind than just her beauty."

"What do you think about when you see a beautiful girl?"

"Her confidence and strength as a fine example of femininity."

John laughed. "Who are you kidding?"

"I'm being serious."

"Uh-huh."

"So, it went fairly well tonight, don't you think?" James asked.

"We got lucky," John said dryly.

"Have you thought about what's next?"

"All I want to think about tonight is drinking a beer and forgetting all this nonsense. I suggest you do the same."

Mae came back and set a mug in front of John. "Do you mind if I sit here?"

"I do not," he said, taking a drink.

"So, how long have you been playing guitar, Barnaby?" Mae said, sitting next to him.

"Oh, since I was but a wee lad sittin' on my pappy's knee."

James shook his head.

"I just love how you took control of the crowd."

"Yeah, well, I am a take-charge kind of guy."

"I can tell," she said, batting her lashes over the top of her mug.

James wasn't sure how much more he could take.

"So, do you dance?" Mae asked.

"Not tonight."

"Why not?"

"Don't feel like it, I guess."

She touched the sleeve of his jacket. "What do you feel like?"

"Drinking this beer."

Marcy and Jerry returned to the table. Jerry frowned at his taken seat.

Marcy sat by James and took his hand.

"It was nice of you to dance with Jerry," James said.

"He is a sweet boy. Are you thinking about leaving soon?"

"You've had enough dancing?"

"I was thinking a walk in the cool evening air might be nice."

"I agree. Hey, John, I will take off if that's okay."

"Go in peace, my son," John said.

James picked up his guitar from the front and left with Marcy, holding hands.

Danny and Mollie returned, and Jerry sat in the chair next to John. Stu returned with Doris and was unhappy to see Mae sitting by John.

"Did James leave?" Stu asked.

"Yeah, with Marcy," Jerry said.

Stu sulked in his chair as he watched Mae flirting with John.

"You could ask her to dance instead of sittin' here fumin'," Jerry said.

Straightening his tie, Stu ran a hand over his messy hair and walked to Mae. "May I have this dance?"

Mae looked at John, who appeared indifferent.

"Yes," she said, taking Stu's hand and following him onto the floor.

John sat his mug down. "I am done here for the evening."

"Can I walk with you, John?" Jerry said.

"Of course, my boy."

Jerry smiled as he followed him to the stage.

"Hey, Barnaby," Danny said, following them. "I was wonderin' if you would go with me to my audition on Thursday."

"Me?"

"Yeah, I could use the support."

"What about Eddie?"

"Eddie is my cousin, but he doesn't understand music like he thinks. Besides, I would like your opinion."

"Well, all right, then."

Danny smiled. "Great."

"By the way, my name isn't Barnaby."

"It is now."

John couldn't help but smile as Danny walked away.

25

HOLDING HANDS, JAMES AND MARCY walked in the crisp night air. The noise from the party had faded, and the only sound was an occasional passing car.

"It's a beautiful night, isn't it?" Marcy said.

"Yes, and quiet," James said.

"The quiet is nice."

"So, do you want to go somewhere and have coffee or ice cream?"

"I thought maybe we could go to my place. It's small but quiet, and we could have a cup of tea or coffee."

"Okay."

Marcy lived at the Morrisey Boarding House on Grant Street. Historically, the large two-story house had been the governor's home, but when a larger house was built, it was converted into a boarding house. The house's large wrap-around porch and ornate gables gave it a distinct character. Two large Magnolia trees were in full bloom, filling the air with a hint of champagne.

James sat his guitar in the front parlor and followed Marcy into the empty large first-floor kitchen, where he sat at the table while she put a teakettle on the stove.

"How many people live here?" James asked.

"Right now, there are four of us. There were five, but the gentleman that lived in the room at the far end of the hall moved out a couple of months ago," she said, sitting across from him. "It's a good group. Everyone is courteous and keeps to themselves. Ms. Moore is a very nice landlady as long as you clean up after yourself and pay the rent on time. Where do you live?"

"I'm currently living with my dad and brother. I was going to live on campus this year, but things just didn't work out that way."

The tea kettle began to whistle, and Marcy got up.

"Besides, my dad needs me."

Marcy took two cups out of the cupboard. "Where is your mom?"

James hesitated. "My mother passed away last fall."

"Oh, James, I am so sorry. I had no idea."

"It's all right. There is no way you could have known."

Marcy brought over the tea and sat down, serving James.

"My dad has just taken it extra hard, and he's withdrawn, so he needs me to help around the house."

"How old is your brother?"

"Sixteen. He will be seventeen in about a month, then he will probably go to college and lead his own life."

"Maybe then you can move out?"

"Maybe," he said, taking a drink.

"So, when do you graduate?"

"Next year, if I can make it that long."

"Why wouldn't you?"

"I have been neglecting my responsibilities lately."

"Because you joined the band?"

"Yeah. I don't even know where that's going."

"You just need to live life one day at a time and take it as it comes."

"What about you?" he said, crossing his legs.

"I want to go back to school. I just don't know if it will work out," Marcy said, fidgeting with the handle on the teacup.

"Why wouldn't it?"

"You could say my financial situation changed."

"Oh?"

"Yeah."

"You don't have to tell me about it. That is your business."

"You're such a kind person."

He smiled shyly.

"Would you like some more tea?"

He looked at his watch. "I didn't realize it was so late. I should try to get some sleep before I have to try to cram a week of studying into one afternoon."

"I understand," she said.

"You know I would love to take you out some time on a real date."

"I would like that."

"Next Friday, then?"

"Yeah."

"I will pick you up here at, say, seven?"

"Okay."

She walked him to the door.

"I am glad we ran into each other tonight," she said.

"Me too."

"Here, don't forget your guitar," she said, picking it up and handing it to him.

"Oh, right."

His hand touched hers gently as she handed it to him. Their eyes met, and the pink hue of her lips tempted him, but he was resolved to remain a gentleman. "I will see you soon?"

"Probably around eleven on Monday morning?"

"Am I that predictable?" he said

"Let's just say I know what time my favorite customers come in."

He smiled.

She opened the door for him. "Goodnight."

"Night," he said, stepping outside. He walked down with a bounce in his step and whistled a tune.

John was reclining on his bed, wishing it was raining. The tapping droplets would lull him to sleep other than the constant sound of his mind's unquieted chaos. He got up, reached inside the pocket of his discarded jacket, and pulled out the small pink book. Holding it gently in his hand, his fingers felt the soft leather cover that carried all the secrets of a young girl's heart. He laid back on the bed, the faint scent of her perfume calming his mind. A tiny gold heart-shaped lock swung from the latch on the side. A file, needle, or pencil in his skilled hands would expose the naked thoughts to his eyes. He smiled as he thought each entry must be sweet and innocent. Stories filled with happiness, sadness, and love. He didn't want to spoil the mystery. He would rather dream about it instead. Setting the small book on his nightstand, he turned out the light.

PART 2

26

I F ONLY THE TAXI COULD fly over the mid-afternoon traffic that jammed the city streets, Carlton's worries would be over, and his stomach wouldn't be burning like a fall bonfire.

By the time he arrived at the club, Joe would be madder than a caged lion. Carlton fumbled through his briefcase, looking for his medication. Beads of perspiration dripped onto the crumpled mess of papers. His doctor had warned him many times about his failing health. *"You need to lower your stress level, Carlton, or you're going to have a heart attack and a stomach with more holes than a golf course."*

Finding the bottle, he swallowed two small pills and then shoved the bottle back into the case.

Why on earth had he signed Joe Delaney as a client? He knew Joe had a reputation for being difficult and demanding. No matter what Carlton did, it would never be good enough. If only his business were stable. If only his wife hadn't put them in debt. If only Joe hadn't offered him more money than he could make signing four regular clients.

The taxi pulled up in front of the Cornby Club and dropped Carlton off. Carlton didn't like the overpriced elite club. He presumed the aristocrats judged him every time he walked through the door.

He glanced at his faded blue tie and cursed under his breath. A vivid yellow mustard blot stood out like a pimple on a young girl's face.

The thin hostess approached him like a sidewinder in a snug black dress. Her matte-painted face held no expression as she greeted him, but he could tell by her eyes that she was unimpressed with his appearance.

"May I help you?"

"Yes, I am here to meet with Joe Delaney."

She raised an eyebrow.

"He is expecting me."

"This way."

He followed the hostess's backless, low plunging dress into the elegant bright main dining room. White linen-covered tables on a lush, dark red carpet spread across the floor like a crimson river. A man dressed in a tuxedo played a listless tune on the piano that the diners ignored.

Joe Delaney was sitting at a table, sipping a gin and tonic. His sandy blond hair was already thinning at twenty-five, and his waistline carried some extra weight, but his narcissistic persona refused to let these minor imperfections define him. From his dark blue tailored suit to his stylish Italian boots, every detail was polished and refined.

Joe Delaney was the leader of the latest hot group named The Dice. Joe formed the group with his friend Will Morris in college. Both boys were eager and talented, but Joe had a natural gift for playing music. He started to learn to play the piano when he was young, and by the time he was twelve, he impressed teachers and other influential people at his recitals. His parents and mentors were confident Joe would become a concert pianist, but when some of his friends began to listen to rock-n-roll, his interest turned to learning the guitar. A few months later, Joe had mastered the guitar and formed a band with Will. His parents had hoped that it was just a passing fancy, and he soon would come to his senses and return to the piano, but he was lost to them. Joe loved the loud, enthusiastic crowd, and all the girls that idolized him. Rock-n-Roll had romanced him, and he would never be the same.

"Hey, Joe, hope you haven't been waiting long," Carlton said when he arrived at the table.

"Anytime I have to wait is too long," Joe said.

"I tried to leave the office on time, but some last-minute problem presented itself."

"Punctuality is important to clients. If you promise to meet them at a certain time, that is the priority, and other problems can wait unless your dog dies. Did your dog die, Carlton?"

"I don't have a dog."

Joe took the last drink from his glass, causing the ice cubes to clink against the sides.

"Did you look over the menu?" Carlton said.

"I'm not hungry."

A cocktail waitress came to the table with another drink for Joe before he set his glass down. "You want your usual, Carl?"

"Yeah, and be quick about it, doll."

She nodded and walked away. Her dress was short and flared out at the back like swan feathers.

"I swear those skirts get shorter every time I come here," Carlton said.

Joe stirred his drink with the swizzle stick. "What news do you have for me, Carlton?"

"You will be glad to know the auditions are set for Thursday. I think we had some decent applicants this time. Are you interested in seeing the applications?"

Joe waved his hand in the air.

"I should warn you, some candidates may be a little green, but we aren't exactly in New York or Cleveland. I promise to do whatever it takes to ensure they are up to your standards."

"You understand that will be coming out of your pocket, not mine."

"Of course, anything to make you happy, Joe."

"What will make me happy is when I have a record contract in my hand."

"I know," Carlton said, nodding his head. "I am on it, believe me."

"Do you know why I have fired my last three managers, Carlton?"

Carlton shifted his weight on the unforgiving chair.

"It's because they couldn't produce the results that I wanted. Do you remember telling me when I hired you that you were a results man?"

"I do."

Joe stared at him, causing more sweat to form on Carlton's brow.

"You better hope the auditions go well, Carlton, otherwise, you will be looking for a new client sooner rather than later."

Carlton's smile faltered.

Joe stood up.

"I'll see you Thursday, then?" Carlton said.

Joe buttoned his suit jacket and put on his shades. He casually threw a hundred-dollar bill on the table and left.

Carlton took a deep breath and then drank from his water glass. Tiny droplets of condensed water cooled his fingertips.

The waitress returned with Carlton's drink and sat it on the table.

"Did Mr. Delaney leave?"

"Yeah."

She picked up the bill with a smile and stuck it between her cleavage. "Can I bring you anything else?"

"Yeah, you can bring me another one of these," Carlton said, lifting his glass in the air. "And make it a double."

27

HER PERSISTENT CLACKING SHOES PURSUED John down the hall
after class. He was taking his time meandering through a maze
of several long hallways before heading toward the front doors
on the first floor. She had spotted her diary sticking out of his jacket
pocket when he walked into class. She was too reserved to confront
him during class, but now she mirrored his every move from six paces
behind.

He walked out of the building and headed toward the park.

"Hey, you!" she called out to him, but he ignored her and kept
walking.

She ran to catch up with him. "Hey."

He finally stopped. "Are you addressing me?"

"Yes," she hissed at him. "Give me my book back!"

"Book? What book?"

"You know very well what book!"

"No, I'm afraid I don't."

"It's my diary," she said, squinting her eyes.

John folded his arms. "Your diary? Hmm...I don't remember
having a diary."

"I know you have it because I saw you with it!"

"Are you sure?"

"Yes, now hand it over!" She extended her eager hand to him.

"Wait a second now, not so fast. Can you describe it?"

"It's pink."

"Pink?" John pressed his finger to his chin. "What size is it?"

"It's small."

"How small?"

"The size of a paperback."

"Oh." He nodded his head, stoking her fury. "Tell me more."

She sighed. "It says *My Diary* in gold letters on the front cover."

"Gold letters must be important."

Her anger was making her body sway slightly from side to side.

"How do I know it's yours? After all, I did find it lying on the ground. It could belong to anyone."

"It's mine, and you know it!"

"Okay, then tell me what the entry on March 22nd says."

She gave him a blank look. "March 22nd?"

"Yes, you tell me what it says, then I will know it's yours."

Red tendrils of frustration crept up her neck as her mind scrambled for an answer.

He placed his hands behind his back. "I can tell you what it said. Let me see, oh yes. It was late when I got home from my date. The thought of being caught by my parents filled me with anxiety. I ran to my room and closed the door. My heart was fluttering like a hundred butterflies. The heat of his touch when he pulled me closer still lingered on my quivering body."

John took a silent step closer.

"My mouth was dry as I anticipated the moment I had waited for so long to come. His dark lust-filled eyes stripped away my inhibition as he slipped his strong arm about my middle." John placed his arm around her and looked into her dazed eyes.

"He was so close to me. How could I breathe?"

He could feel her breath getting shorter.

"Was he going to? Was he going to leave me wanting his kiss?"

John leaned in, and her eyes fluttered.

"That is the correct entry, isn't it?" he said.

Abruptly, her eyes flew open, breaking the spell. She pushed John away as he started to laugh.

"You are a mean, hateful person!" she spat; her face flushed

He pulled her diary out of his pocket and handed it to her. She snatched it from him and held it protectively to her chest.

He took a step backward. "I must admit, I did enjoy the entries you wrote about me."

"I would never write about you!"

"No, but you will," he said with a smirk.

"You'll pay for this!"

"Is that a promise?"

She flashed one more hateful look at him before walking away. His laughter followed her down the path.

28

JOHN STROLLED THROUGH THE PARK, jumping up occasionally to touch a tree branch. His thoughts were still on the blonde from class. Her creased brow, scornful eyes, and pouty lips meant to display her displeasure, had only made her more appealing. He began to whistle as he stuck his hands in his jacket pockets.

He wasn't ready to go home, but there wasn't anything else to do except maybe go bug Jerry. He looked across the park to see James immersed in the book he was reading. A mischievous grin spread across his lips.

"What's shakin', Professor?" John said, tapping James on his back, causing him to whirl around with a frightened cartoonish expression. Grabbing James's apple off the table, he stepped onto the bench, walked across the table, jumped down, and then sat on the opposite bench with a smile.

"I guess you know you scared me half to death!"

"Yeah, but I didn't," he said, taking a large bite out of the apple. "Do you ever read anything other than boring accounting books?"

James slammed his book shut. "I do."

John noticed that James's fingers were still stuck in the book, and he was holding it tightly.

"So, uh, what you got there?"

"Nothin'," James said, closing his lips into a tight smile.

"Come on, what are you looking at?"

"Accounting."

John smiled. "Who is it? Miss March?"

"No, no, no. Nothing like that."

"You know I'm going to find out," John said, twirling the half-eaten apple in his hand.

"It's just a novel."

"Let me see it," John said, holding out his hand.

"You're nosier than an old lady."

John smiled, taking a bite out of the apple.

James sighed and opened his book. "Don't lose my place."

James handed him the book.

"*One Lonely Night*. James, you dog," John said with a sly smile.

"It's not like that," James said, grabbing the book from John.

"You know you're allowed to read about something other than finance," John said, lying back on the bench.

"What are you doing on this side of the park?"

John shrugged. "I'm bored."

"Don't you ever study?"

"Sure, I do."

"When?"

"When I'm sleeping," he said, placing his arm under his head.

James shook his head. "I don't see how you pass your classes."

"Neither do I."

John looked to his right to see Danny coming up the path.

"Well, I'll be doggone," John said.

"What is it?"

"It's not an 'it'—it's Danny."

Danny walked up to the table.

"Hey, fellas."

"Hey, Danny. What are you doing in the park?" James said.

"Looking for Barnaby."

"How did you know where to find me?" John said, sitting up.

"Eddie said he thought you might be goofin' around in the park," Danny said, sitting cross-legged on the table. "What are you doin', James?"

"He's reading a tawdry novel," John said.

"Really?" Danny said.

"No, it's Mickey Spillane," James said.

"Oh, cool."

"So, what's up, Danny boy?" John said.

"I thought we could go to Be-Bops, drink milkshakes, and maybe spin some platters," Danny said.

"Sounds good to me," John said.

"You want to join us, James?" Danny asked.

"Oh, I don't think I can," James said.

"Why not?"

"Because I need to finish my assignment for tomorrow."

"What are you studyin'?" Danny asked.

"Finance," James said.

"Why?"

"It's a steady living."

"Yeah, but what a bore," Danny said, resting his arm on his knee. "I wouldn't want to sit cooped up in an office all day, that is for darn sure."

"What do you want to do?" James said.

"What do you think?"

"Be a vagabond?" John said.

"No, I am gonna be a rock-n-roll star."

"Really?" James said.

"Yeah, Danny is gonna have his mug in the teen magazines so the girls can swoon over him," John said, batting his eyes.

"Is that so bad?"

"I guess not if you like that sort of thing," John said.

"What? You don't like girls swooning over you?"

"Not if they're still in pigtails."

"Good point. While we're on the subject of girls swoonin', how did it go the other night with Marcy?" Danny asked James.

"Marcy?" John said.

"You know Marcy, the girl he was with at Len's party?"

"Oh yeah, I only remember the blonde."

"That is because she was flirting with you," James said.

"Oh yeah," John said, returning to his reclined position.

"You didn't like her?" Danny said.

John put his arm over his eyes. "She was all right, I guess."

"What? She was pretty and really into you."

"I thought we were talking about Marcy."

"So, how did it go, Professor?" Danny said.

"Good," James said, not wanting to give any details.

"He wants to know if you kissed her," John said.

James looked at Danny, who had a grin on his face.

"No, I didn't kiss her."

"Why not?"

"Because it's not proper to kiss a lady on the first date."

"Woo, Barnaby, she is a lady. Sounds serious."

"Indeed, it does."

"Are you seeing her again?"

"Maybe."

"Come on, Professor, we need details," Danny said.

"If you two really must know, I am taking her out this Friday."

"That a boy, Professor," Danny said, patting James on the arm.

"Where are you goin'?" John said.

"I don't know yet."

"You want my advice?"

"No!"

John sat up. "Come on, Danny, let's leave the Professor to his studies."

Danny jumped off the table.

"We will talk soon, hey John?" James said.

"Sure, you know where to find me."

"Good luck on your date, Professor," Danny said.

"Thank you."

"Remember, we want the details."

James watched John and Danny walk away, engaging in playful banter. Part of him wanted to join them, to forget about responsibility just once. James turned to his accounting book, but his eyes fell on the novel lying next to it. His thoughts turned to Marcy and how pretty she looked in her party dress, her soft, warm hand in his. It would be useless to try to return to his studies. So, he packed up his books and went home.

29

THE BEAUMONT WAS THE NUMBER one nightclub in Madison to dance and see a live show. Its large vertical neon sign spelled Beaumont, one bold red letter at a time, as three rows of smaller golden lights zipped around its borders. Frank Sinatra was the only famous person to perform at the Beaumont at the start of his career. A large autographed portrait of him hung in the front lobby as a reminder of his momentous show. Joe Delany's personal goal was that someday his portrait would replace Frank's.

A group of young men with guitars and ducktails were beginning to form on the front steps of the Beaumont. A young woman with glasses and a clipboard stood in front of the entrance, checking in the hopeful candidates eager to become the next member of The Dice.

Danny's confidence began to shrink as he looked at the ornate intimidating building and the crowd in front of it.

"Boy, I don't know about this," Danny said.

"You gettin' cold feet?" John said.

"Well, look at, um', they're all dressed to the nines. I didn't know there was a dress code."

"If all they are interested in is your clothes, you don't want to play with um, anyway."

"What do you think I should do?"

"I think you should go in there and knock um dead. Then tell um they're all a bunch of squares, and you don't want to play with um, anyway."

Danny laughed. "I could do that."

Danny and John walked up to the door. The young woman looked at them over her large, round glasses. "Name?"

"Danny Bruer."

She looked through the checklist and checked off his name. "You'll be number fifteen. And you are?" she said to John.

"I'm his agent," John said, pulling his shades out of his jacket pocket and putting them on.

She made a clicking noise with her tongue and made a note on the paper. "You can go in and have a seat. They will call your number when they are ready for you."

"Thank you, ma'am," Danny said.

They walked into the main event room of the club, where the stage was. Young anxious contestants were sitting on stools, leaning up against the wall, or sitting at the tables. Sounds of different guitar chords cluttered the atmosphere as participants tuned their instruments.

John and Danny stood near the back, not far from the bar. "You ever been to an audition like this before?" Danny asked John.

"Nope."

The room continued to fill up, and anticipation began to build as everyone waited for the auditions to begin. John saw Patrick walk in, adjusting his thin blue tie. Thankful for his shades, John pulled up the collar on his jacket and hoped Patrick wouldn't recognize him.

Carlton and Joe entered the room from the stage entrance. Joe walked in wearing an expensive tailor-made navy-blue suit. Without acknowledging his surroundings, he walked in front of the awe-struck crowd, adjusting his cuffs. He sat down at a table in front of the stage.

Carlton walked onto the stage and held up his hand to shade his eyes from the glaring spotlight.

"Hello, everyone. My name is Carlton Gates. I am the manager of The Dice. We would like to thank you all for coming in today, and we will do our best to make this process as painless as possible. When we call your number, you just need to come up on stage and tell us your number, name, and what song you will be playing. After you have played your song, you are free to leave, and if we're interested in pursuing an interview, we will call you. Okay?"

"Do we get free booze?" someone yelled from the audience.

Everyone laughed.

"Ha-ha, very funny," Carlton said. "Okay, let's start with number one."

The long, tedious process of finding a new member for The Dice had begun. One by one, young men took the stage. Some were nervous, some were cocky, some were offbeat, and some attempted to compensate for their lack of talent by gyrating or bobbing their heads. Much to everyone's relief, a break was called after number ten.

"Who do you think that is sitting next to the manager?" John asked Danny.

"Dunno."

"He's someone important."

"A member of the band, maybe?"

"He thinks he's better than everyone else," John said, folding his arms.

"Judging by that suit he has on, he probably is. Whadda, you think of the talent so far?"

"All I can say is, you have them all beat hands down, Danny boy."

Danny gave him a half-smile.

John noticed Patrick was looking over at them.

"Oh no," John said, wanting to crawl under one of the tables.

"What's wrong?" Danny said.

"I see someone I don't want to talk to."

"Which one?"

"That guy over there," John said, nodding toward Patrick.

"The one that is coming over here?"

"Great."

Patrick walked up to them with a smooth smile. "Hey, John, is that you?"

John smirked at him.

"Well, what do you know? I didn't expect to see you here. Nice shades."

John didn't respond to him.

"Are you auditioning too?" Patrick said.

"No, not me," John said.

"Oh, so why are you here?"

"None of your business, actually."

Patrick chuckled. "So, it's like that, huh?"

John was not about to start a conversation with Patrick.

"You know, I saw you guys play the other night at Len's party, and I thought you all did a fair job, considering."

John kept his mouth in a tight line. Danny looked at him sideways.

"So, are you a new member of The Hound Dogs?" Patrick said to Danny.

"Maybe," Danny said, leaning up against the wall and trying to be cool.

"You were amazing," Patrick said.

"Thank you."

Patrick looked at John again. "I guess I should have known it would be too much for you to be civil to me."

John didn't say anything.

"See you around," Patrick said, walking across the room.

"Who was that?" Danny asked John.

"No one," John said.

The auditions were about to resume when a tall young woman walked in. The entire room fell silent, and all the eyes were fixated on her. Her lithe figure walked effortlessly across the room as her long blonde hair swayed gently behind. A wide-brimmed hat and rhinestone-studded cat's eye sunglasses enhanced her mystery. She sat next to the man in the dark suit and kissed him. An audible groan of disappointment at her dating status was expressed by the group.

Danny resembled a pubescent boy seeing a woman for the first time.

"Hey, Dan, you okay?" John said.

"Uh-huh," he managed to stutter.

John snapped his fingers in front of Danny's face. "Snap out of it."

Dan looked at him through his infatuated stupor. "Did you see her?"

"Yes, I saw her," John said, disinterested.

"She's a goddess."

John rolled his eyes.

"What? You don't think so?"

"Girls like that are after only one thing… money, and by the looks of things, she got what she wanted."

"Number thirteen," Carlton called out.

Patrick walked up onto the stage. Now John had two reasons to be thoroughly irritated.

"Hello," he said. "I am number thirteen."

"How appropriate," John said.

"My name is Patrick McNeil, and I will sing a song I wrote with a friend called 'Walkin' with Baby.'"

John's hands rolled up into rigid fists, and it was all he could do to control his seething temper. If he could have, he would have walked up on stage and busted Patrick's guitar into a million pieces as each note of the song tore at the fabric of his patience.

At the song's end, Patrick strolled off stage, giving one of the better performances anyone had seen all afternoon. He glanced over at John as he walked out of the club. John wanted to follow him and unload his rage on him in the alley, but he kept it together and turned his attention back to Danny, who was still moonstruck. John stood in front of Danny and took off his shades.

"You need to pull it together. You need to pull your mind out of her panties and focus on what you came here to do. You can play circles around any of these jokers we have seen this afternoon. Don't you dare mess this up because you are thinkin' about somethin' you can't have."

Danny felt the back of his neck. "Yeah, yeah."

Number fourteen's audition gave Danny enough time to refocus his attention on what he did best: play rock-n-roll.

"Number fifteen."

"Knock um dead," John said.

Danny walked up on stage with his usual sway.

"I am number fifteen. My name is Danny Bruer, and I will play a song I first heard the other night called 'Crawlin' Dog.'"

John's anger was soon swept away when Danny started to play. He played the song perfectly, his added flare captivating the remaining candidates, and Joe watched Danny with great interest. When Danny finished the song, the other candidates clapped. Danny exited the stage, smiling at the blonde.

⬛⬜⬛⬜⬛⬜⬛⬜⬛⬜⬛⬜⬛⬜⬛⬜⬛⬜

Danny and John left the audition laughing.

"Danny, my boy, you kicked everyone's ass!" John said, setting his hand on Danny's shoulder. "You are the only one that asshole paid attention to."

"Really, Barney?"

"Yes, sir. I am so impressed I will let you buy me a beer tonight!"

Danny smiled, but John could tell that, for some reason, he didn't seem very excited.

"What's wrong, Danny? You don't look like a guy who just gave the best audition of his life."

Danny shrugged. "I dunno, guess I am just not sure this is what I want."

"Really?"

"I've always been solo and played for fun, you know?"

John chuckled. "I do know."

"I just don't know if I am ready to join a band," Danny said, sitting on the short stone wall that divided the grassy slope from the sidewalk.

"Who says you have to?"

"No one."

"Well?" John said, leaning up against the wall.

"It's just that I have a better chance of making it into the music business with this band than on my own."

"You haven't tried to do it on your own."

"I don't have time."

"What?"

Danny swung his foot. "If I don't get a job and strike out on my own, my uncle will make me go back to school."

"You haven't graduated high school?"

Danny shook his head while picking blades of grass.

John jumped up on the wall next to Danny. "When I went back to high school, I didn't have a choice."

Danny looked up at John. "If I play in this band long enough to make a name for myself, then I can quit and go solo, right?"

"Of course."

"Or maybe even join another group, and we could all be successful."

"Yeah," John nodded.

"Can I buy you a milkshake instead?" Danny said.

John jumped off the wall. "The milkshakes are on me, Danny, my boy."

Danny smiled and jumped off the wall.

"Here is to the bright and promising future of Danny Bruer!" John said.

"And Barnaby Dillianthorpe."

John frowned at Danny, and he started to laugh.

30

J AMES WALKED OUT OF THE classroom talking with a fellow student when he saw John in the hallway with his back against the wall. Several students gave John an odd look as they walked by. He twisted his face into a bizarre contortion, making them walk faster.

James stopped. "Hey."

"Hey," John said.

"Are you waiting for me?"

"Nah, I like hangin' around on the second floor so I can watch all the wisenheimers gawk at me."

"They are attracted to your unique sense of fashion," James said.

"I am a trendsetter."

"You can go ahead up to the library, Gilbert. I won't be long," James said to the young man beside him.

"You know that guy?" Gilbert whispered to him.

"Yeah."

"And you talk to him? On purpose?"

"Yeah."

"Wow." Gilbert walked away, shaking his head.

"What's up?" James said.

"I wanted to talk to you, but I see you already have a date."

"Haha. We can go outside if you want."

142

"What I have to say won't take long."

"Okay."

"I've ... uh, been doing a lot of thinking."

"About?"

"What we talked about the other day."

"What did I say?"

"The part about the hard work needed to become a serious rock-n-roll band."

"Yeah?"

John put his hands in his pockets. "I want to work hard."

James smiled. "What about Jerry and Stu?"

"I don't know. I guess that will have to be their choice now, won't it?"

"How did Danny do yesterday?"

"How do you think he did? He blew everyone else away."

"I bet."

John glanced down the hall. "He is going to be big someday, Professor."

"You think he is going to get the job?"

John shrugged.

"Is everything all right?"

"Yeah. You can tell Stu we're meeting on Monday. Can you handle that?"

"Sure."

"Have fun at the library."

"Thanks."

John smiled and walked away.

31

J AMES COULDN'T REMEMBER THE LAST time he had been on a date. He had casually dated a couple of girls in high school, but it never turned into anything serious. He consulted his brother about what to wear because Mark was popular and dated a lot of girls.

"Are you sure this sweater matches this shirt?" James said, looking in the mirror.

Mark was leaning in the doorway, smiling with amusement at his brother. "I have told you five times already, it looks smart."

"Yeah, I don't think the green and blue quite fit."

"Look, the blue stripes on the shirt are so small and faint they're hardly noticeable."

"I guess you're right," James said, slipping the sweater vest over his head. He checked his side reflection.

"So, where did you say you met this girl?" Mark asked.

"At the Coffee Grounds."

"Wow, you mean one of those old ladies?"

"No, you dork. She is young—she started there a while back," James said, pushing past his brother and walking down the hall to the bathroom.

"Sounds like I may need to check out the coffee shop again."

"Real funny," James said, combing his hair.

"She must be really special for you to go to this much trouble. The last time I saw you fuss so much over your hair was when you rubbed Dad's black shoe polish in your hair because you were trying to look like the guy on your fake ID."

James frowned at Mark.

"Would have worked too, except you started to sweat and had black streaks running down your neck."

"Shut up, Mark."

"Boy, was Mom mad because you ruined your best Sunday shirt."

"Don't you have anything better to do?" James asked, picking up his toothbrush.

"Not really. So, do you need any other dating advice? Like maybe the birds and the bees?"

James slammed the bathroom door. Mark smiled and went back to his room.

☐■☐■☐■☐■☐■☐■☐■☐■☐■☐■☐

James bounced up the steps of the boarding house with an assorted bouquet of fresh flowers. Glancing at his distorted face in the brass mailbox, he smoothed his hair before pressing the doorbell. A few moments later, Marcy answered the door. Her ponytail was held by a red and white polka dot bow, and a soft rose tone highlighted her cheeks.

"Hi," she said.

"Hi."

Her soft smile enchanted him, and he forgot all about the flowers.

"Are those for me?"

"Oh, yeah," he said, handing them to her.

"Oh, James, they're beautiful. Thank you," she said, kissing his cheek.

"I'm glad you like them."

"Like them? I love them! Let me put them in water, and we can get going."

"Okay."

"I will only be a moment."

She disappeared into the back of the house. He swung his arms and rocked back and forth on his feet.

She came out of the house and locked the door. "So, where are we going?"

"Anywhere you want to go."

"I would love to go down Main Street and maybe walk around the lake?"

"You don't want to go to the picture show or Be-Bops?"

She took his hand. "I want to walk and see where the night takes us."

"Okay."

Holding hands, they casually window-shopped as they walked down Main Street.

The warmer spring weather made the central part of town come alive, with teenagers looking for something exciting to do on Friday and Saturday nights. The Madison Theater and Be-Bops were popular hot spots, but Lucky's Penny Arcade was also a popular attraction during the season.

Lucky's was located a quarter mile from Main Street on Fair Lane. Lucky, a large weathered clown, stood on top of the building. His once vibrant colors were fading, and he tilted to one side. When the arcade first opened, his jubilant laugh could be heard from a block away, but when his voice box began to fail, the sound that came out was more like a wounded hyena, so his voice box was disconnected and was never replaced. The orange and white blinking lights trimming the building illuminated the clown in an eerie glow.

When James and Marcy reached the end of the street, James turned to her. "Where to now?"

"You know, James, I think Lucky's is open. Can we go?"

"You want to go to Lucky's?"

"Yeah, it would be fun. I love to play Skee-Ball."

"Fine by me, if that is what you want to do."

The two crossed the street and walked down to the crowded arcade. The two pinball machines already had a line of anxious players waiting for their chance to keep the silver sphere on a roll. Onlookers watched as their friends jumped up and down or leaned in weird positions, trying to keep the ball from rolling down grooved gutters of doom. Skee-Ball was also popular, and it took a while for a lane to become available. James and Marcy took turns throwing the balls up the ramp. As balls fell into point-marked holes, red one-point tickets emerged in a rhythmic progression from the machine. They played until their sides hurt from laughing, and their arms felt like Jell-O. The cheesy prizes hardly seemed worth the effort, but Marcy's smile when she picked out a small kewpie doll made it worthwhile.

On their way over to the concession stand, Marcy stopped.

"Look, James, it's one of those photo booths. We need to take our pictures."

"Really? My hair is a mess."

"So is mine," she said, pulling on his hand. Reluctantly, he got into the cramped booth. She was practically sitting on his lap when the blinding light began to flash. The result was some very kooky pictures that made them laugh.

"Are you going to let me see them?" James said to her as they left the arcade with their ice cream.

"I thought you didn't want to take the pictures."

"I just didn't want to look like a goof."

"I can't imagine that you have ever looked like a goof," she said, passing him the pictures. "Why, I bet you wake up in the morning without a hair out of place."

"Hardly."

"Do you like the pictures?"

"I do. As a matter of fact, I am taking the last two." He ripped them off the strip before handing them back to her.

"You want to walk down by the lake?" she said.

"In the dark?"

"Why not?"

"Well, it's getting late and kind of cold."

"I don't care. Besides, you can keep me warm," she said, taking his hand.

"Okay."

The lake was a popular spot for fishing and swimming during the summer, but at night, it was a favorite place for couples to spend some quiet time away from the lights and wagging tongues.

Several cars parked along the shore. Soft music filled the air from the car radios. James and Marcy walked along the path that circled the lake slowly.

"I am so excited for summer. I love the warmer weather and walking barefoot through the grass."

"I love being able to sleep with the window open and listen to the frog's croak."

They sat on the shore and watched the moonlight bounce along the water's flowing ripples.

"Isn't it beautiful out here?" Marcy said.

"Yes."

She looked up at the sky. "It's amazing how many stars you can see out here. Have you ever made a wish on a star?" she said, turning to him. The light from the moon illuminated his face in a soft ray of silver.

"Yes," he said softly.

He was sitting close to her, and she saw a faint trace of desire in his eyes.

"What did you wish for?" she said.

He reached up and felt the side of her face, and her eyes rested on his mouth.

"What do you think?" He pulled her to him and kissed her firmly, letting her blissful full lips comfort his lonesome soul.

"I didn't think you were ever going to kiss me," she said.

"What?"

"I have been waiting forever to be with you. Whenever you came into the coffee shop, I hoped you would ask me out."

"I'm sorry. I am kind of slow that way."

"I thought I dropped enough hints."

"You're so pretty—you could have anyone."

"I don't want anyone. I want you," she said, putting her arms around him.

They shared a few more intimate kisses before slowly walking back to the boarding house.

"I have had such a good time. I don't want it to end," she said, holding tightly to his arm.

"Either do I. But the good news is, we will do it again soon."

"Promise?"

"Of course, I can stop by the coffee shop after school."

"It's been a long time since I've had a boyfriend."

"It's been a long time for me too."

"So, we'll just have to spoil each other."

"Exactly."

"So, have you gotten together with the band lately?"

"No. I saw John today, and we agreed to get together on Monday. He's been hanging out quite a bit with Danny."

"Danny is a wonderful guitar player," Marcy said. "All my girlfriends have a crush on him."

"Do you?"

"Don't be silly," she said, laughing. "He's cute but young and not as handsome as you."

James grinned.

Rounding the corner, the boarding house came into view.

"You want to come inside for a while? I could make us some sandwiches?"

"Okay."

The first floor was empty, and only a few table lamps lit the darkened rooms. James sat at the table as Marcy made them sandwiches. They enjoyed the rest of the evening, making small talk and laughing.

"It's getting late," James said. "I should be getting home. We will go out again next week?"

"Maybe you could come over, and I could make dinner for us."

"Umm, that sounds good," he said, pulling her into his arms.

"What do you like?"

"Anything you make would make me happy."

"I wish you didn't have to go."

"Me too."

"It's so easy being with you."

"I feel the same way."

They kissed a few more times before James finally pulled away and left her standing on the porch. He turned around once, and she waved to him and then watched him disappear out of sight.

32

JOHN WALKED OUT THE SCHOOL's front doors into the throng of students on their course to afterschool activities. He contemplated which route he wanted to take to Stu's house, when he spotted the blonde from class. She was chatting with a group of friends at the park's edge. Tucking her hair behind her ear, she laughed. Her playful, honest expression accentuated her innocence. Then, as if she could sense him watching, she turned to meet his eyes across the chaos. Shying away from his gaze, she tugged at the ends of her hair before glancing back at him. His intense, uninhibited look brought a blush to her cheeks. Flustered, she walked to the other side of the group. John's attention returned to his objective, and he began to walk up the east path.

"Barnaby."

John turned to see Danny walking toward him.

"Hey Danny, what are you doin' here?"

"Looking for you."

"Oh, yeah?"

"It feels weird comin' here, but I don't know where you live."

"Yeah, well, your chances of finding me at home are slim."

"You're not there very often, are you?"

"As little as possible. Did you have something you wanted to talk to me about?"

"Carlton called me. They want to interview me on Thursday."

"Well, congratulations, my boy. I knew you blew the other dimwits away."

Danny shifted from one foot to the other.

"Will you come with me?"

"Oh, come on, Dan, you're a big boy. You don't need me to tag along with you. I barely got in the door the last time. I will be happy to meet you afterward, though."

"I don't want to go alone."

"Why not?"

"I'm scared, I guess."

"Scared? Of what?"

Danny shrugged his shoulders. "I don't know. Sayin' somethin' dumb."

"You're not gonna say somethin' dumb."

"I might."

"Well, I might say my opinion, then you would be in a pickle. I need to get goin'," John said.

"Oh, yeah, I shouldn't keep you. Where are you headed?"

"I'm on my way over to Stu's. We're having a group meeting."

"Oh, yeah?"

"Yeah."

"You mind if I tag along?"

"No, not at all. I would like the company."

Danny smiled and walked with John to Stu's house.

❑■❑■❑■❑■❑■❑■❑■❑■❑■❑

James and Stu were listening to records when John and Danny came bounding down the stairs.

"Hello, kiddies," John said,

"You made it in the house this time without terrorizing Carly?" James said.

152

"She was too busy doin' the hula," John said, making Stu move to the other side of the couch.

"It's a hula hoop, John," James said.

"A wha?"

"Never mind."

"So, you brought Danny along?" Stu said to John.

"He kinda tagged along with me."

"Like a puppy?"

John turned to Stu with a frown.

"So, what's new, Danny?" James said, sitting between Stu and John.

"Not much," Danny said, sitting on a footstool.

"He's got big news," John said.

"Really?" James said.

"No, not really." Danny said.

"He has an interview on Thursday," John said.

"An interview?" Stu said.

"He passed the audition," John said, smiling.

"Oh, wow, Danny, that's great. Congratulations," James said.

Stu's shoulders slumped.

"So, James. Barney and I want the details," Danny said.

John put his feet on the coffee table. "Don't leave none of the nasty little details out."

"Details about what?" Stu said.

"Well, the Professor had a date the other night—with a girl, I might add," John said.

"You did?"

"I did," James said, not wanting to discuss it.

"I have to hear about my best friend's date from these guys?"

"I was going to tell you, but you wanted me to listen to your new album."

"Oh yeah, blame it on me."

"Are you two havin' a lovers' quarrel?" John said.

"Stuff it, John," Stu said, getting up and moving across the room.

"So, how was your date?" Danny asked James.

"It was good. We went for a walk down Main Street and played in the arcade."

"And what else?" John said, sitting up.

"We … uh … we walked down to the lake."

John let out a whistle. "We know what goes on at the lake."

"What goes on at the lake?" Danny said.

John was grinning at James. "Tell him, James."

James hesitated.

"Backseat bingo, Danny," Stu said, sitting on the floor.

"Except the Professor doesn't have a car," John said.

"There are bushes down there," Stu said.

"Well, all right, Professor," Danny said.

"There was no bingo or bushes!" James said, his face red.

"Gentlemen don't kiss and tell," Danny said.

"Gentlemen have no fun," John said, sitting back.

"So, what is the plan for tonight? Are we going to rehearse or anything?" James said.

"Where is Jerry? You did tell him about tonight, didn't you, Stu?" John said.

"I did. He said he would try and make it. He's been staying at the house again."

"Let me try and call over there," John said, going upstairs, the rest following behind him. He dialed the phone. It rang a few times before a man's voice answered.

"Whadda you want?" he snapped.

"Is Jerry there?" John said.

There was a long pause. "No, he ain't."

"Do you know where I can find him?"

"Nope." The man hung up with an abrupt click.

John slowly hung up the phone.

"John?" Stu said.

"I am goin' over there."

John headed for the door.

"Are you sure that's a good idea? Jerry's stepdad is like a rabid dog," Stu said.

"If Jerry is in trouble, I am gonna help him," John said.

"I am goin' with him," Danny said, following John out the door.

"He's gonna get himself killed. Damn it!" Stu grabbed his coat and left, running to catch up with John and Danny.

James's better judgment told him not to follow, but he did.

33

Jerry's mother's house was more of a hovel than a home. Ever since his father died, Jerry's mother crawled into a bottle and never came out. She married Gus Palmer because she thought he was the solution to her problems. He had been nice enough initially, but once he moved in, he turned into a horrible tyrant who beat her and Jerry. Every time she got strong enough to throw him out, things would be good for a while until he managed to manipulate her into letting him come back. It was a nightmare that Jerry thought would never end.

When the boys arrived at the house, the porch light was off, and a dim light showed through the dirty front window.

"John, what are you gonna do?" Stu said.

"Find my friend."

"You know that bastard is probably drunk and meaner than a hornet."

"I don't care."

"You're gonna care when he punches you!"

"Oh, I hope he does punch me because then I'll have an excuse to beat his ass so bad, he'll never get up again."

Stu wanted to say more, but John was on the porch ringing the doorbell. No one answered, so John knocked on the door, but there was still no answer.

"Open this damn door! I know you're in there," John said.

Still no response.

"If this door doesn't open in the next five seconds, I will kick it down! One, two, three, four . . ."

The door opened before he could say five, and a prune-skinned, middle-aged, balding man answered the door. He swayed unsteadily on his feet and glared at John through his bloodshot, yellow eyes.

"Who the hell do you think you are comin' over here and beatin' on my door?" Gus said, spittle oozing from his rotting mouth.

"I'm lookin' for Jerry."

"I told you he ain't here."

John could see Jerry's mother in an old ragged house dress leaning against the wall in the background. She was holding the side of her dirty face and crying.

"Is Jerry in there?" John asked her.

Gus stepped into John's line of sight. "He ain't here."

"I ain't askin' you. I'm askin' her."

Gus turned his glare on her. "I thought I told you to get in that kitchen and make me somethin' to eat! You stupid cow!" He stomped his foot on the floor, and she scurried away like a startled spider.

"I am only gonna ask you one more time. Is Jerry inside?" John said.

"No."

"You're a damn liar."

"And you're a low-down rotten stinkin' punk, and you better get your sorry ass off my property before I call the police!"

"You think I'm scared of you callin' the police? I wish you would. Then they could see how you beat on poor, defenseless women and boys!"

"I didn't beat on her. She is just a whore who got what she deserved."

John grabbed Gus and slammed him into the doorjamb that threatened to crack.

"Let go of me," Gus snarled.

John glared at him as he let him go.

"Get off my property."

"Not without Jerry," John said, pushing his way inside the house. Gus followed him. Grabbing a bottle off a table by the door, he lifted the bottle over his head, but a hand grabbed his wrist.

"I wouldn't do that if I were you," Danny said.

"Jerry!" John called, walking through the house.

"He's outside," Jerry's mother said, tears streaming down her face.

"Where outside?" John said.

"In the cellar," she said, falling to her knees.

John went outside. The boys followed him to the locked cellar with a rusted chain and padlock.

John pulled on the cellar doors. "Jerry, are you in there?"

"John?" a meek voice answered.

"It's okay, buddy. I am gettin' you out of there." The boys frantically hunted for something to break the chain with.

"John," Stu said, bringing him an ax. It didn't take John long to break through the chain and pull back the doors.

Jerry was lying on the earthen floor in a cold tight ball, holding onto his arm.

John jumped down the stairs and kneeled by Jerry's side. "Jerry? Are you all right?"

Jerry gazed at him through weak, swollen eyes. "I think he broke my arm."

John's anger raged through him like oxygen through a blast furnace. "It's gonna be all right, Jerry. We're gonna get you to a hospital."

"Gus won't let us use the phone," Stu said.

"*What?*" John said.

"I can call from your house, Stu," James said.

"Let's go," Stu said.

"I'm faster by myself."

"True." Stu handed James the keys, and he took off on a dead run. "He was on the track team in high school," Stu said.

"No kiddin'?" Danny said.

"Yeah, he lettered."

"Help is comin', Jerry. Just hold on," John said.

"Am I going to die, John?"

"Hell no, you're not gonna die."

"I don't know how long I've been down here. I must have passed out when I hit my head."

John shut his eyes tight.

"I did what you told me to. I tried to stand up to him."

John's heart cracked as he looked down at Jerry's pale, swollen face. "I am proud of you. You did good."

It seemed like forever before the ambulance came to take Jerry to the hospital.

"Don't leave me, John," Jerry said.

"Not gonna happen," John said as they loaded Jerry into the ambulance.

"Can I ride with him, please?" John asked the paramedic.

"Only family is allowed to ride in the ambulance," the paramedic said.

"What hospital are you takin' him to?"

"Madison Central."

"Can I tell him goodbye?"

The paramedic sighed. "Make it quick."

John got into the ambulance. "Hey, buddy, they won't let me ride with you."

"But . . ."

"It's gonna be okay. I promise I am gonna be there."

"I'm scared. What if they make me come back here?"

"We are gonna figure somethin' out—I swear it. You be brave, okay?"

Jerry nodded, and John got out of the ambulance.

Jerry's mother rubbed her arms on the porch as flashing red and blue lights illuminated her in a hollow, lonely glow.

"Isn't she gonna ride with him?" John asked Stu.

Stu shook his head.

"You gotta be kiddin' me!"

"She told them he fell down the stairs."

John closed his eyes. "What is wrong with that woman?"

"Fear."

John, Danny, and Stu left the yard after the ambulance pulled away. Jerry's mother was leaning up against one of the porch posts. No one could bear to look at her because they all knew the hell that waited for her inside.

34

THE STARK WHITE, BARREN ATMOSPHERE of the hospital was depressing. The smell of rubbing alcohol and bleach was enough to churn even an iron stomach. John spent as much time with Jerry as he could during his first few days in the hospital. Jerry was slowly getting his strength back, and his head was feeling better. He was lucky to have only suffered a moderate concussion, but the doctor monitored his condition closely. Most of the hospital staff were pleasant. A few nurses frowned at John's presence, but he didn't care. Supporting Jerry was important.

James, Stu, and Danny visited a few times, but his mother visited only once. She tried to cover up her injuries with rouge, but no amount of makeup would hide the black eye from view. She promised Jerry that she would throw Gus out for good, but he knew that no matter how badly she wanted to, it wouldn't happen.

"You don't have to stay with me, you know?" Jerry said to John, who was doing his best to be comfortable in a straight-back wooden chair.

"You tryin' to get rid of me?"

"No, I'm pretty sure you have better things to do than sit with me all day."

"Nah."

"You're missing school."

"So."

"So? It is gonna get you into a lot of hot water. How are your grades this semester?"

"Can't we talk about something else?" John said, picking up one of the comic books he had read five times.

"Do you want to end up like Stu or me?"

John frowned at Jerry. "What does that mean?"

"You know what that means. You'll have to get a job pumping gas or somethin'."

John went back to his comic book.

"You're ignoring me."

"Am not."

"Are too."

"Let's play cards," John said, pulling the cards out of the bedside table drawer.

"I'm done playin' cards with you."

"What?"

"You cheat."

"I do not cheat," John said, shuffling the deck.

"Do too."

"Do not."

"Hey, fellas," Danny walked into the room, smiling. "For a minute, I thought a couple of old ladies occupied this room."

John sneered at him.

"What are you doing here, Danny?" Jerry said.

"I came by to see how you were."

"You're bored," Jerry said, putting his healthy arm behind his head.

"I am not."

"Yeah, you are," John said.

"Can't I care about my friend?"

Jerry shrugged.

"He's feeling better, actually," John said. "He's gettin' feisty."

"You're just mad because I told you to go back to school."

Danny started to laugh. "Your parents tell you that, not your friend."

"See, listen to Danny," John said.

A nurse entered the room, and John sat up straight. Her stiff white uniform matched her rigid, pinched face.

"It's time for your nap, Mr. Price. You need to rest so you can regain your strength."

John stood up. "I'll see you later, Jerry."

"Yeah, get some rest Jer," Danny said.

"Thanks for coming by, Danny."

"I'll see if I can't get some different comics for you," John said.

"Thanks, John."

Danny and John left the hospital. It felt good to be outside, where the air was fresh, and the sun shone.

"Boy, that nurse looked like a drill sergeant," Danny said.

"Yeah, she doesn't like me much. She told Jerry I was a reprobate."

"We all know that."

"Ha, ha."

"He seems to be doing a lot better," Danny said as they walked down the steps of the building.

"Yeah, I guess so."

"You haven't gotten much sleep the last couple of days, have you?"

John shook his head. "I'm worried about what will happen when he gets out of here. I can't stand the thought of him going back there."

"Yeah, I thought living with my parents was hard."

They walked along in silence for a few blocks.

"You know what? I got an idea," Danny said.

"You do?"

"Yeah."

"What is it?"

"Well, I can't guarantee anything, but there is a small attic room at my aunt and uncle's house. My uncle might agree to let him stay there if he helped around the place doing some odd jobs."

John's eyes lit up. "Oh, Danny, do you think he would go for it?"

"Maybe—it would be worth a shot."

"I would be indebted to you."
Danny gave him a sly smile.
"What?" John said.
"You know what I want."
John sighed.
"Please."
"You know they aren't gonna let me in."
"You're my agent."
"All right, I'll go," John said reluctantly.
"Great, and I will talk to my uncle."
"Deal."
"Are you hungry?"
"What do you think?"
"I'll buy you lunch. It's the least I can do for my agent."
John smiled.

35

JOHN DIDN'T WANT TO LEAVE Jerry to go back to school. Even though he knew Gus would be a fool trying to cause trouble in a hospital, he was still worried.

Composition class was boring, and John was only half paying attention. His book was open, but he was thinking about having to pretend to be Danny's agent that afternoon. He was making progress on his paper when Mr. Miller came over to his desk.

"Mr. Chandler, Miss Merriweather, from the front office, would like to see you in the hall for a moment."

John's brows drew together. "What for?"

"I didn't ask her for details. She said it was important."

John's heart leaped into his throat. What if something was wrong with Jerry? He got up and went out into the hall.

"Are you John Chandler?" Miss Merriweather said.

"Yes."

"I have a message for you from your girlfriend."

"My girlfriend?" John said.

"Yes, she said it was important for you to contact her after class."

"Did my *girlfriend* leave her name?"

"No. I figured you would know who she was."

"Okay, thank you."

Miss Merriweather nodded and left.

John stood alone in the empty hall for a minute. Who in their right mind would be trying to pull some kind of prank on him? He wasn't the least bit amused, and whomever it was would be sorry. He went back inside the classroom.

36

DANNY AND JOHN CAUGHT THE bus that would take them to Carlton's office in the city. The bus was hot and crowded, and a fussy baby was fraying all the passengers' last nerve. Danny was fidgeting in his seat. His leg was bobbing up and down, adding to John's aggravation.

"Danny, you need to calm down," John said.

"I'm trying."

"You must not be trying very hard because your leg is going a mile a minute."

"Oh, sorry."

John sat back in his seat.

"Do I look okay?" Danny said.

"You look fine."

"I combed my hair. Now it's flat or flatter. Is flatter a word?"

John raised his eyebrow.

"I had to borrow my uncle's jacket. It doesn't fit right, but it looks respectable, right?"

"Yes," John sighed.

Danny's leg started to move again.

"So, did you talk to your uncle?" John said.

"About?"

"Jerry."

"Oh, yeah, I did."

"And?"

"And he said he would think about it."

"When do you think he will make up his mind? Jerry doesn't have a lot of time, you know."

"I figure he will talk to us tonight."

John looked sideways at Danny, but he refused to meet his eyes. "What do you mean, talk to us tonight?"

"I told him we would have dinner with them after my interview."

"Who is *them*?"

"My aunt and uncle."

John crossed his leg. "Okay, I'll do it, but I'm not sitting next to Eddie, got it?"

"What is your beef with him?"

"I don't know. He's a goof, and he is a know-it-all."

"He only says good things about you."

"He does?" John said.

"Yes. He is the one who told me about you."

"Okay, I will give him a chance, but I'm still not gonna sit next to him."

Danny laughed.

❑◼❑◼❑◼❑◼❑◼❑◼❑◼❑◼❑◼❑

John and Danny walked into the tiny reception area of Carlton's third-floor office. The room was sparsely decorated with a couple of old chairs, a small table covered with outdated wrinkled magazines, and a plant with yellowed leaves desperately looking for the sun.

A middle-aged woman sat at a small desk. She didn't look up at them while threading the ribbon on the typewriter.

"Excuse me," Danny said.

She held up her finger, which was smudged with black ink. She continued to argue with the stubborn machine.

Danny looked at John, who shrugged.

The phone rang, and she picked it up without even looking at it. "Mr. Gates's office. Uh-huh ... uh-huh ... uh-huh. . .."

She reached up, pulled out a pencil from her stiff reddish bouffant hair, and wrote a note on a piece of paper. "Ten-thirty? Yes, yes, bye." She hung up the phone and stuck the black smudged pencil back in her hair. She looked at Danny through her narrow cat-shaped glasses.

"Name?" she said.

"Danny Bruer," he said.

She looked at the list and checked off his name. "Have a seat. Mr. Gates will be with you shortly."

John was relieved that she didn't say anything to him. Five minutes later, the office door opened. Carlton came out with a young man. He shook his hand, told him they would be in touch, and showed him out the door. Carlton went back into his office for a few minutes before returning.

"Sorry to keep you waiting. Danny Bruer, is it?"

"Yes, that's right," Danny said, standing.

"Good to meet you, Danny. I am Carlton Gates," he said, shaking Danny's hand. "Come on back."

John stood.

"Wait, who is this?"

"He's my agent," Danny said.

"Your agent?"

"That's right."

"Does your *agent* have a name?"

"Mr. Dillanthorpe."

John grinned at Carlton. Carlton raised his eyebrow, but Danny's face was serious.

"Come in."

Danny looked at John, but he couldn't see much of an expression because John was still wearing his shades. They went into Carlton's messy office. Three filing cabinets were set up against the wall with mounds of paper on top. His large desk took up most of the room. It, too, was loaded with miscellaneous documents, files, and dirty coffee mugs. Joe was sitting in one of the chairs in front of the desk. His neatly pressed appearance painted quite the contrast to his surroundings.

"Danny Bruer, meet Joe Delaney."

"Hello," Danny said.

Joe didn't move or attempt to shake Danny's hand. He merely nodded.

"Who's your friend?" Joe asked Danny.

"This is my agent, Mr. Dillanthorpe."

Joe looked at John, who nodded.

"Won't you sit down, Danny?" Carlton said. Danny sat down in the other vacant chair.

"I wasn't expecting another guest. There's a box over there you can sit on," Carlton said to John.

John pulled the box over next to Danny and sat on it.

"Okay, now that the formalities are over, we can move forward with this interview," Carlton said, sitting behind his desk. "First off, we were impressed with your performance, Danny."

"Thank you," Danny said, smiling.

"We are looking for someone to play the rhythm guitar and, you know, kind of back up Joe here."

"Whadda, you mean, kinda back up, Joe?" Danny said.

"Well, being the group leader comes with special privileges that the other members don't have. You understand?" Carlton said.

Danny's face was blank.

"What Mr. Gates is trying to say is, you're gonna be Joe's doormat," John said.

"Well, I wouldn't put it exactly like that," Carlton chuckled.

"Danny will have the privilege of playing in my band and learning from the best," Joe said. "He hasn't established a name for himself yet, so the fact that he won't be in the spotlight really won't matter. No one knows our drummer, Boyd Markham, but if you say he's Joe Delany's drummer, that means something. Understand?"

John's teeth clenched tightly, but he didn't say anything.

"You're a good guitarist, Danny, and I like you," Joe said. "You have a raw talent that needs to be developed. I'm not going to candy-coat anything. Working for me is hard, very hard. I don't tolerate any foolishness, laziness, or incompetence. I expect you to be on time every time and follow my direction without question. But it isn't all hard work. We play hard too, don't we, Carlton?"

"Oh, yes."

"So, see? It's not all bad news. You give me what I want, and I will take good care of you."

Danny gave him a small smile.

"I am having a party at my house on Saturday. Nothing formal. Just a casual cocktail party with some friends. I would like you to come and meet the rest of the group. It will allow us to get to know each other better in a less formal setting."

"Do I have to come alone?"

Joe smiled. "Of course not. Your agent is welcome to accompany you if you wish."

John's face was a cold, hard line.

"Carlton, arrange for a car to pick my guests up."

"Of course, Joe," Carlton said.

"Leave your address with Beverly, and I will see you Saturday around seven?"

"Okay," Danny said.

John waited in the hall for Danny while he left his information with Beverly.

They left the building and stopped by the market to grab a soda and peanuts before boarding the hot bus.

"Are you going to eat all the peanuts?" Danny asked.

"They're my favorite," John said.

"I see that."

John handed what was left of the peanuts back to Danny.

"How do you think the meeting went?" Danny said.

"Good, I guess."

"What did you think of Joe?"

"Do I have to answer that?"

"I thought he was fine. A bit arrogant, maybe."

"Maybe?" John scoffed.

"I guess if I had the money he does, I would be arrogant too."

"One thing is for certain, if you join the group, you will have a shot at the big time. That's what you want, right?"

"I guess so."

"You guess so? You don't want fame, money ... girls."

"Maybe," Danny said.

"You would love it, and you know it."

"Okay, maybe just a little."

John looked at Danny sideways, and he laughed.

37

DANNY'S AUNT AND UNCLE LIVED about a mile west of Main Street. The lovely two-story house occupied a spacious piece of land not encumbered by close neighbors. Everyone in town knew the Bruers because they owned the record shop and the mercantile. Still, they were genuine, kindhearted people whose contribution to the community was heartfelt and appreciated. Danny could tell that John wasn't thrilled about having dinner with his family. He had been quiet and withdrawn on the bus while staring out the window. Danny knew very little about John's home life. The few times Danny had mentioned coming to his house, John had quickly dismissed the idea. So, Danny left the subject alone and figured when John was ready to talk about it, he would.

"Are you nervous about tonight?" Danny asked.

"I don't do so good with meeting relatives," John said, putting his hands in his jacket pockets.

"They're really nice, you'll see."

"Yeah, yeah."

"My aunt is a terrific cook, and I think she's making apple pie."

"Sold," John said.

The amazing aroma of a home-cooked meal greeted them at the door. The hardwood floors had braided throw rugs, and pictures of country farmhouses decorated the walls.

"Aunt Mable, Uncle Bob, I'm home," Danny called out, making his way toward the kitchen.

A plump lady in a checkered housedress smiled at him from behind glasses as round as her pleasant face.

"Daniel," she said.

John hung back behind Danny like a lost waif.

"This is Barn...uh...I mean John," Danny said, pulling John into the room. "John, this is my Aunt Mabel."

"Hello," John said with a lopsided grin.

"Well, hello, John. We have heard so many wonderful things about you."

"You have?"

"Yes. Eddie can't stop talking about the birthday party and how wonderfully your group played."

"Well, Danny played a big part in that."

"It was nothin'," Danny said.

"Would you like some lemonade? I made it fresh this afternoon."

"Sure. You want some...John?" Danny said, tripping on the name.

"Yeah...I mean, yes, please," John said.

A teenage girl with short brown hair came down the stairs and walked past John without noticing him.

"Mom, Eddie's locked himself up in the bathroom again. I think he's putting more Vaseline in his hair because he's singing 'Peggy Sue.'"

"Well, never mind him. You need to set the table, please."

"Yes, ma'am."

Danny handed the glass of lemonade to John. He took a drink, and suddenly his cheeks sucked up into his mouth as he tried to breathe.

"Are you all right, dear?" Mable said.

"Yes," John managed to squeak.

"Oh, I guess I didn't add enough sugar."

John smiled, his eyes watering.

"Betty, will you add more sugar to the lemonade, please?" Mable said.

Betty turned her mouth open to speak, but when she saw John, words failed her.

"Don't stare, dear," Mable said as she scrubbed the potatoes.

Betty looked away, embarrassed, and ran into the other room.

"Maybe you should introduce your cousin to John, Danny," Mable said.

"Oh yeah, I forgot he didn't know her."

"Why don't you boys go out in back? Bob is trying to get that old lawnmower to work. I told him to get a new one, but he won't hear of it."

"Okay," Danny said.

John and Danny went out the back door to the garage. A portly, balding man with glasses that sat half-down his nose was standing with his arms crossed, studying a lawnmower with an unopened toolbox beside it.

"Hey, Uncle Bob."

Bob turned to see Danny and John.

"Hello, son."

"Uncle Bob, this is my friend John. John, my Uncle Bob."

"Hello," John said.

"Well, hello, young man. I have heard a lot about you," Bob said, offering John his hand.

"That's what I've heard," John said, shaking his hand.

"Yes, sir, sounds like you have a lot in common with Daniel here."

"Yeah, except Daniel has way more talent than I have."

"Aunt Mable said you're having trouble with the lawnmower again?" Danny said.

"Yeah, it's like me. It has a hard time getting started."

"Did you change the sparkplugs?"

Bob felt his jaw but didn't say anything.

"You want me to look at it?"

"To tell you the truth, I would be fine if you waited till this weekend to look at it."

"Are you sure?"

"Yeah. I think so."

"You're not in a hurry to cut the grass?"

Bob smiled. "Well, I have been procrastinating a bit, yes."

"I don't mind cutting the grass, Uncle Bob."

"I know, but Eddie promised to cut the grass."

"Oh."

"I gave him an advance so he could buy an outfit for the party. He told me he would work it off by doing extra work around the house."

"He hasn't done any extra work?"

"He said something is wrong with the lawnmower."

"He could push the manual one," Danny said.

Bob smiled and sat his hand on Danny's shoulder. "Now, why didn't I think of that?"

Danny smiled.

◻■◻▦◻▦◻■◻▦◻▦◻■◻▦◻▦◻

Bob, Danny, and John returned to the house to wash for dinner. Betty and Mable were busy serving the food. Bob sat at the head of the table. Danny sat next to him, and John sat next to Danny. Betty kept her distance from John and wouldn't look at him directly. Eddie came into the room and snatched a dinner roll off the tray that Betty was carrying.

"Eddie, you need to wait until after Daddy and our guest have been served."

He took a big bite out of the roll to spite her and sat next to his father.

"Daddy," Betty said.

"Edward," Bob said, taking a roll from the platter. "You know the rules."

"Sorry," Eddie said, laying the half-eaten roll on his plate. "They're extra good when they're warm."

"You can dry the dishes tonight," Bob said.

"But Dad, I have important things to do."

"You want to wash them too?" Mable said, bringing in the mashed potatoes.

"No," Eddie said, barely opening his mouth.

Betty brought the platter over to John.

"Which one should I take?" he asked her.

"Whichever one you want," she said, still avoiding eye contact.

"Did you make these?"

"No, but I helped."

"Would you hurry up?" Danny said. "I don't want an extra cold one."

John took one and sat it on Danny's plate.

"Hey, what if I didn't want that one?"

"Well, it's yours now."

Betty giggled.

John looked back at her, and for the first time, he saw her small oval face concealed behind a thick pair of glasses that magnified her hazel eyes. John smiled at her and took a roll. She turned and left before he could see her blush.

"Your cousin is sure shy," John said to Danny.

"Yeah, she doesn't get out and socialize much."

"Why not?"

"She's self-conscious about her glasses, and other kids tease her a lot."

John shook his head.

After Bob said the grace, John listened to the chatter among the family. He started to relax slowly.

"So, how was the interview?" Eddie said.

"It was fine," Danny said, as he took a bite of mashed potatoes.

"That is all you're gonna say? 'It was fine?'"

"There wasn't much to it. Joe did most of the talking."

"Joe Delaney? You met Joe Delaney? Oh, Dan, how cool is that? What's he like?"

Danny shrugged. "I dunno. He was, okay."

"Okay? Okay? He is like the ginchiest," Eddie said.

Bob's brow wrinkled. "Did you just say, ginchiest?"

"Yeah."

"What does that mean?"

"You know, cool, hip, gear, with it."

"Oh."

"What did you think of him, John?" Eddie said.

"Me?" John said.

"Yeah."

"I thought he was a . . ." John looked around the table and realized he was in polite company.

"The ginchiest?" Bob said.

Everyone started to laugh. John looked at Bob, smiling, and decided to go with it.

"So, when are they gonna decide?" Eddie said, not missing a beat.

"Eddie, calm down. Let the boy enjoy his dinner," Bob said.

"I'm sorry, Dan," Eddie said. "I am just so excited for you! You're gonna make it big! So big!"

"I wouldn't say that," Danny said.

"I would."

"Is that what you want, Danny?" Bob said.

"Well, sure. I mean, who wouldn't like to make a lot of money?"

"Is he a good man?" Mable said.

"Of course he is," Eddie said.

"Edward, let Danny answer his questions," Bob said.

Eddie poked at his green beans.

"I think so. I don't know him yet," Danny said.

"We just want to ensure you're not getting involved with someone with a low moral character," Bob said.

"I know," Danny said.

"So, Danny tells me you have a friend who needs a place to stay for a while," Bob said to John.

"That's right, sir," John said.

"Apparently, he has had a rough go of it."

"Yes."

"Both Danny and Eddie have told me he is a good boy and won't be causing any trouble."

"He is very quiet and reserved and just needs a chance to get out of a bad situation," John said.

"I have talked it over with Mable, and we think it would be fine for him to stay with us until he can get on his feet."

"I can't thank you enough, sir. I will pay his rent while he is here," John said.

"Oh, no need for that. He can help around the house, and we always need help moving products around at the mercantile. It won't be charity if that is what you're afraid of."

"I just want him to have a chance at a fair shake."

"I respect that," Bob said.

"Come on Betty, help me serve the pie," Mable said.

◻◼◻◼◻◼◻◼◻◼◻◼◻◼◻◼◻◼◻

Later, after the dishes were cleared away, John pulled Eddie aside. "Hey, Eddie, thanks for putting in a good word for Jerry. It means a lot to me."

Eddie nodded. "I know he's had a rough time."

"Friends?" John said.

Eddie smiled. "Of course!"

John thanked Mable and Bob for their hospitality, and Danny walked him to the front gate.

"Thanks again for going with me today. It meant a lot," Danny said.

"Sure and thank you for introducing me to your family. They're good people."

"So, do you think I should take the job if they offer it?"

"I don't know, Danny. I guess it's up to you and what you want. It really doesn't matter what I think."

"It matters to me."

"I just want you to be happy, and if being a member of The Dice is what you want, then I say go for it."

Danny put his hands in his pockets. "I wish you would come with me on Saturday night."

John shook his head. "That I can't do, but you better believe I will be there for your first show."

"I'll make sure you get tickets."

"Fair enough. I'll see you later."

Danny watched John disappear down the road. The night was suddenly quiet and somehow empty. Danny sighed and went back inside the house.

❑■❑■❑▨❑■❑■❑▨❑■❑■❑▨❑

John took his time walking home. He was hoping the long walk would make him feel better about Danny joining The Dice, but for some reason, it didn't. John knew Joe only wanted to use him, but he had no proof, and he didn't feel right about influencing Danny's decision.

John was thankful for the solitude of his small bedroom. He quickly changed into his favorite T-shirt and dungarees and sat on his bed. Fumbling through his books, he pulled out his notebook. There was something different about it. It was so ... new, and none of his doodles were on the front. Acute panic surged through his being. He thumbed frantically through the pages, hoping that his eyes were mistaken. The pages were ... blank. His temper threatened to tear the book in half. He flipped to the last page, where a note was scribbled. "Oh, where, oh, where has my notebook gone? Oh, where, oh, where can it be? I wonder how many days you will have to wonder what happened to me." John glared at the page. His muscles tightened, his jaw clenched, and his mind was a whirlwind of fragmented thought until suddenly, the pieces clicked into place, and he knew. Closing his eyes, the rage subsided. Clicking his tongue, he set the imposter aside, and a large grin crossed his face.

38

THE BUS TO DAVENPORT CREPT along its regular route. Jostling along, squeezed in next to a sweaty stranger was never pleasant, but even the crammed hot bus couldn't spoil Anne's mood. She was worried that John might figure out what was going on when he left the room to talk to Miss Maxwell, but he was in the hall long enough for her to take the notebook off his desk. Now his notebook was in her hands. She closed her eyes and imagined the look on his face when he discovered his notebook was gone. Now he would know what it felt like to have his privacy invaded, his intimate thoughts exposed to a foe's eyes. She never felt so powerful, so avenged! She would enjoy laughing at him as he had laughed at her.

The bus dropped her off two blocks away from her house on Lincoln Street. Flowers were budding on the trees that canopied the lush green lawns. A small group of girls were jumping rope on the sidewalk. Crouching down like a frog, Anne jumped into their game, causing them to squeal with laughter. Missing a skip, she thanked them for the game and skipped home.

"Anne is that you?" her mother said when she heard the front door close.

"Yes, Mother."

Her mother came out of the kitchen with a dishtowel in her hand. A freshly pressed apron covered her light green dress. "How was your day, dear?"

"Good."

"Would you mind helping me chop the vegetables?"

"Sure, Mom. I just need to wash up first."

"That's fine."

Anne bounced up the stairs to her bedroom. The sun's rays cast a lazy glow through the sheer pink curtains. Setting her things on the small white desk, she went into the Jack and Jill bathroom she shared with her little sister, Tracy. Humming, she brushed the tangles out of her hair. Tracy listened to the radio while she lay across her bed doing her homework.

"What are you so happy about?" Tracy asked.

"Me? Nothing," Anne said, twisting a band around her ponytail.

"Are you seeing Steve tonight?"

"No."

"You want to know what happened in school today?"

"What?"

Tracy jumped off her bed, excited to tell someone the story.

She came into the bathroom and shut the doors like she genuinely had a piece of juicy gossip. "Well, Miss Ramsey, you know, the Home Ec teacher?"

"Yes."

"Well, she was showing us how to make a cake, like none of us know, right? Anyway, Buzz Carmichael and Curt Dorsey put a rubber spider in the cake pan, and when she went to pour in the batter, she screamed and threw the bowl in the air, and chocolate batter flew everywhere!"

"Really?"

"No joke. Some of it even stuck to the ceiling! Gosh, that was the best."

"How do you know it was Buzz and Curt?"

"Who else, silly?" Tracy said, looking at herself in the mirror. "How come my hair isn't blonde like yours?"

"Well ... I don't know."

"I got Mom's hair color," Tracy said, looking in the mirror. "Mousey brown, yuck."

"I think it's very pretty," Anne said, lightly touching the curls.

"It's too darn short. I look like a freshman."

"You could grow it."

"Oh, what does it matter?" Tracey said, jumping off the counter. "What boy is going to look at a girl with braces?"

"You only have another year."

"But by then, Buzz will be a senior, and it will be too late!" Tracy stomped her foot and went back into her room.

"Why?"

"Because Jane Davis will have sunk her claws into him," Tracy said, flopping onto the bed.

"If this Buzz can't like you for who you are, he isn't worth your attention."

"Now you sound like Mom."

"Don't worry. When the time is right, you will meet the right boy," Anne said, returning to her room.

"But Buzz is the right boy," Tracy said, following her.

"He sounds like a troublemaker."

"Yeah," Tracy said, looking up at the ceiling.

Anne shook her head and left the room.

❑■❑■❑■❑■❑■❑■❑■❑■❑■❑■❑

Anne went back downstairs to join her mother in the kitchen. She sat at the counter, and her mother brought her a bowl of carrots and potatoes.

"Make sure you cut the carrots about half an inch thick and the potatoes into fourths. You know how fussy your father is about his vegetables."

"Yes, ma'am." Anne picked up the knife and started to chop the carrots.

"Are you going out with Steve tonight?"

"No, I have too much studying to do."

"You two haven't been seeing a lot of each other lately. Did you two quarrel?"

"No. We've just been busy with school and homework."

"We should have him over for dinner some night soon."

Anne ignored the comment.

Tracy came downstairs and attempted to sneak an apple off the counter.

"You know it's almost dinnertime," her mother said, not even looking up from stirring the pot.

"I know, but I'm hungry now."

"Well, don't spoil your appetite, and make sure you brush all the apple pieces out of your braces."

"Yes, ma'am." Tracy rolled her eyes at Anne and went back upstairs.

"Honestly, your sister," Anne's mother said, salting the gravy. "Why can't she be more like you?"

"I'm not so great."

"You just need to be more disciplined about your routine. You dawdle too much. Make sure the pot doesn't overflow. I will be right back."

Anne tried not to let her mother's criticisms and constant corrections bother her because she knew nothing would ever be good enough in her mother's eyes.

39

THE CLARK FAMILY GATHERED IN the dining room for dinner an hour later. Anne's father had come home from work promptly at five-thirty and expected a warm meal to be on the table by six o'clock sharp. Her mother never disappointed him because she lived to make sure that his every need was catered to. Every month, she would study *Good Housekeeping* and the *Ladies' Home Journal*, ensuring she was current on all the latest recipes and fashion trends. She was the envy of every woman because her hair and makeup were always impeccable, despite being a mother, wife, committee chairman, and volunteer.

Arthur Clark sat at the head of the table. His chiseled narrow face looked stern even when he was happy. He was an intimidating, no-nonsense man who didn't tolerate foolishness of any kind. The girls ate quietly. They did not speak unless they were spoken to. Tracy chased a carrot around her plate because she didn't want to eat it.

"Tracy, eat your carrots, and don't put your elbows on the table. It isn't ladylike," Florence said.

"Yes, ma'am," Tracy said, upset that her mother had drawn attention to her.

"How was school today, Anne?" her father said.

"Huh?" Anne said, looking up from her plate.

"We don't use slang at the dinner table, Anne," her mother said, taking a tiny bite from a piece of potato.

"Yes, Mother," Anne said. "School was fine, Daddy."

"Did anything exciting happen?"

"No."

"I told Anne how we need to have Steve over for dinner again soon," Florence said.

"That sounds like a good idea," Arthur said.

Anne continued to concentrate on her eating.

Her parents exchanged a concerned look.

"How was your day, Tracy?" Arthur asked.

Tracy looked at her father. Her mouth was full of extra tough carrots that she struggled to chew.

Her father glowered at her bloated mouth.

Tracy swallowed the hard lump. "Fine," she managed to mutter.

Arthur quietly resumed eating.

Anne helped her sister clean up the kitchen after dinner before retiring to her room for the evening.

The solitude of her bedroom was comforting. It felt good to slip into her pajamas after the confines of her dress and girdle. Subconsciously, she nibbled on a fingernail as she attempted to compose her essay for composition class. The notebook sat on the edge of the desk, distracting her.

She thought about putting it back in her book bag and forgetting about it, but the temptation to look at it was too strong. She picked up the notebook. Slowly, she opened the cover and began to explore its pages. She wasn't expecting to uncover anything of genuine interest, maybe some doodles, chicken scratch, a lewd picture or story, but instead, she found the naked musings of a visionary's soul. Page after page was full of poems, thoughts, and striking breath-taking sketches of what would appear to be an ordinary subject but lying beneath the surface was a complex depth of emotion.

Suddenly, the joy of taking the notebook faded, and guilt and shame remained. She realized that the crude, harsh, unfeeling person he portrayed was not the man he was inside. Turning to another page, she saw her image on the page. Every detail of her facial features was captured perfectly. Knowing he had been moved enough to sketch her made her stomach tingle.

The ring from the telephone shocked her back into reality, and when Tracy knocked on the door to inform her Steve was on the phone, she wished she wasn't home.

Anne picked up the extension in her room.

"Hello?" she said.

"Hello, darling. How are you?" Steve said.

"I'm fine. How are you?"

"Swell. I thought you were going to call me last night."

"Oh, yeah, I lost track of time," Anne said.

"You're immersed in your studies, then?"

"Yes, that's it."

"You know you can't avoid me forever."

"I know," she said, twisting the phone cord around her finger.

"Most girls would be excited if they thought their boyfriend might be ready to pop the question."

"I know."

"I would like to think you will say yes when that time comes."

"Of course, silly," she said with a shaky laugh.

"May I take you out to the movies on Saturday?"

"Yes."

"Great, I will pick you up around six, okay?"

"Okay."

"I love you."

She hesitated. "I love you too."

"Good night."

Anne listened to the dial tone for a while before hanging up.

He was right. Most girls would be thrilled by the thought of being engaged to someone like Steve. He was educated, attractive, and intelligent. He would be a marvelous provider, and her future would be safe and secure. She closed the notebook and tried to think about her other studies, but her thoughts drifted back inside the notebook. She would enjoy her last few hours with it. Tomorrow she would have to face the confrontation that she knew was coming. Sure, she could be a coward and leave it for him to find, but she would face him and admit her crime. Turning to the last blank page, she picked up her pencil.

◻◼◻◼◻◙◻◼◻◼◻◙◻◙◻◼◻◼◻◙◻

When Florence came in, Arthur was sitting in the living room reading the evening paper.

"Arthur, I am worried about Anne. Her behavior has been so odd lately."

"I am sure there is nothing to worry about. It's probably just growing pains," Arthur said, not looking up from his paper.

"I don't know, dear. She is almost a grown woman now."

"Once she is committed to Steve, she will settle down into her place, and everything will be fine. You'll see."

"I suppose you're right. She does need to settle down."

"Of course she does."

"Thank you, dear."

Arthur smiled, not having looked up from his paper once.

40

ANNE'S SWEATY HANDS TWISTED AROUND each other as she watched the clock's minute hand slowly creeping toward the top of the hour. The noise level increased as other students entered the classroom leisurely. The later it got, the more upset she became. Where was John? She had psyched herself up to deal with the situation, and he was nowhere to be seen. Typical, she thought.

The hour struck, and her heart sank. Mr. Miller was closing the door when John came in. Anne held her breath as he slowly walked across the room, each footfall sounding like a death knell. Having John out of eyesight was maddening. He had snuck up on her before. What if he did it now? She gripped her pencil and moved it back and forth between her fingers like a pendulum.

"Good afternoon, class. I am assuming you all finished your narrative essay due today. It would be nice if a few of you shared your essay with the class. Do I have any volunteers?"

No one raised their hand.

"Miss Clark," Mr. Miller said.

Anne didn't move. She was trying to make herself disappear.

"Miss Clark?"

"Huh?" Anne said, noticing Mr. Miller was standing by her desk.

"Will you please share your essay with the class?"

Blood drained from her face. "Uhh … uhh. . .."

Mr. Miller raised his eyebrow. "Is there a problem?"

"Uhh … I am just not feeling well today."

"Do you need to see the nurse?"

"No."

"Then please take the podium."

"I didn't realize we had to read it in front of the class."

"I mentioned on Tuesday to be prepared to share your essay with the class."

"I know. I just didn't think it would be me."

"Your work has always been exemplary, and you are studying to become a teacher."

Anne didn't want to share the theme of her paper with the class. They would all think she was a silly little girl, giving John another reason to laugh at her. Fate was punishing her for taking his notebook, and she would deserve whatever cruelty he unleashed on her.

Slowly, she willed her heavy feet forward. Each step felt like walking through a tar pit. Once at the front, she stood behind the podium. Her shaking hands made the paper rustle. Setting the paper down flat, she gripped the sides of the podium until her knuckles were white.

"My Grandmother's House," her voice squeaked. "One of my fondest childhood memories is the summer trips I took with my family to visit my Grandmother Jean." The following five minutes were complete agony for Anne. It was as if time were moving in slow motion. Every sentence, every word, sounded stupid and dull. When she finally finished, the classroom clapped politely.

"Thank you, Miss Clark. You may take your seat," Mr. Miller said.

Anne walked toward her desk, and to her horror, John was sitting at the desk next to hers. He looked at her with a stern face. A gasp froze in her throat. She wanted to run from the room as fast as possible, but medicine was medicine, and it was time she took hers.

John didn't bother her while another student read his essay, but his presence was stifling.

"Very good, Mr. Meyer," Mr. Miller said. "You may take your seat. Would you like to go next, Miss Thomas?"

"Actually," John said. "I would like to go next."

Mr. Miller raised his eyebrows. "You, Mr. Chandler? You want to read your essay?"

"I do," John said, standing.

Whispers passed between students. Mr. Miller's expression lent to realizing he thought it would be a mistake to let John read his essay, as he had never volunteered for anything the entire semester.

"You may read your essay, Mr. Chandler."

John walked confidently up to the podium, set his notebook down, rolled his sleeves, and cleared his throat.

"The title of my essay is, 'The *Thief*.'"

"Once over an under time, there existed an unscrupulous thie*fff*. Now this thief wasn't no ordinary thief, no siree. This was a very clever thief, or at least they believed they were."

Anne sunk into her chair.

"Now, this thief stole a priceless possessedtion that belonged to a sweet, handsome innocent young man. A young man who would never do such a deceitful thing to another hummus bean

. . . *ever*."

Anne's stomach churned.

"This young man was quite upset, tormented, and as a matter of fact, he was, excuse me, I mean *is* furious over the loss of his most prized possessedtion. For it is foul indeed to steal a possessedtion that does not belong to you! Woe be to him, who has committed this heinous of deeds!" John slammed his fist onto the podium, causing everyone to flinch. "For strike out my words, the punishment will be severed once I have slain my hands on the pulpit!"

Anne looked up to see John staring straight at her with narrow, foreboding eyes.

John raised his hand. "Can I get an Amen!"

The class began to laugh.

"Mr. Chandler!" Mr. Miller said, walking up beside him. "You were supposed to read your essay, not preach a sermon."

"Sorry, sir, I guess the spirit swept me up in the moment."

"You may sit down," Mr. Miller said.

As John passed by Anne, he laid a note on her desk.

Dreading to read the note, she opened it. *Meet me by the large oak tree after class.*

She sighed heavily.

At the end of class, everyone left, including John. Anne was headed for the door when Mr. Miller stopped her.

"Miss Clark, may I talk to you for a moment, please?"

"Yes, sir."

"Miss Clark," he said, sitting on the edge of his desk, "you know I consider you one of my brightest students."

"Thank you, sir."

"I have noticed that your work has been dropping off lately, and I felt it necessary to express my concern."

"Yes, sir," she said.

"Is there something you would like to talk to me about? Maybe I can help."

"No, sir, there is nothing you can do. I promise I will bring my grade up."

"I certainly hope so. I would hate to see someone as promising as yourself take a turn for the worse."

"Yes, sir."

"You may go now."

She nodded and left.

□■□■□■□■□■□■□■□■□■□■□

Anne trudged up the path that led to the oak tree with heavy feet. She didn't see him. Was she too late? Leaning up against the solid old trunk, she let her breath out.

"So, you *did* show."

She put her hand to her chest and blinked her eyes. Had he materialized out of thin air?

He folded his arms. "You have something that belongs to me, don't you?"

"I don't know what you're talking about."

"Don't play dumb with me."

"How do I know it's yours? Can you describe it?"

He chuckled. "So, this is your revenge, is it? Because I found your diary?"

"For reading it."

"You know damn well I didn't read it."

She glowered at him.

"I could have, though. I could have broken its five-cent lock if I was that desperate to read about how mummy and daddy took you to Grandma's house. Or how your boyfriend holds your hand but never kisses you like you need him to."

"You're a hateful man."

"Why? Because I know the truth?"

She felt tears burning her eyes. "Why do you have to be so mean to me? What did I ever do to you?"

"Okay, tell me I'm wrong. Tell me the stories in your diary are not about an innocent girl."

"So, what if I happen to want to document my life? So, what if it makes me feel good to write about my thoughts and experiences? Sorry, they don't read like some sleazy dime store novel. That's not who I am! Does that make me horrible?"

"Not at all. If anything, it's commendable. You will make some young man very happy someday."

"What does that mean?"

"It just means you will make a good, dutiful wife. Most men with a good wife don't even know how lucky they are. Sometimes they take her for granted. They treat her like she is their property and that her mission in life is to serve him. They forget how valuable she is, and after a few years, so does she."

Her eyelids drooped.

"Enjoy your innocence while you still have it. It dies all too soon."

Reaching into her satchel, she pulled out the notebook and handed it to him.

He took it from her. Its worn, comforting surface quieted the clamoring. "You didn't spray any perfume on it, did you?"

"Of course not!"

"So, what did you do with it? Sleep with it under your pillow?"

"No."

"You looked at it, didn't you?"

She avoided his eyes.

"I figured as much."

"You are very talented, John."

His stern features were unmoving.

"I truly mean it. Your work is more than just ramblings or doodles. They are true pieces of art because I could feel them breathe. Most of us can only dream of having that talent."

Their eyes touched. A crack in his rock-hard surface, revealing a sliver of empathy.

"I should get going. I have a bus to catch." Anne turned to leave. "By the way, I love the butterfly picture in the field. It reminded me of being free." She walked away, celebrating the small victory of leaving him speechless.

41

JERRY'S HEALTH WAS IMPROVING, AND he was returning to his old self. He was able to get out of bed and do some light activities, like walking or sitting in the common room with some of the other patients. John still went and visited him as much as possible. Hopefully, staying with the Bruers would positively influence Jerry's life, and he would never have to live in the horrible situation again.

Jerry was sitting in one of the common areas playing checkers with another patient when John showed up for his visit.

"Hey, Jerry."

"Hey, John," Jerry said.

John pulled over a chair and sat down next to Jerry. "Are you winnin'?"

"Some."

"How do you play this crazy game?" John said, looking at the checkerboard.

"You mean to tell me you have never played checkers before?"

"Nope."

"I don't believe you."

"Believe what you want."

Jerry moved his piece. "What did you play as a kid growin' up?"

"The bug-n-run."

"The what?"

"The bug-n-run."

"I don't even want to know what that is."

John watched the other patient studying the board.

"What are we waitin' for?" John whispered to Jerry.

"He is contemplating his next move," Jerry said.

The other patient picked up his piece and moved his hand toward a square.

John shook his head. "Oh, I wouldn't do that."

The patient frowned at him, then decided to set his chip down in another spot.

"Oh, I wouldn't do that either."

"That's it. I can't play under these conditions. I am leaving." The patient got up and left.

"He's no fun, is he?" John said, taking his seat. "So, you about ready to bust out of this joint?"

Jerry shrugged and rested his head on his hand. "At least I get three meals a day here, and I don't have to worry about sleeping on the ground."

"What if I told you I have some good news for you?"

"You do?"

"Yeah. Danny and I found somewhere else for you to stay."

Jerry lifted his head up. "Really? Where?"

"At his aunt and uncle's house."

"You mean Eddie's parents?"

"Yeah."

"Oh, John, I don't think I could stay there."

"Oh, come on, why not?"

"Because," he said, rubbing his arm. "Those people are you know."

"No."

"Like Eddie."

"They are not like Eddie."

"How do you know?"

"Because," John said, moving checker pieces around.

"Because how?"

"I had dinner with um."

"You did?"

"Yeah, it was nice. His aunt is a great cook."

"I don't know. . .."

"Look, you'll have your own room in the attic, and his Uncle Bob said he could use your help around the stores, so it's not like it would be charity."

Jerry crossed his arms. "I dunno. What if they don't like me?"

"You don't have to stay there forever. It's only until we can figure somethin' else out. I will probably need to get a job … eventually … someday."

"You workin'?"

"Could happen," John said, offended.

"Remember that one summer you had that job at the corner store?"

"Let's not talk about that."

"They banned you for life."

"Okay, I said let's not talk about it. Come on, Jerry, you can't go home."

"You really think I would be all right?"

"I wouldn't have agreed to it if I didn't think so. Tell me you'll give it a chance."

"I will see you?"

"Of course. We gotta start rehearsin' again here soon."

Jerry held his arm up. "I don't think I am gonna be playin' much of anything."

"So? You will still have to come to rehearsal. It's not like I am gonna let you slide."

Jerry gave him a half-smile. "All right, I guess I could give it a shot."

"That's the spirit!"

"So, you want me to teach you how to play checkers?" Jerry said.

"Right now?"

"Why not?"

John scratched behind his ear. "Can't we just play cards? I promise, I won't cheat."

197

Jerry grimaced.

John clasped his hands together. "Please."

"Oh all right, but were goin' to play gin rummy."

"What?"

"You heard me," Jerry said, picking up the checkers.

"You know I don't like that game."

"I don't care. I'm the one with my arm in a cast."

"Okay, but I'm only doin' it because you're my best friend, Jerry."

"Yeah, yeah," Jerry said and pulled out the deck of cards.

◻◼◻◼◻◼◻◼◻◼◻◼◻◼◻◼◻◼◻

John was sitting on his bed at home, thankful for the return of his notebook. As he gazed at it, he thought of Anne and everything she had said about him. Was she saying all those things because she felt guilty about taking the book? He then thought of her brown eyes and lovely blonde hair that framed her sweet face. What had she done with the book while she had it? Did she just look at it? He smelled it, and there wasn't a hint of perfume. He opened it up and carefully examined the pages, ensuring nothing had changed or been ripped out. Everything was accounted for. He picked up his pencil and turned to the last page; to his surprise, it wasn't blank. She had drawn a picture there. It was a sketch of him sitting in his favorite spot, and a butterfly was sitting on his book. Beneath the image, it said, "Dear Diary, what will I dream of tonight?"

42

JOHN, STU, JAMES, DANNY, AND Eddie stood on the hospital's front steps, cheering for Jerry when he walked out the front door.

Jerry grinned. "Thanks for comin', guys."

"Are you kiddin'?" John said, putting his arm around Jerry's neck.

"Hey, don't pound on my head."

"I wasn't gonna."

"So, you glad to be outta that place, Jer?" Stu said.

"Yeah, I am."

"No more hospital food," John said.

"It's good to see you, Jerry," James said.

"It's good to see you, too, Professor."

"Tonight, we are takin' you out to celebrate," John said.

"You are?"

"Yep. Your choice."

"Really?"

"Yep, most of us will be there," John said, glancing sideways at Danny.

"Danny is on his way to the big time!" Eddie said.

"You gonna join The Dice?" Jerry said.

"Maybe," Danny said, running his hand over his hair.

"Wow, that's neat."

"Thanks, Jer," Danny said.

"So, what are we doin' tonight, bud?" Stu said.

"I wanna go to the pictures," Jerry said.

"You can go anywhere you want to tonight, and you wanna go to the pictures?" John said.

"Come on, Jerry—don't you want to go see the girlies?" Stu said, nudging him.

"I don't think I am up for watchin' you and John get lucky."

"Tonight might be your night, Jer. You never know," Stu said with a wink.

Jerry frowned.

"If Jerry wants to go to the pictures, then that is what we're gonna do," John said.

"As long as it has an X," Stu said.

"Stuff it, Stu!"

They all laughed and walked down a few steps and stopped. Jerry's mother stood at the bottom of the stairs dressed in an old moth-eaten felt coat and a hat with a faded yellow flower. She waved at Jerry.

"I gotta go talk to her, fellas," Jerry said.

John put his hands in his pockets, and Jerry went down the steps.

"Damn it," John said.

"You think he'll go home with her?" Danny said.

"If he does, that bastard will just beat him again," Stu said.

"Poor Jerry," Eddie said. "He deserves better than this."

"He has to know that he's got someplace better to go," James said.

"One would hope," Eddie said.

Jerry walked over to where his mom was standing.

"Hello, Jerry," Martha said in a meek voice.

"Hi, Mom."

"How are you feelin'?"

"Better."

"You look better," Martha said, brushing the hair from his brow.

He looked at the fading bruise on her cheek. "How are things at home?"

"Fine."

"Is he still there?"

She absently touched her hat with a slight nod.

Jerry sighed.

Martha looked up the stairs. "They all hate me, don't they?"

"That's not true, Mom."

"They blame me."

"Mom . . ."

"I know it's my fault, Jerry."

Jerry sat his hand on his mother's shoulder. "It's not your fault. You just need to leave him for good."

"And then what? What would we do, then? We can't make it on what I get paid at the diner."

"I got a job."

"You do?"

"Yep. I will be workin' with Eddie's dad at his stores, and what I make, I am givin' straight to you. I am gonna get you out of that place."

"Oh, Jerry, if only that were true," she said with a tear in her eye.

"It will be. You'll see."

Martha felt his cheek. "My boy. I don't deserve you."

"I am gonna stay at Eddie's house for a while. Just until I can get enough money saved to get our own place."

She nodded.

"I hate to think of you bein' all alone with him."

"I know, but it's best to stay away for a while. He's been workin' extra-long hours, and his mood isn't the best."

Jerry hugged her. "I love you, Mom."

"I love you too, Jerry."

"I will come to see you at the diner."

"Okay," she said, pulling away. "Now, you be a good boy."

"I will."

He squeezed her hand, and she walked away with her head down.

The guys came down and joined Jerry.

"You okay, Jerry?" Stu said.

"Yeah. I told her I was stayin' at Eddie's for a while."

"She okay with it?" Danny asked.

"I guess so. I got to get her away from him."

John set his hand on Jerry's shoulder as they turned and headed for the Bruer's house.

43

JERRY WAS APPREHENSIVE ABOUT MEETING the Bruers, but being with his friends uplifted his spirits and helped ease his fears. Bob and Mable did their best to make Jerry feel at home. They cleaned out the attic room and arranged it nicely for him. Curtains hung over the small window, and the bed had a homemade patchwork quilt. Betty placed a small vase of flowers on the chest of drawers to add cheer, and Eddie donated some of his clothes because Jerry didn't have any.

The large group gathered around the dining room table for a special welcome lunch for Jerry. Bob said a special grace in Jerry's honor, and Mable ensured that the chicken platter was passed to Jerry after Bob. Jerry had never felt so special as his apprehension melted away.

"So, we hear you play guitar?" Bob said to Jerry.

"I do, but I'm not as good as Danny."

"You do just fine, Jerry," Danny said. "If you want, when your arm gets better, we could practice together."

"Really?"

"Of course."

"It would be great to have Danny sit in on some of our practices, wouldn't it, John?" James said.

"He'll probably be too busy bein' famous," John said.

"I will always make time for my friends," Danny said.

John smiled at him.

After lunch, John sat on the porch steps with Danny while Jerry played cards with Stu and Eddie. James had left for a date with Marcy, but he promised Jerry, he would see him soon.

"So, you ready for the big party tonight?" John asked Danny.

"I guess so," Danny said, glancing off into the distance.

"You don't seem very excited."

"I just don't know what to expect or how to act."

"You just need to be yourself."

"Myself doesn't have a bunch of expensive clothes or fancy manners."

"Maybe not, but you know how to play the guitar better than anyone I have ever met. This is your big shot, Danny. You got a chance to get out there and be somebody. You just wait. We'll turn on the radio one day, and you'll be—a star."

"What about you? Don't you wanna be on the radio?"

John shrugged. "Sure, I mean, who wouldn't?"

"You could do it, you know?"

"Yeah, maybe."

"You just need a drummer."

John chuckled. "We need a lot more than that."

Betty came out with a plate of fresh-baked cookies.

"Would you like a cookie, John?" she asked.

"Did you make these?"

She smiled. "I did."

"Then yes, I would love one."

Her cheeks turned pink as he took one off her plate.

"Can I have one?" Danny asked.

"Of course."

He took one. "Thank you."

"It's almost four."

"Thanks."

She nodded and went back inside the house.

"I guess I need to get ready soon. I would much rather go to the movies with you guys tonight."

John laughed. "You want to go watch B-horror movies?"

"I do."

"Well, it is a double feature."

"When does the second movie start?"

"Maybe nine."

"Well, maybe I will drop by."

"Cool, we'll be sitting in the balcony."

Danny nodded and went inside the house.

44

THE MOVIE THEATER WAS ALWAYS busy on Saturday nights, especially if it was a double horror feature. Many young couples liked to sit in the back or in the balcony to neck. Young kids sat in the front because they thought it made the monsters look bigger. Rowdy, disruptive teenagers sat in the middle, throwing things at the younger kids and trying to scare them. If any older people came to the theater, they sat at the end of the row in case the crowd got too rowdy. Ushers walked up and down the aisles, attempting to keep the peace. They were the perfect target for practical jokes and general tomfoolery. It was a thankless job.

John loved to sit in the front row of the balcony because it gave him the perfect view of the entire theater audience. If someone were sitting in what he considered *his* seat, he would politely ask them to move, and if they refused, it was their misfortune.

John sat between Stu and Jerry with his feet on the ledge. The boys were thankful that Eddie mingled with his friends instead of bothering them.

Jerry's arms were resting on the ledge. He was busy watching the people come in and choose their seats.

"You see any cute girls down below?" Stu said.

"They all look the same to me."

"Oh, come on, Jerry. Do you need glasses or somethin'? All girls do not look the same, do they, John?"

John shrugged.

"You have seen naked girls, right Jerry?" Stu asked.

"Of course I have," Jerry snorted.

"In pictures," John said, looking up at the ceiling.

"That ain't true."

"What girl have you seen naked?" Stu said.

"I dunno."

"That's what I thought," Stu said, putting his feet up.

"I ain't gonna tell you her name."

"That's cause you saw her in your dreams."

"Did not!" Jerry said.

"I told you we should have taken him to see some titties," Stu said to John.

"Payin' money to go see girls you can't touch ain't no fun. It just leaves you frustrated," John said.

"What do they feel like?" Jerry said.

"What?" John said.

"You know . . ."

John frowned at him.

"He wants to know what boobs feel like," Stu said.

John looked at Stu. "Why don't you tell us?"

"He asked you."

"And I am askin' you."

"Maybe he's never felt, um," Jerry said.

Stu gave him a disgusted look. "I have felt plenty of um."

"You still haven't answered our question," John said, crossing his hands across his middle.

"I dunno. They feel like water balloons."

"You felt up a water balloon?" John said.

Jerry started laughing.

"Ha, ha," Stu said, standing.

"Where you goin?" Jerry said.

"To concessions," Stu said, leaping over his seat and walking away.

"You ever think I'll have a girlfriend, John?" Jerry said.

"Sure you will," John said, sitting up.

"I've never had a real girlfriend before."

"You just need self-confidence."

Jerry rested his chin on his hands. "I'm not attractive."

"Whatever."

"Well, it's true."

"Have you ever tried to talk to a girl?"

Jerry was quiet.

"Well?"

"No."

"See, you have to talk to them first."

"I don't want to be rejected," Jerry said, picking at his cast.

"None of us do."

"When have you been rejected?"

"Lots of times."

"Name one?"

"Really, Jerry?"

Jerry blinked at him.

John sighed. "Linda Hobbs. You happy now?"

"You asked out Linda Hobbs?"

"Yeah, sure," John said, looking over the side of the ledge.

"Wow, I thought Linda Hobbs made out with everyone."

"Can we please talk about something else?"

"Linda Hobbs," Jerry said again.

John was hoping Jerry would move on to another subject when he saw Anne walk in. His whole attention was drawn to her. She walked down the aisle, looking for a seat. Was she alone? Maybe she was with some girlfriends, but John's jealousy stirred when her boyfriend joined her. He watched their interaction with great interest. Was she genuinely interested in that bozo? He could hear her light laughter as kernels of buttered popcorn passed her pink lips.

"Hey, roomie," Eddie said, plopping in the seat next to Jerry. He was eating hot tamales out of a small box.

"Haven't you had enough sugar, Eddie?" Jerry said.

"Nah," Eddie said, eating a handful.

Suddenly, it became clear why Eddie could never sit still.

"Hey, give me some of those," John said to Eddie.

"Sure," he said, giving him two.

"Give me a few more."

"You're kinda greedy."

John glared at him.

"Gee whiz," Eddie said, reluctantly giving him a few more.

"I wonder where Stu went?" Jerry said.

"He's downstairs flirting with Karen," Eddie said, propping his feet up.

"Who's Karen?" Jerry said.

"The girl workin' the concession stand. She's a fine-lookin' skirt," Eddie said, twitching his feet.

Jerry looked back at John, who still had his eyes transfixed on Anne. Her boyfriend put his arm around her, and John stretched out his tight fingers.

The crowd began to hoot and holler as the lights started to go down and the cartoon started. Stu came back and sat down with a smile on his face.

"What are you smilin' about? Did you see some water balloons?" John said.

Stu smirked at John.

45

DANNY RESEMBLED AN UNDERTAKER STANDING in front of the house. His dark suit was stiff, and his toes were cramped in an old pair of his uncle's shoes. He wished he was heckling a lousy movie with his friends instead of trying to impress a bunch of people at a party he didn't want to attend. All he had to do was take a step down the path, and he would make the first show, but when he saw the black Cadillac limousine pull into the drive, he knew he was committed.

The shiny car pulled up next to him, and he sat in the back seat. The chauffeur was a brooding Black man with broad shoulders and chiseled features.

"Hi," Danny said. "I'm Daniel Bruer, just in case you were wonderin' who was sittin' in the back of your car."

The chauffeur didn't acknowledge that he had even heard Danny.

The quiet ride was unsettling. The only sound was the hum from the engine, and the chauffeur kept his eyes on the road.

"What's your name?" Danny asked.

The chauffeur didn't answer, but he did glance at Danny through the rearview mirror.

Danny rested his arms on the seat in front of him. "I figured we could talk since you're giving me a ride. You see, I have no idea where you're takin' me. Could you give me some idea?"

"I'm taking you to Mr. Delaney's house."

"Is it truly his house? Or does he live with his parents?"

"It belongs to his parents."

"Do they live there?"

"I try and stay out of his business. They pay me, and I do my job."

Danny ran his hand over the back of the seat. "Do you like your job?"

"It helps to keep a roof over my family's head."

"You know I'm nervous about this party. I've never had to wear a suit before except for my brother's wedding. I normally wear jeans, you know. I am a simple guy."

"Me too."

"Hey, is there a radio in this car?"

"Yeah."

"Do you listen to it?"

"Sometimes."

"What do you like to listen to?"

"The blues."

Danny smiled. "Oh. I like the blues. I haven't heard that much of it, though."

"That's because they don't play it on the radio."

"I know you have to go looking for it."

"Yeah."

"Maybe you can tell me where to find it."

The chaffer began to laugh.

"What?"

"I don't know if a white boy like you wants to go where they play the blues."

"Why not?"

The chauffeur pulled down his glasses to reveal his wide eyes.

Danny gave him an innocent smile.

"You're not like the rest of um, are you?"

"I don't understand?"

"Never mind."

The car passed through a gated entrance. Perfectly trimmed emerald green Arborvitae bushes lined the long, winding gravel driveway. The house was mid-century modern with a long-gabled roof. A large fountain with a half-naked woman holding a jar over her shoulder was in front of the imposing house.

When the car stopped, the chauffeur got out and held the door open for Danny.

"Are you gonna be the one who takes me home?" Danny said.

"Yes, sir."

"I'm just Danny."

He smiled.

"I would like to know your name."

"I'm Clive."

"I'm glad to meet you, Clive," Danny said, extending his hand.

Clive smiled and shook his hand before getting back in the car.

46

JOHN WAS TRYING TO WATCH the movie, but his attention kept drifting back to Anne. He was waiting for her boyfriend to make a move on her, but so far, all he had done was put his arm around her.

John turned to Stu.

"How's your aim?"

"What?"

"I said, how's your aim?"

"Whadda you talkin' about?"

John pointed to the boy sitting next to Anne. "You see that pecker head down there?"

"Which one?"

"The one next to that blonde girl in the fifth row."

"Yeah."

"You think you could hit him in the back of the head with one of these?" John said, showing Stu his hot tamales.

"I dunno. Why do you wanna hit him in the head?"

"You think you can do it or not?"

"Maybe."

"Okay, I am gonna throw the first one, and when he turns around, I'll duck down. Then when he turns front, you hit him again. Cool?"

"You're gonna get us kicked out of here with your antics again, and Jerry will cry."

"What?" Jerry said.

"Nothin'," John said.

"Are you wantin' to start trouble for us, John?" Jerry said.

"No, now just watch the dumb movie."

Jerry gave him a knowing look and turned back forward.

"Come on, Stu," John said.

"What if the usher sees?"

"He ain't gonna see unless you hit him in the head instead," John said, crouching down.

"I still don't understand why we're doin' this," Stu said.

"Just shut up and do as I say, or I'll knock you upside the head."

"You're missin' the best part," Eddie said.

"You mean you've seen this terrible movie before?" Stu said.

"Twice."

Stu rolled his eyes.

"Here we go." John aimed and sent the tamale into orbit before ducking down behind the barrier. "Well?" he said to Stu.

"Bull's eye."

John smiled. "What's he doing?"

"Lookin' around like an idiot."

Stu threw the next tamale and nodded.

"Let me know when he gets up and leaves his seat," John said, throwing the next one.

"He's getting' up now."

"Great." John jumped over Stu's legs and ran toward the left exit.

"Where is he going?" Jerry said.

"Beats me."

Anne was eating popcorn and watching the movie when she felt someone sit beside her and reach into her popcorn.

"Everything all right?" Anne said.

"Fine."

Startled, she turned to see John. "What are you doing here?"

"What are you doing here?"

"Watching a movie."

He took another handful of popcorn. Anne didn't know what to do. Her eyes darted, looking to see if Steve was somewhere close.

"You can't sit here," she said.

"Why not?"

"Because . . ."

"Because your boyfriend is comin' back?"

She blinked at him.

"That's your boyfriend, isn't it?"

"Um. . . ., was all she could answer.

John put his arm on the back of her seat. "Are you serious about him?"

Her mouth was full of cotton. "Well. . . ."

He leaned closer to her. "Do you love him?"

Her thoughts were frozen, but her mesmerized eyes conveyed her desire.

"Do you want somethin' to write about in your diary?"

She nodded breathlessly as he leaned into her. Her eyes closed as his lips captured hers in a warm, gentle kiss. He pulled back slightly; her glazed eyes mesmerized by the golden hue encompassing his pupils, and for the first time, they truly saw each other through a clear lens.

Her hand rested on his forearm, and her lips parted as he leaned in to kiss her again.

"Hey, you! That's my seat!"

They both turned to see a fuming Steve.

"It is?" John said.

"Yes!"

"Shh!" the people around them said.

"Is there a problem?" the usher said, coming down the aisle.

"This ruffian is in my seat!"

"Can you be quiet already?" the man sitting in the row behind them said. "We're tryin' to watch the movie!"

"Sir, you'll have to move," the usher said to John.

John stood up. "Hold onto your pants. I just got lost, is all."

"Shh!"

John glanced at Anne, who was smiling at him. He winked at her and walked away.

47

DANNY WALKED UP TO THE large double doors dwarfed by two narrow full-length windows. Straightening his jacket, he smoothed down his hair and took a deep breath. He pressed the doorbell. A tall, thin butler answered the door.

"Hi, I'm Daniel Bruer."

"Welcome. Mr. Delaney is expecting you."

Danny followed the butler down the ornate hallway toward the back of the house. The open patio area was filled with clusters of people dressed in expensive cocktail party attire and sipping drinks out of crystal glasses. Another large fountain sat in the center. In the middle of it was a statue that resembled Atlas.

"You made it."

Danny turned to see Joe's smooth smile.

"I see your agent decided not to join you this evening."

"No, he was busy," Danny said.

"What do you think of my house?"

"It's impressive."

Joe chuckled. "Indeed. Why don't we get you a drink, and I will introduce you to the rest of the group?"

Danny followed Joe to the bar.

"What would you like to drink?" Joe asked him. "The bar is fully stocked, so don't be shy."

"Could I get a glass of water?"

Joe's brow wrinkled. "Are you joking?"

"No."

Joe handed Danny a glass of water, and then Danny followed him to where two men were standing near the fountain with mixed drinks.

"Gentlemen," Joe said to them. "I have someone here I would like you to meet. Daniel, this is Will Morris. He plays the bass."

"Hello, Daniel," Will said, shaking Danny's hand.

Will was a few inches shorter than Joe, and his thick brown hair was styled in a pompadour. His oblong face was pleasant, and his smile revealed a row of perfect white teeth, but something unsettling about his deep-set chestnut eyes made Danny uneasy.

"And this is Boyd Markham, our drummer," Joe said.

"Hey, Daniel," Boyd said, taking Danny's hand in a firm handshake. Boyd's build was thick, and his curly brown hair was combed over to one side in a lazy wave. He wasn't as flashy as his counterparts and seemed more genuine, but Danny decided to remain reserved.

"We thought tonight might be a perfect opportunity to play a few tunes together since we have a small crowd here," Joe said. "Nothing complicated. You think you can handle that?"

"I didn't know that you would want me to play. I didn't bring my guitar," Danny said.

"You don't need it. If you join my band, you will have a better one," Joe said, setting his hand on Danny's shoulder.

"You mind if I see what guitar I am playing so I can get familiar with it?" Danny said.

"Of course. Will, you don't mind showing Danny the stage, do you?"

"Not at all."

"I will leave you with them and see you in ten." Joe smiled at Danny and walked away.

"So, tell us about yourself," Will said.

"What do you want to know?"

"Like, where you live?"

"Madison."

"You live there your whole life?"

"No, I'm originally from Kansas."

"Oh? Lots of farms up that way. Cows, chickens, and corn," Will said, taking a drink from his glass.

Danny noticed his manicured nails and hid his hands in his pants pockets. "I suppose so."

"I don't make it out to the country often, do you, Boyd?"

"No, can't say that I do."

Will swirled the liquid around in his glass. "Joe says you're pretty good on the guitar."

"I like to think so."

"Joe is excellent. I'm sure you'll learn a lot from him." Will said with a smirk.

"I'm sure I will."

"Follow me and we'll show you the stage," Will said.

Danny wasn't expecting to see a full-size stage. It was part of the permanent landscape of the yard and was covered by a green and white retractable awning.

A young man was on stage, putting a mouthpiece on a saxophone. His suit was dark grey like Boyd's, and his light brown hair was combed into a perfect ducktail.

"Daniel Bruer, this is Eric Haverstean, also known as the Saxman," Will said.

"Nice to meet you," Eric said, shaking Danny's hand.

"Daniel will be playing with us this evening," Will said.

"Well, good luck," Eric said.

Eric appeared not to be as arrogant as the other members. He seemed to be an average guy whom Danny thought he could be friends with.

"Joe thought you might like this guitar," Will said, opening a guitar case and pulling out a highly polished sunburst Gretsch. Danny blinked his eyes in disbelief.

"Is something wrong?" Will said.

"No, I've just never seen such a flawless instrument."

Will looked at Boyd, who shrugged his shoulders.

"Well, you can't play it unless you touch it," Will said.

Danny wiped his damp hands on his pants before taking the guitar from Will. He strapped it on and played a few perfectly toned chords.

Joe joined them on stage. "Well, what do you think of it?"

"It's stunning."

"I thought you would like it. So, as we discussed previously, you will play rhythm, correct?"

"Yes."

"Good. Now you just stand left of the drums, and if you can't keep up or get lost, I would rather you stop playing than ruin the song for the rest of us, agreed?"

"Sure," Danny said.

"Are we ready to entertain this crowd?" Joe said.

"You know it," Will said, strapping on his Rickenbacker, and Boyd sat behind the drums. Joe picked up his Stratocaster, put on a pair of shades, and stepped up to the mic.

Joe spread out his arms. "Good evening, friends and neighbors, and welcome to the party!"

Some guests came closer to the stage, and others shifted their attention from where they stood.

"I thought it might be fun for us to play a couple of tunes for you all tonight. I would like to welcome Daniel Bruer. He will be accompanying us on the rhythm guitar. Let's give him a round of applause."

The audience clapped their acceptance.

"I thought we would kick off the night with a Big Joe Turner tune, 'Shake Rattle and Roll'!"

Joe took command of the stage with flair and charisma. His playing was extraordinary and effortless. Eric and Will moved in unison behind Joe, and when Eric wasn't playing, he was snapping his fingers and bobbing his head. The group was polished and undeniably smooth.

Danny struggled to play the song, not because it was difficult, but because blending into the background stifled his character. Eric came bopping over to Danny and smiled at him.

"Move with me and pretend like you're having the time of your life," Eric said as he started to play the sax and move from side to side. Danny misunderstood the direction. He thought a shackle had been taken off his ankle. He was on the move. His double sidestep and turn were perfectly executed. Eric blinked in surprise. Danny had no idea he had stepped over the line, but when he saw Joe's disgruntled stare at the song's end, he knew he had.

"Well, you can't say that Danny doesn't have spunk," Joe said to the crowd. "I think he forgot this isn't a dance audition."

The crowd was laughing, and Danny's face turned red.

"I guess you could say he's got 'A Whole Lotta Shakin' Goin' On'!" Joe set down his guitar as two stagehands rolled out a piano. This time, Danny kept his place, and Joe played the song as if he was Jerry Lee Lewis. Danny glanced out at the audience. Some people were dancing, and others were clapping, which was more movement than they had displayed all night. The song ended with some enthusiastic clapping, but nothing like the night of Len's party. No one said anything to Danny, as band dispersed to join the party. He walked over to Eric, who was putting his sax in its case.

"I guess I messed up, huh?" Danny said, setting the guitar down.

Eric looked at him and shrugged. "I wouldn't worry about it."

"I guess I am just used to being the front man."

"Is this the first time you've played in a band?" Eric said, setting his sax case next to the speaker.

"I've sat in with a couple of bands, but I usually play solo."

"Well, if you hang around long enough, you'll learn that no one upstages Joe." Eric and Danny left the stage.

"How long have you been with the band?" Danny asked.

Eric lit up a cigarette. "Couple of months. I only play with them when they need me. I prefer to play jazz, but I play a little bit of everything until I can find a permanent gig."

"That sounds cool."

"Yeah. I am saving up some money so my fiancé and I can move to Chicago. There are more jazz bands there."

"Do you mind if I ask what happened to the guy before me?"

Eric leaned up against the wall. "He got tired of putting up with Will and Boyd. They can be real jerks."

"I can see that."

"Yeah, I would suggest you stay clear of them. They're nothing but trouble."

Danny nodded.

"I got to go, man, check you later," Eric said, walking away.

Danny felt awkward and out of place. He thought about leaving when he noticed Joe's girlfriend sitting by herself, sipping a glass of wine. Her long hair was wound around her head in a loose braid, and her short, white lace dress complimented her slender legs. Joe was talking and laughing with some of the guests. How could anyone ignore something so beautiful? Danny walked over to her.

"Hi," he said.

"Hi," she said, looking up at him. Her blue eyes were even more enchanting up close.

"I saw you sittin' over here all by yourself, and I thought you might like some company."

She half-smiled.

"The name's Danny."

"I know who you are," she said coolly.

He sat down next to her. "What's your name?"

"Monica."

"Pretty name."

She took a sip from her glass.

"So, what did you think of the show?"

"Show?"

"Well, I guess the two songs we played."

"Fine," she said.

"You think I did all right?"

"You did fine."

"I guess moving was a mistake. It's part of my style."

She smiled pleasantly and turned her head.

He figured she wasn't interested in talking to him and wanted to be left alone. He looked at his watch; it was eight. If he hurried, he could meet up with the guys at the movie.

"I guess I should be taking off now," he said. "It was nice meeting you."

Monica tilted her head. "Can I be honest with you?"

"Sure."

"You seem like a nice guy, and this band isn't for nice guys."

"Oh?"

"I didn't mean it to sound like a bad thing. You're a wonderful guitar player, and I can see you have great potential, just not with him."

Danny looked into her eyes, which didn't shine as they should. Before he could say anything further, Joe came over.

"I was wondering what happened to you," he said to Danny.

"I was just thinking about leaving."

"So early?"

"I am helping my uncle clean out the garage tomorrow."

"How domesticated."

Danny forced a smile.

"Let me walk you to the front door."

"Thanks. Goodnight," he said to Monica.

She nodded and took another drink from her glass.

"So, how did you feel being up there with us?" Joe said.

"It was great. I am sorry I overstepped my bounds."

"No problem. It's not like anyone noticed."

The two finished their walk to the house. Joe stopped in the hall to call the car and then walked Danny to the door.

"I want to thank you for coming out tonight," Joe said.

"Thank you for having me."

"I will be in touch."

Danny smiled and shook Joe's hand. Once inside the car, Danny took a deep breath and closed his eyes. He was glad to be in the car and pulling away from the house.

"Hey, Clive, would you mind droppin' me off at the theater on Porter Street? I'm meeting some friends there."

"Not a problem," Clive said.

Danny took off his tie and stuffed it into his jacket pocket. Settling back into the seat, he stared out the window and tried to put the night behind him.

48

THE LIGHTS CAME UP FOR intermission between movies. Jerry, Eddie, and Stu all went downstairs, leaving John alone with his smile. Anne was still sitting with her boyfriend. On the surface, it appeared as if nothing had changed, but John knew differently.

A pair of hands squeezed John's shoulders. "What kicks?" he turned to see Danny and smiled wide.

"You made it."

Danny sat next to John. "Told you I would."

"Look at you all dressed up in your Sunday best."

"I wish I had my leather and dungarees."

"So, how did it go? Are you an official member now?"

Danny loosened his collar. "I don't know."

"Whadda, you mean, you don't know?"

"I kinda doubt it, actually."

"You do? Why?"

Danny shrugged. "I just don't think we clicked. So how was the first movie?"

"Pretty dumb. It's hard to believe a girl would be so frightened of a man in a rubber monster costume."

Danny propped his feet up. "True."

"Eddie said he's already seen it twice."

"Yeah, he likes the theater because he can talk to other goofs like him."

John laughed.

Eddie and Jerry came back upstairs.

"Dan-o!" Eddie said, sitting by Danny.

Jerry sat down in his seat, munching on some popcorn.

"How did it go? Bet you blew um away, right?" Eddie said.

"I wouldn't say that."

"You're just modest."

"You mind gettin' me a soda and some corn?" Danny said, fishing around in his pocket for money. "I haven't had a thing to eat or drink since lunch."

"You didn't eat at the party?" John said.

"Nah, they didn't have anythin' edible. You want somethin', Barnaby?" Danny said. "It's on me."

"I'll take a soda, too, Eds."

"Comin' up," Eddie said, jumping up and running downstairs.

"You havin' a good time, Jerry?" Danny asked.

"Yes."

"You're not disappointed you didn't go to the peep show?"

"Nope," Jerry said, stuffing his mouth full of popcorn.

Danny smiled at John.

Stu returned upstairs and was mad to see Danny sitting in his seat.

"Hey, Danny, that's my seat," Stu said.

"There's a seat next to Jerry," John said.

Stu frowned at him and sat by Jerry.

"You want some of my corn?" Jerry said.

"No," Stu said, pouting his lip out.

"I'm glad you're sittin' by me. Now I don't have to sit by Eddie," Jerry said.

Stu smiled at him.

"Bet you're glad I won't be sleepin' on your floor no more."

"Are you kiddin'? I loved you sleepin' on my floor. It was like I had a little brother."

"You mean it, Stu?"

"Yeah, you ding-a-ling," Stu said, sticking his hand in the popcorn.

Eddie came back up just as the second feature started. John was happy that Anne and her boyfriend had left because now he could enjoy hanging out with Danny and watching the second show, even though it wasn't very good. Danny was happy, too, now that he could relax and be himself and be with his true friends.

49

ANNE WATCHED THE STREETLAMPS FLASH by as the car rolled down the road. The radio was turned on low, and she was thinking about John. Steve was talking, but she had no interest in what he was saying to her.

"You haven't heard a word I've said," Steve said, breaking her concentration.

"Huh?" Anne said.

"Your mind is wandering again."

"I'm sorry. I guess I'm just tired."

"It's not even ten o'clock."

"I know—I just had a long week."

"Well, I'm sure a stop at Be-Bops will perk you right up."

"Do we have to stop tonight? I think the popcorn may have upset my stomach."

"Oh, well, I will take you home, then." He drove down to Barton Street and made a left. She was glad when they pulled up in front of her house.

"I'm sorry about cutting our night short," she said, gazing at her hands.

He scooted closer to her and gently pushed her hair from her shoulder. "I'm worried about you. You've been so distant lately."

"I've just been working hard to bring my grades up."

"You shouldn't be worried about any of that when you're with me," he rested his hand on the back of her neck and leaned in to kiss her.

She turned away. "I should go inside."

"What's your hurry? It's been a long time since we have seen each other. Don't you want to spend some time with me?"

"Of course I do, but I just don't think it would be very romantic if we were kissing and I burped."

"Oh," he said, pulling back.

She smiled demurely. "I'm sorry. I wish I felt better."

"No, I understand if you don't feel well."

Steve got out of the car and walked around and opened her door for her. He took her hand and walked her up to the door.

She turned to face him. "I had a good time."

"So did I. The weather is turning nicer now, we should plan a picnic for next weekend. We could take a long drive, find a secluded spot and make up for lost time," he said, rubbing his hand up and down her arm.

"That would be wonderful," she said

"I'll call you this week," he leaned over and kissed her cheek.

She forced the corners of her mouth to rise.

"Say hello to your folks for me," he said, bouncing down the stairs.

"I will," she said, giving him a small wave.

Anne walked into the house, hoping her parents wouldn't ask many questions.

"Darling, is that you?" Florence said from the living room.

"Yes, mother," Anne said, stepping into the room.

"You're home kind of early, aren't you?"

"I am."

"Is everything all right?"

"Yes, I am just tired. I will see you in the morning."

"Goodnight, dear."

Anne was glad to be in her room where she could be alone with her thoughts. She knew she had given Steve the brush-off, but she didn't want to kiss him when all she could think about was the kiss she shared with John. It was only one kiss—how could that mean anything? She got ready for bed and looked at her diary on the nightstand. For some reason, she couldn't write tonight. She needed to put any thoughts of John out of her mind and focus on her relationship with Steve. All she needed was a good night's sleep, and everything would be back to normal in the morning. With a determined mind, she shut out the light and tried to sleep, but thoughts about the kiss and how its tenderness had warmed her core floated through her mind. Pulling the pillow over her head, she forced the thought aside. He was not going to haunt her dreams! But sadly... he did.

50

I T WAS LATE WHEN THE second feature was over. Stu had left with Karen, so John walked home with Danny, Eddie, and Jerry.

"Why don't you stay the night with us, Barnaby?" Danny said.

"Would you, John? It bein' my first night and all," Jerry said.

John nudged him. "You afraid you're gonna get scared?"

"I might."

They laughed.

"You don't think your mom and dad will mind?" John asked Eddie.

"Nah. Oddly enough, they like you."

John turned to Danny. "Well, I really don't want to walk home this late, so okay."

The following day, after breakfast, John sat on the porch with Danny, Eddie, Jerry, and Bob. They were teaching John how to play checkers when Mable stepped onto the porch.

"There is a call for you, Danny."

He went inside. "Hello?"

"Hello, Danny, it's Joe."

"Oh, hi, Joe."

"I talked with the boys, and we would like to make you an offer to join the group."

"Really?"

"You sound surprised."

"I just thought after I goofed. . .."

"Don't be ridiculous. I have forgotten all about it. So, do you accept?"

Danny looked at his family, who had followed him to the phone, but he didn't see John.

"Ah, yeah, I accept."

His family was smiling at him, and Eddie jumped up and down.

"Wonderful. Practice is tomorrow afternoon. I'll meet you at Carlton's office at noon, and we will go over the contract. Does that work for you?"

"Yes."

"Good. Welcome aboard, Daniel."

"Thank you." Danny hung up the phone.

John was on the front porch with Jerry, and they could hear the celebrating inside the house.

"Sounds like Danny is a member of The Dice," Jerry said.

"Yup," John said, not even looking up from the board. "It's your move, Jerry."

Jerry made his move and nothing more was said.

51

THE NEXT FEW WEEKS WERE quiet and uneventful. Jerry settled into life with the Bruers, and Danny met with Carlton and Joe to review his contract. He would have felt better if John had gone with him, but John had school and wanted to stay clear of the whole affair.

James studied and spent his free time with Marcy. The last few evenings they spent together, they played bridge with her landlady and another tenant, Mr. Nichols. It wasn't very romantic, but it was light-hearted fun.

On this particular evening, after the older couple had retired, James and Marcy cuddled on the small couch in the common room and watched a movie. It was ten-thirty when Marcy turned off the TV.

"Wow, it's already getting late," James said, sitting up straight.

Marcy sat close to him and lazily touched his hair. "It's not that late, James."

"It is if you have to study."

"Is that all you ever think about?" she said, nuzzling his neck.

Heated goosebumps prickled up his spine.

She unbuttoned the top button on his shirt.

"Marcy . . ." he whispered.

She brought her face up to his. Her mouth was slightly parted, seductively inviting his kiss. He pulled her into his arms and held her close as they kissed. Her hands were tangled in his hair as she pressed tightly against him. James's hand traveled up her back to the base of her neck as they shared several long, suffocating kisses.

"Why don't we go upstairs?" she whispered in his ear.

He was so caught up in the moment that he didn't fully comprehend what she was saying. She stood up and took his hands. Dazed, he followed her until they reached the edge of the stairs. She put her foot on the first step, second, and third.

"Uh, Marcy, wait for a second," James said, struggling to clear his muddled mind.

"Is something wrong?"

"Uh ... I, um ... just don't know."

She chuckled. "Know what?"

"What about the other tenants?"

"What about them?"

"Well, what if they hear us?"

She touched his collar. "Are you planning on being noisy?"

"No, I just am . . ."

"What?"

"Not sure that I'm ready," he said, defeated.

"You feel ready to me," she said, putting her foot on the next step.

"Marcy, I'm serious."

She stopped and blinked at him in disbelief.

"I'm sorry."

"No, I understand," she said, walking down the steps and into the kitchen.

James sighed and followed her. "Marcy . . ."

"No, I'm sorry, I thought you wanted the same thing I did."

"I do," he said, taking her arm.

"Then why are we here in the kitchen?"

"I'm just not ready. Can you please try and understand?"

"Is it because you aren't attracted to me?"

"Are you kidding?"

"We have been dating for a while, and you haven't even made a pass at me."

He averted his eyes.

"Are you a . . ."

"No," he said firmly.

She searched his eyes.

"It's just been a long time for me and . . ."

She took his hands.

"I just don't want to disappoint you."

She felt his face. "You are so sweet. You could never disappoint me," she said, kissing him tenderly.

"I don't know why you're with an idiot like me."

"Because you are the kindest man I have ever known. Most men I've dated haven't cared if they disappoint me."

"I want it to be special," he said, putting his arm around her. "Can you just give me a little more time?"

"Of course," she said with a smile.

He kissed her. "I hate to leave you."

"I know your studies are important."

"They are, but so are you. You do know that, don't you?"

"Yes, of course."

She walked with him to the door, and they kissed goodnight. When she closed the door, James's shoulders sank. He wondered if she honestly did know how important she was to him. Just because he didn't spend the night with her was not some rejection. He just needed some time to build up his confidence. Surely, she understood, and everything would be fine. He dismissed any thoughts of losing her aside, but sadly, they would haunt his mind.

52

DANNY QUICKLY LEARNED THAT BEING a member of The Dice would bring more challenges than he thought.

Every day, he got up early and made the long trek back and forth to the studio at Joe's house for rehearsals. Most nights, he got home late and was exhausted, but Mable always set a dinner plate aside for him. Joe had offered to lend Danny one of his cars, but he didn't feel right about it.

But the biggest challenge was trying to fit in with the group. Joe was highly critical of Danny's playing and constantly berated his performance. Will and Boyd snickered behind his back.

It was quite a blow to his confidence, but Danny refused to give up. He paid close attention to Joe's criticism, and the situation improved once he figured out his style and expectation.

Eric was the only one that treated Danny like a person, and unfortunately, he wasn't around very often, but when he was there, he would spend time with Danny, which was a refreshing change to his typically lonely days.

Occasionally Monica would visit the studio, but she was always with Joe. Sometimes she would look over at him, and he would smile, but it was rarely returned.

One morning, Danny took an earlier bus than usual because he wanted to spend some extra time practicing without the other group members there to bother him. He was walking through the foyer when he heard someone playing a lonesome tune in the studio. He figured it was Joe, but when he walked around the corner, he saw Monica playing the guitar. He hung back so that she wouldn't see him watching her. Her eyes were closed, and she swayed sensually with a rhythm wrapped around her graceful figure. He was drawn in with every note of the hypnotic music, her image taunting his desire enough to where he was about to forget himself. Just then, the studio door opened, and Joe walked in.

She didn't stop playing, and he didn't seem interested. She finished the song and set down the guitar.

"I hope you didn't mess up the tuning," Joe said. "I just did it the other day."

"I was careful."

"Check it. If I have to retune it, I will not be happy."

She picked it up with a frown and sat down.

"I'm going out tonight, so don't wait up for me."

"Where are you going?"

"None of your business," he said, picking up his Stratocaster.

"Who is she this time, Joe?"

"See, that is your problem. You're always suspicious."

"That's because you can't keep your dick in your pants."

"You expect me to believe you're some saint or something?"

She set the guitar down. "I have always been faithful to you, Joe."

"I didn't ask you to be."

"You mean you want me to sleep with other men?"

"You can do whatever you want but know this: if I find out about it, you will be back where I found you in the gutter with all the rest of the trash."

She stood up and slapped him.

He gave her a hateful glare.

She grabbed her coat and purse and headed for the door.

"Where do you think you're going?"

"Anywhere you're not!" She left, slamming the door. Joe wiped his thumb across his mouth. The door opened behind Danny, and he could hear Will and Boyd. Danny walked into the studio with Will and Boyd behind him, laughing.

"Mornin', country boy," Will said to Danny. "Did ya shuck any corn before ye came in today?"

"Lay off of him, Will. I am getting tired of your stupid jokes," Joe said.

"Why are you in such a sour mood today? Did Monica cut you off again?"

Joe glowered at him.

"I don't know why you put up with her. You could have any woman you want, and you mess with the ice queen."

"And you would know all about that, Will?" Joe sneered.

Will's jaw tightened.

"What about you, Huckleberry Finn?" Boyd said, looking at Danny, who wanted to stay out of the whole mess.

"What about me?" Danny said.

"What do you think about Monica?"

"I don't know her well enough to have an opinion."

"You don't have to know her to have an opinion."

"This conversation is over," Joe snapped. "Now, let's get to work." Joe turned on his amp. "You're slipping, Will. You've been drinking too much again."

"Look who's talking," Will said under his breath.

"And your timing is off again, Boyd," Joe said.

Boyd wrinkled his nose at Will, who gave him a smirk.

"I mean it. I am sick and tired of you two drinking and carousing all the damn time. Now you need to step in line."

"Or what—you're gonna ground us?" Will said.

"Do you think I can't replace you?"

"You're nothing without me."

"You wish."

"Come on, guys," Boyd said.

"Vanessa is joining us to practice next week, and I don't want to hear any comments from either of your smart mouths!" Joe said to Will and Boyd.

"What did you have to promise her to get her to agree to this?" Will said.

"Don't worry about it."

"Are you trying to get in her pants?"

"I said shut up. Now let's get to work."

Danny went home from practice that night with a headache. Once again, he wondered if he had made the right decision. Playing the music was one thing, but the constant bickering and fighting was another. He reminded himself that this was only temporary until he could establish himself. He just had to hang in there, no matter how hard things became.

53

THE AFTERNOON COULDN'T HAVE BEEN more perfect. The radio was on, the window was open, and a lazy spring breeze teased the curtains. Tucked away in the sanctuary of his room, John was lazing on his bed, reading a book. While turning the page, 'All I Have To Do Is Dream' came on the radio. His eyes rested on the paragraph before him, a faint memory of peonies and a taste of strawberries split his concentration with a snap. Sitting up straight, John closed the book and thumped it against his head. Exasperated, he laid back on the bed with a sigh. What was it going to take to get Anne off his mind?

How could one kiss turn his entire world upside down? He had been with several girls, and none of them had this kind of effect on him. Turning off the radio, he picked up the book again, determined not to let foolish thoughts ruin his peace, and it would work for now.

54

JOHN WASN'T THE ONLY ONE struggling with bothersome thoughts. Without realizing it, Anne looked forward to composition class. She would stop in the washroom to comb her hair and freshen her lipstick before class. Seated at her desk, she would wait for John to walk in and then sneak a glance at him. She wasn't sure if he was looking at her because he always sat at the back of the room, but sometimes, an unsettled sensation touched her skin, giving her goosebumps.

❏■❏■❏■❏❏■❏■❏■❏■❏■❏■❏■❏

The afternoon composition class was busy taking a test. The only sound was the occasional cough or someone shifting in their seat. Anne's head was resting on her hand when a crumpled piece of paper landed on her desk.

She glanced over her shoulder at John, but he was looking at his paper. She opened the note and softly giggled at the amusing doodle. Mr. Miller's head popped up, looking around the room suspiciously over the top of his glasses. Putting her arm over her head, Anne worked on the test until he looked down again. Writing a response, she threw the note back to John. A little while later, the paper returned with a message on the page.

"Did you write about me?"

"No," she wrote, sending it back.

Five minutes ticked by, and the note hadn't returned, making it impossible to concentrate on the test questions. What was wrong? Was the note coming back? Had she made him mad? A few more agonizing minutes went by before the message returned.

"The blush on your face doesn't lie."

She stuffed the note in the back of her book and concentrated on the test.

The bell rang, signaling the end of the class and the end of the test.

"Pencils up," Mr. Miller said.

Anne quickly checked the last few questions before waiting in line to turn in her paper. She was almost to Mr. Miller's desk when she felt a tap on her shoulder. Whirling around, a gasp of surprise escaped her lips. John was right behind her. Unable to hide, her cheeks betrayed her. A rakish grin slowly lifted the corners of his mouth. Cutting in front of her, he turned in his paper, and Mr. Miller's eyes followed him out of the room.

55

JAMES RAN OUT OF CLASS and down a flight of stairs, nearly knocking over three people. He had tried several times to catch John coming out of class and had failed each time. Today nothing would stand in the way of his goal. Today he was lucky, and something delayed John long enough for James to catch up with him.

"John," James said, setting a heavy hand on his shoulder.

"Professor, imagine seeing you here," John said.

"John, have you heard of a telephone?"

"What?"

"Do you know what a telephone is?"

"Of course, I know what a telephone is."

"It would make everything so much easier if I didn't have to hunt you down whenever I want to talk to you."

"Now you want my number?"

James sighed. "Why do you have to make everything so hard?"

The two walked outside to John's table and sat down.

"So, what's on your mind, Professor?"

"I haven't seen you in a while and wanted to know what is going on with the group."

"Well, not much right now with Jerry's arm in a sling."

"How is he doing?"

"Good. He's workin' with Mr. Bruer at the mercantile and learnin' a lot."

"How about Danny?"

"Good. I haven't seen him much since he started rehearsin' with The Dice. I think I'll see him on Sunday, though."

"Wow, he's really on his way."

"I guess so."

"We will have to go check them out."

"Yeah," John said, picking at his fingernails.

"Have you seen Stu?"

"Wait a second, isn't he your best friend?"

"Yeah."

"But you've been busy pursuing other interests?"

"I guess so," James said, rubbing his neck.

John brought his knee up to his chest. "So, how are things goin' with the little lady?"

"Good ... sort of."

"Sort of?"

"It's complicated."

"She can't want a ring already?"

"No, no, it's not that. It's about you know," James said, rolling his hand.

John gave him a blank look.

"What comes next?"

"Oh?"

"I don't know how to talk about it."

"I'm your friend, not your dad."

James chuckled.

"So, what happened? You made a pass, and she told you no?"

"Not exactly."

"She told you she was saving herself for marriage?"

"No."

"Then what?"

"It's hard to explain. We had been necking, heavily, and then. . . .."

John blinked at him.

James took a deep breath. "Then she took my hand and wanted me to go upstairs with her, and I froze. I didn't know what to do. My first time was, shall we say, awkward at best."

"It's that way for everyone."

"Even you?"

John laughed. "You think I was born with experience?"

"No, but. . .."

"My first time was not some great thing. The only thing that kept it from being a total disaster was that she was older."

"I'm just so worried that I will disappoint her. Do you understand at all?"

"I do. You just need to take it slow and let her set the pace. She'll let you know what she wants without you even havin' to ask. Just relax and let it happen."

James nodded and rested his head on his hand.

"Now, I need your advice, Professor."

"Okay."

"This conversation stays between us, right?"

"Of course."

John began to rock back and forth slowly. "So, say like you kinda like some girl and say you wanted to maybe spend some time with her. How do you do that?"

James furrowed his brow. "Are you wondering how to ask a girl on a date?"

"Somethin' like that."

"You have never asked a girl out on a date?"

"Not really."

James blinked his eyes. "You mean you've never had a girlfriend?"

"Well, no."

"Most of the girls you've been with have been a onetime thing?"

"What is this? Twenty questions? I just don't want to get all tangled up in that relationship stuff, you know? Worryin' about if she is happy or not, or if I said the wrong thing, or what is she thinkin'? You know, girl stuff. They're a whole mess of troubles. It's best to be honest with them upfront, so they know what they are gettin' into from the beginning. That way, there are no expectations or wasted time wonderin' if I'm gonna call them or want to see them again."

"So, you're used to girls that chase after you, and you can manipulate. This one is different. She isn't some empty-headed girl who is infatuated with you. She has some substance. You like her . . . a lot."

John narrowed his eyes.

James smiled. "I think I hit the nail on the head."

"If you don't watch it, I'll hit you on the head."

"You need to start a conversation with her. Ask her how she is doing or talking about something trivial. Then you say something like, 'Hey, I was wondering if I could take you out sometime?'"

"And then what?"

"Well, if she says yes, you take her somewhere like out to dinner, a movie, a walk, or something like that."

"Oh."

"You think you can just spend time with a girl without taking her to bed?"

"I spend time with girls all the time that I don't take to bed."

"I'm not talking about your aunt."

"Ha-ha."

"We should get the group together soon," James said.

"Agreed."

"I'm afraid we might be losing our rehearsal space."

"Yeah, I thought about that too."

"Maybe we could communicate directly instead of me having to stalk you."

"I'm not good at the phone thing."

"So, I've heard."

"They annoy me."

"They cut in on your private time."

John nodded. "By jove, I think you're catchin' on, Professor."

"I promise if I call you, it won't be to chat, and if you call me, I won't expect to chat. Agreed?"

"Don't tell Stu I agreed to talk to you on the phone. I don't want him callin' me."

James laughed.

"Also, don't call after nine p.m. or before eight a.m., my stepmom doesn't like phone calls at odd hours. She can also be abrupt sometimes."

"I understand the rules."

John ripped a piece of paper out of his notebook, wrote down his number, and gave it to James, and James did the same.

James smiled and got up. "Does this mean you're going to call me later?"

"Wise ass."

James walked away, laughing.

56

Vanessa Walker was a talented, remarkable Black woman. Her beauty and impeccable appearance got her attention, but her sultry singing voice made her unforgettable.

As a child, she sang in the church choir, then later in her twenties, she sang in local clubs for pennies. Over the years, her popularity grew, and she even sang backup on some amateur recordings. Her dream was to have a recording contract someday, but it has been hard to find the proper representation.

Several groups asked her to sing with them, but she graciously declined; however, Joe managed to convince her to guest star in a few Dice shows with a promise that he would talk to Carlton about representing her.

Danny was alone in the studio when Vanessa walked in. She was tall and thin, wearing a fur wrap and the longest fingernails Danny had ever seen. Her dark, exotic eyes looked Danny over.

She lazily placed her hand on her hip. "What is a wholesome white boy like you doin' in the devil's den?"

"I figured this was as good a place as any to play the devil's music."

She threw her head back and let out a hardy laugh. "You are pretty cute for a skinny white boy. What's your name, sugar?"

"Daniel Bruer. Danny for short."

"Well, I am Vanessa Walker. Vanessa for short."

"It's nice to meet you, ma'am."

She raised her eyebrow. "You can call me Vanessa."

He smiled at her. "Okay."

"So, where are Joe and the rest of the group?" she said, sitting down and crossing her legs.

"They stepped out for a moment to get some refreshments."

"What instrument do you play?"

"Right now, the rhythm guitar."

"What do you mean right now?"

"I normally play the lead."

"Oh," she said, nodding her head. "You're riding in the back seat right now, are you?"

"Just gettin' some good experience."

She smiled at him.

Joe returned from his break to see Vanessa.

"Vanessa, when did you get here, darlin'?"

"Hello, Joe."

"Stand up and let me look at you," he said, pulling her to her feet. "My, you're a vision."

"You look mighty fine yourself," she said with a flirty smile.

"Why thank you," Joe said, puffing up like a rooster.

"I swear all your money must be spent on your wardrobe. Are your suits made of silk?" Vanessa said, fingering his lapel.

Joe laughed. "Some of them."

"Ooo, I wish I could afford such finery."

"Stick with me, darlin', and you will."

Danny rolled his eyes.

"So, what are we singing?" Vanessa said.

"Baby," Joe said, setting his hands on her hips.

"You got what it takes," she said, swaying her body.

"Mmm. You know you got just what it takes," Joe said, easing his arm around her waist.

The two crooned the rest of the song to each other, and Danny averted his eyes.

Will and Boyd returned at their leisure.

"Look who's here," Will said. "A vision of perfection."

"Hello, Will," Vanessa said.

He took her hand and kissed it. "So, when are you going to stop hanging around Joe and let me take you for a ride in my new Cadillac Convertible?"

"You got a new convertible?"

"I did. I would love nothing more than to take you out in style."

"Ooo Will, you sure know how to tempt a lady," she said, winking at him.

"Let's get to work, shall we?" Joe said possessively, taking Vanessa's hand.

She walked away from Will, but she let a wicked smile linger.

Joe flirted with Vanessa for most of the afternoon before they left together. Danny decided to hang back for a while and spend some time with the guitar that he still wasn't used to playing.

Will sauntered over to him. "Hey, Huck, Boyd, and I just want to apologize for our abhorrent behavior toward you."

"Forget it," Danny said.

"No hard feelings?" Will asked, offering him his hand with a smile that Danny knew wasn't genuine.

Danny reluctantly shook his hand.

"Boyd and I are going out for a drink. Why don't you join us? My treat."

"No thanks. I should be getting home."

"What? Are you on a curfew?" Will said with a chuckle. "We're bandmates and want to get to know you better."

"It's a long walk to the bus stop."

"All the more reason I will give you a ride home later. Come on, give us a chance."

Danny truly just wanted to go home, but he did want to try to make an effort to be friends with them. So, against his better judgment, he agreed to go out with them.

57

WILL DROVE A FLASHY 1958 burgundy Cadillac Convertible that people couldn't help but notice. He took several backroads into the city so that more people would see him and think he was important. Danny didn't mind the illusion because it helped him deal with his being with Will and Boyd.

The Cadillac pulled into the parking lot of an expensive elite club called the Starlight. The valet parked the car while the three went inside. The cocktail waitresses wore large feather caps and skimpy silver sequin outfits that barely covered their bodies. Royal blue carpet covered the floor, and ornate crystal chandeliers hung from the ceiling.

"What can I get you, gentlemen?" the waitress said, giving them a red-painted smile.

"I'll have a gin and tonic," Will said.

"Me too," Boyd said.

"I'll have a beer," Danny said.

"A beer?" Will chuckled.

"Yes."

"Okay then," Will said, smiling at the waitress. "Is Vern in tonight, doll?"

"Why, yes, sir."

"Can you please tell him Will and Boyd are here?"

"Of course," she said, walking away.

"Not bad," Boyd said.

"Her ass is a bit big for my taste," Will said.

"Just the way I like, um," Boyd said, hanging his tongue out.

Will laughed. "What kind of girl do you like, Huck?"

"I like nice girls."

"Nice girls aren't much fun," Boyd smirked.

"You do like girls, right?" Will said, crossing his legs.

"Why sure I do."

"Just making sure."

Boyd laughed.

A man wearing a loud, flashy suit came over to the table. He had slicked-back dark hair and an oily handlebar mustache. "Will! What a surprise! Always a pleasure to see you!" He fervently shook Will's hand. "You should have called ahead. I could have reserved some seats for you in the VIP lounge."

"It was kind of a last-minute deal. I want you to meet Daniel Bruer. He is the newest member of The Dice."

Vern smiled at him. "Hello, Daniel, welcome to my club."

"Thank you, sir."

"So, you see, Vern, it's a special night, and we want to celebrate Danny being part of the group. I would hate to disappoint him. Do you think you could find some room for us?" Will said, slipping some money into Vern's hand.

"For you, Will, anything!" the greedy man said, stuffing the money in his pocket.

"I knew I could count on you, Vern," Will said, playfully shooting his finger at him.

"I assume you would like some party favors as well?"

"You read my mind!"

The two shared a fake laugh.

"I will see what I can arrange, and Marla will take you back."

"Thanks, Vern," Will said, winking at him.

Danny had no idea what to expect when Marla came over to the table wearing a dark velvet burgundy dress with a long slit up the side.

"Come this way, gentlemen," she said.

Will smiled at Boyd and tapped Danny on the shoulder. "Come on."

They all followed Marla to the back of the club, where she led them down a narrow hallway and into a private back room. The room had several luxurious royal blue overstuffed couches and glass tables. Several men laughed and talked to women in short, low-cut dresses sitting next to them or on their laps. The blatant display of aberrant behavior made Danny uncomfortable.

Three young women came into the room dressed in shimmery short evening dresses carrying a tray of drinks.

"Good evening, gentlemen," the girl with black hair and sharp features said, sitting next to Will.

A dishwater blonde woman with long nails sat beside Boyd, and a younger, petite blonde sat beside Danny.

"Did you order the beer?" she said, her playful green eyes twinkling.

"I did."

She handed the beer to Danny. "I'm Vickie. What's your name?"

"Danny."

"Cute name. Is this your first time?" she said, scooting close to him.

"Excuse me?"

"You know, at the club?"

Danny bobbed his head. "Oh, as a matter of fact, it is."

"That would explain why you seem so nervous," she said, setting her hand on his knee.

"I'm not nervous," Danny said, leaning on the couch arm.

"Do you want me to sit in your lap?"

"What?" Danny squeaked.

"I just want to get to know you better."

"I'm fine with you sitting by me."

"Are you sure?"

"Yes," Danny said, crossing his foot over his knee.

"Hey, Vickie, why don't you go get the tray?" Marla said.

"Are you gentlemen ready?" Vickie said.

Will shared an evil grin. "I'm always ready."

"I'll be right back," Vickie said, leaving the room.

Danny let his breath out and loosened his shirt collar.

"Would you like another drink?" a waitress asked Danny.

"Can I get a glass of water?"

"Of course."

Boyd leaned over to Will. "I don't think Huck knows what to do with Vickie."

Will sipped on his drink coolly. "Yeah, he seems a little green."

"You think he'll go upstairs with her?"

"What do you think, Marla?" Will said.

"I think little boy blue doesn't know what to do."

The three of them laughed.

"Hey, I want to hear the joke," the blonde on Boyd's lap said.

Boyd whispered in her ear, making her laugh.

Danny heard them whispering, and his stomach contracted.

Vickie returned with a glass tray, set it down on the table, and kneeled beside it. Opening the small bag, she spilled the white powdery substance onto the glass. She took a razor blade and made small rows of the powder. Will pulled out a 50-dollar bill and rolled it up with a smile.

"Who wants to go first?" he said.

"You always do, Will," Boyd said.

"Don't mind if I do."

They all laughed as Danny watched Will sniff up two lines.

"Woooo," he yelled out. "That's the ticket!"

Danny watched each member in the circle take their turn, inhaling a line or two. He knew they expected him to join in, but he had no desire to. He turned his hands over each other in his lap.

"Come on, honey, don't be shy," Vickie handed him the bill.

The entire group was staring at him.

"Come on, Danny," Will said. "Don't you want to fly?"

"Have you never sniffed snow before?" Boyd said.

"It will help you loosen up and have fun," Vickie said.

"I ... I ... don't think I should," Danny said.

"Come on, Huck," Will said. "Live a little! I guarantee it will make you feel more alive than ever."

"You're not scared, are you, Danny?" Marla said.

"It'll make a superman out of you," Boyd said, slapping his girl's bottom. She let out a squeal, and they laughed.

Danny wanted to get up and leave, but Will and Boyd would forever taunt him if he did. Danny kneeled on the floor next to Vickie.

"Danny! Danny! Danny!" Boyd began to chant, and soon the rest joined in as Danny inhaled.

Boyd laughed. "You owe me 500 dollars, Will!"

The laughter faded to a dull, rushing hum as the room spun around. Danny was weightless, floating among the dazzling constellation of stars shooting above his head. Tiny stings like needle pricks shot a blast of electricity that threatened to burst out of his fingers.

"How do you feel now?" Vickie whispered in his ear.

Leaning his back against the couch, he sprawled his legs out and stared at the ceiling. "Amazing." He stuck his hand out, grasping at empty air. "Do you see the stars? There are hundreds of them. I think I could touch them."

Vickie nuzzled his neck, her ample breasts pushed up against him, and he felt a stirring in his loins that he had only felt a couple of times in his short life.

"You need to do another row to continue to feel good."

"No," he mumbled, his lead eyelids threatening to close.

"You don't want the stars to disappear, do you, Danny? You're so close to touching them," she said, licking his ear, which sent a tantalizing shudder down his spine.

His head protested his movement, but he inhaled another mind-numbing line.

"I want you," she whispered, pulling his desire into his throat. Her hand drifted up his pant leg.

He grabbed her wrist. "Not here."

"Let's go to my room," she said, taking his hand.

"I don't want to move," he mumbled.

"I will hold your hand. I promise you won't fall."

He looked over to see Boyd was gone, and Will was making out shamelessly with Marla, who was on his lap. Slowly, Danny rose to his wobbly feet. Vickie led him down a dimly lit hallway. Fixtures drifted unevenly on the walls, and menacing shadows seemed to follow him. They went up some stairs to her small, private room. The room was sparsely furnished with a bed and a chair. A gaudy burgundy draped lamp completed the room. Danny stood swaying on his feet as he blinked at Vickie.

She reached up and tenderly touched the side of his face. "Are you going to kiss me, Danny?"

He wrapped his hand in her hair and gave it a painful tug. When she parted her lips with a groan, he pressed his lips to hers in a suffocating kiss.

"You aren't as timid as you pretend to be."

He kissed her again, this time taking her tongue with his. She unbuckled his pants.

"What are you doin?" he muttered.

"Just relax."

Gently, she pushed him back onto the bed. She unzipped her dress and let it fall to the floor. He gazed at her, his mouth completely dry as she pulled off her stockings. Lying next to him, she nuzzled his neck. One by one, the buttons on his shirt opened, exposing a smooth, youthful chest. Her hair covered him like a veil, releasing butterfly kisses descending. The moment for words and protests vanished as rising waves brought the silent tide. It was useless to fight the domineering, enticing journey of decadence. An intense pull toward a bottomless hole abandoned all reason. Bracing an uncontrollable acute ache for release, shattered into a quivering rapture of vibrant ecstasy.

"Did I make you feel good?" Vickie whispered in his ear.

He nodded, giving her a sappy smile. She pushed the damp hair from his brow. Danny could not keep his eyes open any longer, so he closed them and drifted asleep.

She stood up and pulled on her robe. Walking over to the discarded pants, she pulled out his wallet. Very little money was inside, but an old faded picture of a young, vibrant woman holding a small, grinning boy touched Vickie's damaged heart.

Glancing at the wholesome young man peacefully sleeping, she wished she could have met him under different circumstances, and things might have been different. Kissing his forehead, she left the room, walked down the hall, and knocked on a door.

"Come in."

She opened the door to find Marla sitting on the bed next to Will, who was reclined on some pillows. His shirt was open, and he had a drink in his hand.

"Well?"

"He's out for the night."

"Did he. . .."

"No, but I made him very happy," she said with a small smile.

Will nodded at Marla, who retrieved his wallet out of his jacket.

"What should I do with him now?"

"Let him sleep it off," Will said, handing her some money. "Does that cover you for the night?"

"You are very generous." She tucked the money into her sleeve and left the room.

58

DANNY WOKE UP TO A relentless pounding in his head. Every inch of his body ached, and his stomach rolled. He opened his eyes and peered around a dim-lit room, smelling of stale food and wasted cigarettes. He groaned when he sat up. Rays of crooked sunlight shined through the broken blind slats. Discarded clothes, magazines, dirty glasses, and crusted, moldy TV dinner trays were strewn everywhere. Placing his head in his hands, he struggled to make sense of his fragmented memories of the night before.

"You alive?"

He looked up to see Boyd in his underwear and a dirty T-shirt. His hair was a mess, and his normally clean-shaven face had stubble. He walked over to the fridge and pulled out a bottle of milk that he began to guzzle. Wiping his arm across his mouth, he belched loudly and scratched his ample stomach.

"Where is the bathroom?" Danny asked.

"Down the hall to your right. I think there is some aspirin in the medicine cabinet if you can find it."

Danny got up and staggered down the hall, feeling miserable. The bathroom was a filthy, horrible mess. A dirty towel hung lopsidedly on the rack, and a tube of hair gel oozed goo on the sink's rim. Danny didn't dare look too closely at the toilet, or he would be sick. There were several bottles of pills in the medicine cabinet, and his head hurt too much to try to figure out which was the correct bottle. He walked back out into the living room.

Boyd was sprawled out in his chair, munching on cereal and watching cartoons. Droplets of milk were on his chin.

"What time is it?" Danny asked.

"It's around ten."

"What?" Danny said, horrified.

"You got somewhere to be?"

"Can I use your phone?"

"Yeah, it's in the kitchen."

Danny walked into the kitchen and dialed the phone.

"Hello?"

"Hey, Auntie."

"Danny! Where are you?"

He sighed. "It's a long story. I just wanted you to know I am all right and coming home."

"Do you need Bob to pick you up?"

"No, I need the walk. I will see you soon." He hung up the phone.

Boyd looked at Danny as he shoveled another large spoonful of cereal into his mouth. "If you want to hang around a while, I can take you home."

"No, I'm fine."

Boyd shrugged. "Suit yourself."

"What happened last night?" Danny said.

"Whadda, you mean? You don't remember?"

"Not all of it, no."

"Oh, that's a shame. Vickie is a nice piece of ass."

"How did I get here?"

"Will brought us here."

"I don't even remember leaving the club."

"Yeah, you woke up for a while, but you were really out of it. I had to carry you out."

Danny frowned. "You did?"

"Yup. Over my shoulder."

"I made a real fool of myself," Danny said, rubbing his temple.

"Ah, it wasn't that bad. I have seen worse, believe me."

Danny headed toward the door.

"It gets better after a while, you know."

Danny looked confused at him.

"The snow you get so you can tolerate without losing your cool. You just got to do more of it."

Danny gave him a disgusted look and left.

59

THE JOURNEY HOME WAS MISERABLE for Danny. He sat on the bus hugging his stomach and wishing he could wake up from the nightmare that was replaying in his mind. How could he have been so stupid? He should have kept his wits about him instead of letting them slide. He knew he could never trust Will and Boyd, yet he had fallen into their trap like a hungry mouse.

The long walk to the house hurt his feet, and he thought he might die when he walked through the door. Mable came out of the kitchen, wiping her hands on a dish towel. She couldn't believe it was her vibrant nephew standing hunched over in front of her. His hair and clothes were a mess, and his face was sunken.

"Danny? Oh, honey, you look terrible!"

"I feel terrible."

"What happened?"

"I don't want to talk about it right now."

"Okay, do you want me to fix you something to eat?"

"Nah, I think I just want to take a shower and go to bed."

"I could make you a warm toddy?"

"I'm good. I'll see you later," Danny said, climbing the stairs.

The warm shower water soothed Danny's aching muscles. He let the water pour down on him for several minutes, wishing it would somehow wash away the feeling of shame. Vague memories of the girl and what had passed between them were returning. How could he ever forgive himself for the lack of restraint? He got out of the shower and caught a glimpse of his somber face in the steam-covered mirror. The water condensed and rolled down, distorting his vision. He wrapped a towel around him and staggered to his room. He pulled the shades and noticed the steaming cup his aunt had left on his nightstand. He sat down and took a drink of the warm, comforting liquid. It made him feel better, but it could not stop the loathing he felt for himself. Lying on the bed, he rolled up into a ball and prayed to the Lord for the forgiveness he couldn't give himself.

◻◼◻◼◻◼◻◼◻◼◻◼◻◼◻◼◻◼◻

Later that evening, Danny came downstairs for dinner. Eddie was out with some of his friends, so it was just Mabel, Bob, Jerry, and Betty at the table.

Danny didn't say anything to anyone as he ate without looking up from his plate. He knew his aunt and uncle were watching him, but he could not bring himself to face them. After dinner, Jerry helped Betty clear away the dinner dishes.

Mable was at the sink preparing to wash.

"Why don't you sit down and relax?" Jerry said. "I can help Betty with the dishes."

"Oh, Jerry, that is nice of you, but I can do it," Mable said.

"I can never repay you for all the kindness you have shown me. So please, let me do this for you," Jerry said, gently touching her arm.

"You are such a good boy, Jerry," she said, smiling at him. "I will go tend to the mending." She grabbed her basket of clothes and left the room.

Danny went straight up to his room. He sat on his bed with his guitar. It was a comfort to hold it in his hands. He strummed it gently, hoping it might help relieve the heaviness in his heart.

A few moments later, there was a knock at his door.

"Come in," he said.

Bob opened the door. "Hey, Danny, mind if I come in for a minute?"

Danny set his guitar aside. "Of course not."

Bob came in and shut the door. "I guess you know your aunt and I are concerned."

"I know," he said, averting his eyes.

"We were very worried about you last night."

He nodded.

"We realize you're almost a grown man, but we are responsible for you. You know you can't run around all hours of the night and not let us know where you are. You have come so far to mess up things now."

"Yes, I know that."

Bob put his hands in his pockets. "Were you with John?"

"No," Danny said, resting his guitar back on his lap. "I was with the other members of the group."

"And they are older?"

"Yes."

"Did they pressure you to do things you wouldn't normally do?"

Danny plucked at the strings absently.

Bob sat on the bed. "I know you don't need a lecture from me, and you know what is at stake. You are doing so well here. We would hate to see you go down a dark road again."

Danny met his uncle's eyes. "You have no idea how much I love it here, and if I let you and Aunt Mable down, it would destroy me. I apologize for causing you both to worry, and I swear to you on my word that it will never happen again."

Bob looked at Danny's dark, heavy eyes. "I trust you, Danny, and your word is good enough for me."

"Thank you, sir," Danny said, his bottom lip quivering.

"Do you want to come down and watch the telly with us? I think we could talk Mable into making some popcorn."

"No thanks. I am gonna play for a bit, then go to bed."

Bob stood up. "You know I am here for you if you need to talk."

"I appreciate that."

"Goodnight, son."

"Goodnight."

Bob left the room quietly, closing the door.

60

JERRY DRIED AND PUT AWAY the dishes while Betty washed. She was a reserved girl and hardly said anything to him. He only saw her at mealtimes, otherwise, she was busy with chores or in her room.

"Dinner was sure good tonight," he said to her.

She nodded, scrubbing a dish.

"Did you make the pie?"

"No, I helped."

"Your mother is an amazing cook."

She rinsed another dish.

"Do you like to cook?"

"Yes, but mostly, I like to sew."

"You will have to show me your work sometime."

"I made this dress."

"You did?"

"Yeah."

"It's nice."

She pulled at her hair, then grabbed a serving dish.

"I was wondering, since Eddie isn't home tonight, if you would like to play a game of checkers with me."

She looked at him, blinking her eyes. "You want to play with me?"

"Yeah, I mean, if you want to. You don't have to. I just thought maybe since we . . ."

"I would love to," she said with a shy smile.

"Great."

When the kitchen chores were completed, they sat on the porch and played checkers. She studied the board with her hands in her lap.

"How come you have never played with us before?" Jerry asked.

"I didn't think anyone wanted me to."

"Every time I see you, you're either setting the table, doing the dishes, or helping your mother with the housework. I never see you having any fun. Don't you have any girlfriends you like to do stuff with?"

"No, not really. I get teased a lot about how I look," she said, studying her next move.

"What's wrong with the way you look?"

"Mostly, I get called names because of my glasses."

"Your glasses? Let me see your face."

She stared at the board.

"Come on. It can't be that bad."

She slowly looked up at him. He had never really looked at her small, oval face before.

"Oh, I see what the problem is."

"You do?"

"Yeah, you don't look like Buddy Holly."

She laughed, and he saw her wholesome beauty.

"You know, maybe the frames are a little big for your face, but besides that, you're really pretty."

An innocent blush flushed her face.

"I mean it. You shouldn't hide your face anymore, and the people that tease you are just plain bullies. What they say doesn't matter, anyway. You can tell them to go suck an egg."

She laughed.

He smiled at her.

"When do you get your cast off?" she said, moving her piece on the board.

"Another week. I can't wait to get it off. It itches somethin' terrible."

"I broke my arm once."

"You did? How?"

"I was on my bike and took a bad tumble because I hit a rock in the road."

"That's terrible."

"I broke my glasses too."

"Oh?"

They returned to the game, but Jerry's concentration was off, and she beat him.

"You want to watch some telly with your folks?" he said.

"Why? Are you afraid I'll beat you again?" she teased.

"Want to bet?" he said, smiling at her.

"A penny slug?"

He laughed. "I think I can afford that."

They played several more games that night, laughing and talking.

61

DANNY LOVED SUNDAYS BECAUSE IT was his day of rest, but it was also the day he would see John. He was sitting on the porch with Jerry when John entered the gate with his hands in his pockets.

"Hey, Barnaby," Danny said.

"Hey, rock star."

The two slapped hands

"Hey, Jerry, how's the arm?" John said.

"Gettin' better—my cast comes off next week," he said with a big smile.

"That's great news."

"So, how goes it, Danny?" John said, sitting on the step above him.

"Okay, I guess," he said, tucking his hands behind his head.

"I saw the Professor this week," John said to Jerry.

"Oh yeah?"

"Yeah, he hasn't heard from Stu. Have you?"

"No. His mom wants him to get a job."

"Yeah?"

"I think she gave him like two weeks or somethin'. He was pretty worked up about it."

John picked up a twig and ran it across his fingers. "Yeah, well, we need to be getting' together as a band soon."

Jerry felt his arm. "Yeah, about that, I kind of have a problem."

"Okay," John said.

"I don't have my guitar," Jerry said sadly.

"Where is it?" John asked, not wanting to hear the answer.

"It's at the house."

John shut his eyes.

"I asked mom to bring it to me the last time I saw her."

"When was the last time you saw her?"

Jerry shrugged.

"I guess we are just going to have to go over there and get it," Danny said.

"I could go by myself," Jerry said.

"You ain't goin' there by yourself," John said.

"If I go now, he probably won't even be there," Jerry said.

"You ain't goin' alone, and that's final," John said with a stern look.

"You think he'll be drunk on a Sunday?" Danny said.

"The devil doesn't take a holiday," John answered.

"I guess we're goin' for a walk then," Danny said.

"Let me get my jacket," Jerry said, going inside.

"Danny, what's wrong?" John asked.

"What do you mean?"

"Oh, I don't know. Your debut with The Dice is next weekend, and you look like you lost your dog."

"I'm fine," Danny said, forcing a smile.

"You're lying to me."

Danny sat forward. "I don't want to talk about it."

"So, something happened?"

Danny looked down at the ground.

"You don't have to come with us," John said.

"I know, but I want to."

"I could use some backup. Hopefully, things will go smoothly."

"One can always hope," Danny said.

The trio walked to Jerry's house. Jerry mainly talked about working with Bob. John didn't have much to say, and Danny was withdrawn.

"You think he's here, Jerry?" Danny asked.

"I dunno."

John opened the gate. "Let's get this over with."

They walked up to the door, and Jerry knocked. "Hey, Mom, it's me."

They waited a few moments before the door slowly opened. Jerry's mom was standing in the same old faded house coat she was in when the incident happened. Her hair was messy, and a fresh bruise was on her cheek.

"Jerry?" she said, smiling at him.

"Hey, Mom."

She gave him a big hug.

"I hope it's okay we came by."

"He's not here," she said.

"Can we come in?" Jerry said.

"The house is a mess," she said, trying to smooth her hair. "I haven't had time to clean lately. I have been workin' extra shifts at the diner." They walked into the dimly lit, cluttered living room.

She sat on the edge of the easy chair. "Have a seat."

Jerry moved some old newspapers off the couch so they could sit down.

"How are you doing, Jerry?"

"Really good. I love workin' at the store with Mr. Bruer. He's been teaching me a lot."

"That's nice."

"You did put the money away I gave you, right?"

"Yes," she said, twisting her hands in her lap.

Danny looked at John, who gave him a skeptical look.

"I get my cast off next week."

"Good."

"The band is gonna start practicin' again, so I came by to get my guitar."

Her eyes darted back and forth.

Jerry stood up. "I'll just go get it."

"Jerry," she said, stopping him. "Sit down."

"Is somethin' wrong?"

She shifted her feet. "Honey, your guitar is . . .your guitar is . . . gone."

"Gone? Whadda, you mean gone?"

"He didn't mean it."

"What happened?" Jerry said, a tremor in his voice.

"When you two had that fight, he . . . he . . . smashed it."

Jerry's face lost its color, and he froze where he stood.

"He broke it? He broke the one thing in this world I give a damn about? How could you let this happen? You know that guitar belonged to my dad."

"I . . . I . . . couldn't stop him."

"You couldn't stop him?"

"I didn't know until it was too late," she said, tears spilling down her cheeks.

He stepped back, disbelief on his face.

"I'm sorry, honey," she said, reaching out to him.

"You're always sorry. He pulls this kind of junk all the time, and all you can do is cry and say, I'm sorry. Well, you know what? I'm sorry too. I'm sorry that I ever thought things could be different. I'm sorry I believed you would ever leave his sorry ass. But most of all, I am sorry that I ruined your life by being born."

"Jerry, please . . ."

"I'm done here. I don't ever want to see you again." Jerry left the house, slamming the door.

His mother buried her face in her hands and began to cry.

John and Danny left the house. Jerry was halfway down the path by the time they caught up to him.

"Jerry," John said, but Jerry didn't acknowledge him. "Jerry!" he said louder, but he kept walking. John reached out and grabbed him. "Jerry, I think you better go back there and talk to her."

"I have nothing more to say to her," he said, glaring at John.

"Look, I know you're mad—"

"Damn right, I'm mad."

"Will you just listen to me for one minute? I know what happened was shitty, but she is your mother, and you are the only thing she has that is keeping her alive."

"She doesn't care about me! She told me time and time again how I ruined her life. If she hadn't gotten pregnant with me, she wouldn't have married my dad, and his family wouldn't have disowned him. You are so easily fooled by her poor me act. All she has to do is cry and put on those puppy dog eyes, and everyone feels so sorry for her. Well, I don't anymore! She deserves that bastard!" Jerry turned and stormed off down the road.

"Should we go after him?" Danny said.

"No," John sighed. "He probably needs some time alone."

"Poor Jerry."

"Yeah, that guitar was the only piece of his dad he had."

"You wanna go down to the lake for a while?" Danny said.

"Sure."

Danny and John walked down to the lake. The picnic area was full of families enjoying Sunday afternoon. They walked to the far side, where it was quieter, and sat on the shore.

"You ever wonder what it would be like to just get on a ship and sail the world?" Danny said. "Just leave all the problems behind you."

"You probably would be tradin' one set of problems for another," John said, leaning back on his elbows.

"You're a real optimist."

"No, I'm just a realist. Whenever I think I have put my problems behind me, more seem to crop up."

"What's botherin' you?"

"I don't even know where to start," John said, lying down with his hands behind his head, and looked up at the sky.

Danny laid down next to him.

"Now, there is a place to go," John said.

"Where?"

"The moon."

"You're nuts," Danny laughed.

"Why is that so funny?"

"Because it's dark and cold up there."

271

"Then why are so many songs written about the moonlight?"

"Because it's romantic."

"For girls, maybe."

"They would think anything is romantic if the latest glamour magazine told them it was."

"How right you are."

Danny was silent again.

"You ready to tell me what has upset you?" John asked.

"I can't bring myself to talk about it yet."

"It's that bad?"

"It is to me."

"When you're ready, I'm here for you."

"You are gonna be there next Saturday night, aren't you?"

"Of course. Wouldn't miss it."

"I would like for James and Stu to be there too."

"I will pass that on if I can find Stu."

"He'll find a job."

"Maybe. He's not motivated. It also means we are probably going to be without a place to practice again, and now Jerry is without a guitar," John said, sitting up.

"We can solve the guitar problem, and you guys could practice at the house," Danny said.

"Are you sure Bob would agree to that?" John chuckled.

"Why would he object?"

"Because he has already done too much."

"Jerry and I live there. It only makes sense."

John rumpled his brow. "You, uh, wantin' to practice with us, Danny?"

"Yes," he said, looking John squarely in the eyes.

"Oh."

"Do you not want me to?"

"Are you kiddin'? I mean, sure, I want you to. It's just . . ."

"What?"

"Well, you're a member of The Dice now."

"So?"

"Are you sure they wouldn't mind you playin' with another band?"

Danny sat up. "Well, it's not like I am another band member. I'm just playin' with my friends. Right?"

"Right," John said.

"I guess we should head back, huh?" Danny said.

"Or we could sit here and skim rocks," John said, sending a rock into orbit.

Danny threw one next. "You know all this walkin' has made me hungry."

"Yeah?" John threw another rock.

"How about a burger and a shake?"

"You read my mind, Danny boy."

Danny smiled, and they left their problems to sink with the rocks in the lake.

62

DANNY DREADED SEEING BOYD AND Will at rehearsal. He had tried to block out what happened at the Starlight, but it continued to haunt him. He promised himself he would never be so stupid again, but every time he tried to rest, the dreadful memories returned.

The studio was empty when Danny arrived, and he sat down with his guitar. Thankful for the few moments of peace, he strummed a quiet song.

"Hey, Danny," Eric said, coming into the studio.

"Hey, I'm surprised to see you here," Danny said.

Eric sat his case down and opened it. "We open next weekend, so I have to be here every day. How are things going for you?"

"Okay, I guess."

"How are you liking it?"

Danny shrugged.

"Is something wrong?"

"No. I'm fine."

"Is Joe giving you the business?"

"A little bit, but nothing I can't handle."

"It's the other two, isn't it?"

Danny didn't answer.

"They aren't easy to put up with, for sure."

"You said they're the reason the guy before me left?"

"Yep."

"Does Joe know what a nuisance they are?"

"I'm sure he does, but he and Will have been friends since before high school."

Danny nodded.

"Your best defense is not to let them bully you. Stand up to them."

"Thanks, Eric."

A little while later, Will and Boyd came in laughing and being disruptive. Eric was polishing his saxophone when Will came up to him. "Hey, look, the saxman is here! Are you practicing with us this week?"

"Got to be ready for Saturday," Eric said.

"By the way, we're getting new suits."

"So, I heard."

"Joe is meeting with Carlton this week."

"So?" Boyd said. "That guy is a loser. He ain't gonna get us anywhere."

"He's been talking to Capital," Will said.

"Yeah, I'll believe it when I see it," Boyd said, picking up his drumsticks.

Will left the room to get his bass.

"Hey, Huck," Boyd said to Danny. "How's it hangin'?"

"Boyd," Danny said flatly.

Will returned, and Boyd walked over to him. "Hey, man, I think something is wrong with Huck."

Will looked over at Danny. "He looks the same to me."

"He's actin' kinda funny like."

"So? Maybe his mommy didn't read him his bedtime story last night. Who cares?" Will said, walking the bass.

Joe strolled in fifteen minutes later. "Mornin', boys."

"Good morning, Mr. Delaney," Boyd said

Joe walked over to the piano and sat down a briefcase he was carrying.

Boyd leaned up against the piano. "Will says you got a meeting with Carlton this week. Is he giving you good news?"

"If he wants to keep his job, he is." Joe passed out the papers in his hands.

"What's this?' Will said.

"The setlist. You all need to read it over and memorize it."

"We're opening with 'Whole Lotta Shakin' Goin' On'?" Will said.

"Yeah, you got a problem with that?"

"Would it matter if I did?"

"You just want to complain."

"Is Vanessa coming in again this week?" Boyd asked.

"Yes."

"Are you and her hittin' the sheets yet?" Will said.

"Shut up, Will."

"Well, you did leave early with her the other day, and I don't see Monica here this morning."

"Are you and Monica done?" Boyd said, winking at Will.

"Shut your yappers, and let's get to work," Joe said. "We have to leave early today to go in for a fitting."

The practice proceeded as usual, and at the end of each song, Joe would give each of them his feedback. Danny was glad that Joe wasn't finding several things to complain about with his performance anymore.

When the lunch break came, Danny left without a word.

"What is going on with Danny today?" Joe said.

"Beats me," Will said. "Come on, Boyd, let's go grab a sandwich."

"I ain't buyin' today, Will," Boyd said.

"You'll do whatever I tell you to do."

Eric walked over to Joe. "I think those two might be giving Danny a hard time."

Joe rumpled his lip. "That wouldn't surprise me at all."

63

LATER, THE BAND TOOK A break to go to the tailors for the last fitting of their outfits. They took Will's car because it was new and impressive to ride around in. Danny sat in the back with Boyd and made no effort to smile or be part of the conversation. He sat as far up against the door as he could and watched out the window.

"Hey man, are you all right?" Boyd asked.

"I'm fine," Danny said.

"Are you still sore about Friday night?"

Danny didn't answer.

After the fitting, they returned to the studio before breaking up for the day.

"Hey, Danny," Will said, walking over to him. "You want me to give you a ride home?"

"No," Danny said, walking away from him.

Will looked at Boyd, who shrugged.

Will followed Danny. "Is there a problem?"

Danny turned to him. "How much did you pay her?"

"What?"

"How much did you pay Vickie to be with me?"

"What does it matter? You had a good time, right?"

"How much?" Danny said, stepping into him.

"I don't know what you're getting so uptight about. We went out and had a few laughs. So what?"

"I want to know."

Will sighed. "Three hundred. Are you happy now?"

Danny's shoulders fell.

"You need to loosen up, you know that? You're strung tighter than your guitar," Will said, walking away. "Come on, Boyd, Huck's got a bee up his ass."

"Don't call me Huck anymore," Danny said with a scowl.

"I'll call you whatever I want."

Danny walked over to him. "You call me that again, and I am gonna lay you out."

Will stepped up to Danny. "Woo, I'm really scared."

"Come on, you guys, knock it off, will you?" Boyd said.

Danny and Will glared at each other.

"What the hell is going on over here?" Joe said, finally taking notice of the tension.

"Nothing is going on. It's all cool," Boyd said. "Right, guys?"

Will stepped back. "Yeah, it's all cool. Come on, Boyd."

Will glared at Danny one final time before leaving with Boyd.

"You and I are going to talk," Joe said to Danny.

"I'm gonna miss my bus."

"Too bad."

Danny felt like a naughty child following behind Joe into the lounge room. He sat down on one of the dark brown leather couches.

"You want anything?" Joe asked from behind the bar.

"No thanks."

Joe came over and handed Danny a glass of water.

"Thanks," Danny said.

Joe sat down on the couch across from Danny.

"So, what's going on between you and Will?"

"Nothing."

"Don't insult me. You haven't been yourself all day."

"I don't want to talk about it."

"Danny, I can't help you if I don't know what's happening."

"I don't need your help, Joe. I can handle it."

"You expect me to believe that? You two were almost going at it. Now, I will not tolerate that kind of conflict in my group. You need to level with me—what happened?"

"I went out with Will and Boyd on Friday night, and it didn't go well, okay? I did things that went against my morals and my beliefs. I acted like a complete and total fool, and I hate myself for it. Does that explain it well enough?"

Joe sighed. "Did they take you to the Starlight?"

"Yes."

Joe took a drink. "I take it you have never been to a place like that before."

"No, I haven't, and I won't ever go again."

"Aren't you being a bit hard on yourself? I mean, was it your first time with a woman or something?"

"No."

"Well then, you got laid. Why is that some kind of crime?"

"It's not a crime to be with the woman you love."

"Oh, I get it now. My, you're young," Joe said, finishing his drink.

"For some men, love means something."

"What does that mean?"

"Nothing, I just need to go home." Danny stood up.

"I am not letting you go home this late on a bus. I can take you home."

"No. I can walk."

"What is it with you? I am trying to be nice to you. Now sit down."

Danny sat.

"You have been with the group for over a month, and I hardly know you. I would like the chance."

Danny sat back.

"I am sorry about what happened. I will talk to Will."

"I don't want you to talk to him. I will keep my distance from him and Boyd."

"You think you will be able to work with them?"

"Yes, as long as they stop disrespecting me."

"That's fair."

"You know, it's not just the girl. It was the whole night."

"Are you talking about the cocaine?"

"I can't believe I did that."

"A little snow isn't going to kill you. If you made it a habit, then that would be a problem. You did it, you learned from it, now move on. We all do things we regret. Welcome to the world." Joe got up and fixed himself another drink. "You know, Danny, you're a good kid. You have a great talent, and I am glad you joined my group."

"You are?"

"Yes, you seem so surprised."

"I guess because all you have ever done is criticize me."

"You learned a lot, and now you're tight. Am I right?"

Danny didn't say anything.

"I am sorry if I rode you too hard, but it will be worth it. Just wait until Saturday night. We are going to bring them to their knees."

Danny smiled.

"You know I am meeting with Carlton this week."

"That's what Will said."

"I tell you—we are close. You just wait. We will make a record, and every teenager in America will be bopping to it. The money you are going to make is going to make all of this worthwhile."

Danny wasn't thrilled about Joe taking him home, but riding in his black Jaguar XK140 was worth the trouble. Joe pulled up in front of the house. Danny was sure he would make some snide remark about the house.

"Quaint," Joe said when he saw it.

"Thanks for the ride, Joe."

"Danny," Joe said, setting his hand on his arm. "I am willing to help you out."

"I know, and I appreciate it."

"I want to take you to the top with us."

"Thanks, Joe," Danny opened the car door. Eddie was standing in front of the house with his mouth open.

"Who's that?" Joe asked.

"My cousin."

Eddie came quickly down the walk. "Holy sh … gee, Danny! Look at that grand piece of automotive excellence! You could pick up any chick in the world in this!"

"Hey, Eddie, this is Joe Delany. Joe, this is my cousin Eddie."

"Hello, Eddie," Joe said.

"Whoa," Eddie said, his eyes wide.

"You coming to the show Saturday, Eddie?" Joe asked.

Eddie gawked at Joe as if he was in a trance.

"Eddie, did you hear Joe?"

"What?"

"Joe wants to know if you'll be at the show."

"Oh, hell yes!"

Joe smiled. "You like my car?"

"Yeah," Eddie said, nodding his head.

"Hop in."

"What? Me?" Eddie squeaked.

Joe opened the door. "Yes, you."

"Go ahead, Eddie," Danny said.

Eddie got in the car, and Joe pulled away from the curb, taking Eddie for the ride of his life.

64

ANNE LAZILY WROTE MUSINGS IN her notebook in the comforting shade of an elm tree. She looked wistfully over at John's table, but he wasn't there. Maybe he wouldn't come out today, and her chance to watch him unnoticed would be gone as another long weekend loomed ahead. Her attempts to trick herself into believing she could be happy with Steve weren't working because every time she was with him, all she could think of was John.

"Are you lookin' for me?"

Startled, she looked up to see John standing by her table. "No."

He leaned on the table. "You always look over there, do you?"

"Over where?" she said coolly.

"Over at the jocks."

"What?"

"See, um, huddled in a circle, passing a cigarette between them, hoping the coach doesn't come out and catch um?"

Anne giggled.

"There's a place I go to draw sometimes. The view is beautiful, and I thought you might want to come with me."

She blinked at him. "You want me to go somewhere with you to ... draw?"

"Yes."

"Um…I should…uh, probably not miss my bus," she said, fiddling with her books.

"Oh, of course. I will leave you to it then," he said, walking away.

Her heart leaped as she watched him leave, then without another thought, she grabbed her books and ran to catch up with him.

He looked at her. "What about your bus?"

"I can catch another one."

Anne had no idea where he was taking her, and she thought maybe she should worry about it, but she didn't. It was such a thrill just to be walking beside him. They walked in silence down to the lake; ducks quacked at them as she followed him up a hill off the eastern shore. Once they reached the top, she could see what he was talking about. The view of the green valley and the lake was breathtaking. He sat on the grass, and she sat next to him.

"It's beautiful up here," she said.

"And quiet," he said. "It's easy to forget my problems and just create."

She nodded.

He pulled out his notebook. "You got a pencil?"

"What is it with you and pencils?"

"I have one. I just want to use yours."

She frowned at him, dug around in her satchel, then handed it to him.

"Now, I want you to look at that tree over there," he said, pointing.

"You mean the dead one?"

"Yeah."

"Okay."

"Describe to me what you see."

She looked at him, confused. "I—see a dead tree."

"I see a barren, lonely skeleton's arms etched against a parched sky."

She barely moved her head in a dumbstruck nod.

"I want you to take a long good look at it. Focus on every part of it, every detail, no matter how small."

They studied the tree for a few moments.

"Now, close your eyes," he said.

She looked at him apprehensively.

"Go on."

She closed her eyes.

"I want you to think about the tree and let me know when you have it pictured in your mind, but don't open your eyes."

Her hair rustled with the breeze while she concentrated in the darkness.

"I've got it," she said.

"Now, take the pencil and my book and draw the tree."

She frowned. "With my eyes closed?"

"Yes."

"Are you crazy? I can't do that?" she said, looking at him.

"Why not?"

"Because . . ."

"Because what?"

"I can't see it."

"Really? You just told me you have a picture of it in your mind. Do you not trust it?"

She had a puzzled look on her face.

"You think your mind is that limited that it can't create from memory?"

She looked at the tree again.

"You have studied every detail about that tree. You can feel it and let it flow from your hand. Don't listen to the doubt in your mind. Breathe life into the dead tree."

She closed her eyes and thought for another dark moment, and when the tree began to materialize in her mind's eye, she began to draw.

He leaned back on his arm to watch her struggle with the thought of not being able to see the lines on the paper.

"Stop worrying about it being perfect. Just let the lines define their path," John said.

Releasing her feeling of inadequacy, she let her hand drift.

A thin grin crossed her fair features as the outline of her feminine profile left its imprint in his fretful mind.

At last, she opened her eyes and started to laugh. "It's terrible!"

"It's not that bad."

"Yes, it is. I want to see you do it."

"All right," he said, taking the book and pencil from her. "I am not going to draw the tree, though. I am going to draw the crow sitting on the branch."

"I don't see a crow?"

"Exactly," he closed his eyes and began to draw.

She pulled her legs up to her chest and wrapped her arms around them. With his eyes closed, John looked so peaceful. The sun highlighted strands of hair framing his chiseled face. How could she be so attracted to such an unkempt maverick? Everything about him was unconventional, and she wouldn't change a thing.

When his drawing was completed, he opened his eyes. Anne was amazed at the picture of the bird sitting on the branch.

"It's pretty terrible," he said.

"No, it's not."

"Neither is yours."

"Can I have it, please?"

"Sure."

She carefully tore the picture out of the notebook and handed it back to him. He was looking straight ahead.

"What are you looking at?"

"You see that old woman there walking along the path?"

"Yes."

"Her image speaks to me," he said, drawing.

She smiled, pulled out her notebook, and began drawing the landscape because she didn't want to forget it.

Her troubles slipped into the back of her mind as a languid, warm afternoon passed. It seemed only a brief moment before the sun descended into slumber.

"I guess we should be heading back," John said, closing his book. "You gonna be able to catch a bus home?"

"If I hurry," she said with a smile.

He walked with her the entire way to the bus stop.

"You didn't have to walk with me," Anne said.

"You think I would let you walk alone when it's getting dark?"

She gently took his hands. "I had a wonderful time."

"Me too," he said.

"I hope we can do it again sometime. I've never had anyone to draw with."

"Me neither."

He held on to her hand until the bus drove up.

"You be safe goin' home," he said.

"I will."

He watched her get on the bus and waited for it to pull away before he started walking home.

65

THE BRUERS PLANNED A SURPRISE party to celebrate Jerry getting his cast off. James hadn't heard from Stu, and he was worried about him. When he did talk to him on the phone, Stu told James he found a job at the supermarket with Len. Len was promoted to assistant manager, so Stu was hired as a stock boy. James met up with Stu on Thursday night. They headed to John's house so he could walk with them to the party.

"It's good to see you, Stu," James said. "I was beginning to think I wasn't going to see you again."

"Just been busy, is all."

"Too busy to call me?"

"I guess I haven't felt much like socializin' lately. Besides, you have a girlfriend now."

"So?"

"So, when was the last time you wanted to hang out with your buddies on a Saturday night?"

"Saturday is the only night she and I can be together."

"Like I said, you got a girlfriend."

James sighed.

"How's it goin' with her?"

James put his hands in his pockets. "Good."

"Uh-oh. Problems already?'

"No."

"Have you forgotten we've been friends since grade school?"

"It's complicated."

"Most chicks are."

"I don't want to talk about it."

"Oh, I know."

"Know what?" James said, annoyed.

"She wants to get married."

"No, that is definitely not it."

"Well, you just wait. It's only a matter of time till she's hasslin' you for a ring."

"Marcy's not like that, okay? Can we talk about something else?"

"Sure. You're almost on summer break, huh?"

"Yeah, I can't wait."

"Then how much time have you got left?"

"Dunno, maybe six more months."

Stu frowned. "How long does it take to learn to add two plus two?"

"It's a little more complicated than that."

"I hate math."

"I know."

They turned the corner of 12th Street onto Dover. James had never known anyone that lived on the Southwest side of town before. The neighborhoods between Dover and Morrisey were made up of upper-middle-class families. The yards were well-manicured, and no loud cars or late-night shenanigans were tolerated.

"So, what do you know about John's family?" James said.

"Not much. He doesn't like to talk about his home life. All I know is he lives with his stepmom."

"No other siblings?"

Stu shook his head. "He's very private."

"I know. I've never met anyone so aggravating."

"He made Patrick crazy too."

"But they were friends at one point, right?"

"Best."

"How did you meet John, anyway?"

"Through Patrick."

"So you were friends with Patrick first?"

Stu shrugged. "I guess."

"What do you mean, you guess?"

"I dunno, we had a class together, and one day we realized we both liked the same girl."

"Who? Tracy Bartley?"

"No, this was another girl."

"Who?"

"Linda."

"Linda? Hobbs?"

"Yeah."

"What? You had a crush on Linda Hobbs?"

"Didn't everybody?"

"Well ... yeah ... I guess."

"Oh, come on, no one could fill out a sweater like Linda."

James nodded.

"Anyway, we used to sit in the back of the class, you know, and watch her."

"Watch her do what?"

Stu stopped and stared at James.

"What?"

"Sometimes I wonder about you," Stu said, walking forward. "So, one day, Patrick tells me he heard from a friend of his friend's friend that Linda puts out."

"Oh yeah, right," James said, rolling his eyes. "You know she dated Brad the Boulder. He would have smashed in anyone's teeth that got next to her."

"If he knew about it."

James frowned.

"So, Patrick decides he is gonna ask Linda out to see if the rumor is true. His friend, friend's friend, tells him he will give Patrick twenty bucks if Linda shows him her boobs."

"And did she?"

"No, it turns out the only reason she agreed to the date was that her little brother was having a party that night, and she wanted someone to help her wrangle them."

"What?"

"Yeah, Patrick said it was one of the most horrible nights of his entire life. Eight wild little boys are running around the house, flinging boogers and food at each other. They even raided Linda's underwear drawer and ran around with panties on their heads. It was a disaster."

"Sounds like a nightmare."

"Yeah, he didn't even get a goodnight kiss."

"That stinks."

"Yeah," Stu stopped. "This is it, John's house."

James looked at the small two-story house with a small lawn and two lovely rose bushes growing by the porch.

"Are you sure this is where he lives?"

"Yeah. I've only been here once before."

"So, are we going to ring the doorbell?"

"You go ahead. I'll wait here."

"Why?"

"You haven't met his stepmother. She eats little children for breakfast."

James frowned.

"No lie."

"She can't be that bad."

"I am waitin' right here."

"It's not like he doesn't know we're coming."

Stu gave him a sideways look.

"For heaven's sake," James said, going inside the gate and up to the door, where he rang the bell. He waited. Stu mouthed the word "breakfast" to him. Finally, the door opened, and a tall, thin woman answered. Her steel grey hair was perfectly curled and tight against her head. Her glasses sat low on her long, thin nose.

"I'm not interested," she said.

"Excuse me?"

"Whatever you're selling, I'm not buying."

James could see her pushing the door.

"Wait, ma'am."

She looked annoyed at him.

"I am here to see John."

She looked him over like she was judging him. "You know John?"

"Yes, ma'am."

She crossed her arms. "What's your name?"

"James."

She looked at him as if she was also expecting the last name.

"Bennett."

She turned and walked inside and yelled up the stairs. "John, James Bennett is here for you." She walked back to the door. "It might take him a while to come down. He doesn't like visitors."

"I know, but he is expecting me."

"Hmmm," she said through her tightly clenched mouth.

James smiled, hoping John would hurry up for once.

John came downstairs a few moments later. "Hello, James."

"Hello," James said, relieved to see him.

"I see you met James," John said to his stepmother.

"I have. I almost thought he was at the wrong house. He looks very respectable. Not like the usual reprobates that come over here looking for you. Are you going out carousing tonight?"

"No, I am going to a party for Jerry tonight. He got his cast off today."

"Poor boy," she said, looking at James. "Life has been unkind to him."

"Hopefully, it will improve for him now that he is staying with the Bruers," James said.

"Hmmm," she said, looking James over again. "Have you got your key?" she asked John.

"Yes, ma'am."

"I will not get up and let you in if you forget it."

"I know," John said with a strained smile.

"Don't be too late. Lock the door when you come home."

"I will."

"And don't make a bunch of noise. It will be unpleasant for you if you wake me up."

"I know."

James and John walked down the walk.

"Wow, she is kind of harsh," James said. "Not what I expected."

"What did you expect? Someone like Mable?"

"I dunno."

"There is a reason this house looks like a gingerbread house."

James hid a smile and walked out the gate.

66

THE BRUER HOUSE WAS BUSTLING with activity as they finished the last preparations for Jerry's party. The boys did what they could to help prepare, but they were mainly underfoot. Mable had John and Danny hang some streamers and balloons, but they popped most of them and hung the streamers crooked. Betty made a special cake for Jerry, but John kept harassing her, wanting to lick the frosting spoon. She scolded him but was soaking up the attention.

"I see, um!" Eddie said.

They all scattered for a place to hide in the dark living room until Bob and Jerry entered through the front door.

"Where is everyone?" Jerry said.

"I don't know—you better turn on the lights," Bob said.

Jerry flipped the lights and put his hand to his chest when everyone jumped up and screamed surprise!

"You okay, Jerry? You look a little peaked," Danny said.

"I just wasn't expecting ... this!"

Everyone laughed.

Bob set his hand on Jerry's shoulder. "We thought you deserved a celebration for getting your cast off."

Jerry smiled up at Bob. "Thank you."

Bob squeezed his shoulder.

"I think we need to start the celebration with a speech from the guest of honor," John said.

"What? No," Jerry said, shaking his head.

"Speech," John said.

"Speech," Danny chimed in.

Everyone else joined in until Jerry had a red face.

"All right," he said, embarrassed that everyone was staring at him. "I want to thank you all for coming and helping over the last six weeks. I, for one, am glad to have the use of my arm back and to be more helpful to Bob at my job."

Everyone clapped, and Jerry smiled sheepishly.

"Now we eat cake!" John announced.

Betty placed her hands on her hips. "John! You ruined my surprise!"

"Oh, I'm sorry, little lady. Will you please forgive me," John said, taking her hands and kneeling in front of her.

She resisted a smile by rolling her lips.

"Please," he said, batting his eyes at her.

She giggled. "I forgive you."

"But you will help wash the dishes tonight, won't you, John?" Mable said.

John looked up at Mable with his mouth open.

"Thank you, dear," she said, entering the kitchen.

❏■❏■❏■❏■❏■❏■❏■❏■❏■❏■❏

Before dinner, Jerry waited for his opportunity to talk to John, but he was tied up in a conversation with Danny and James.

Jerry wasn't the only one that had observed the trio conversing and laughing. Stu was sitting withdrawn by himself at the far counter of the couch. His head was in his hand, and he was chewing on a fingernail.

"Hey, Stewy, how's it goin'?" Jerry said, sitting next to him on the couch.

"Okay, I guess."

"How come you're sitting over here by yourself?"

"I don't know, just tired."

"Oh? How come"?"

"I got a job."

"You did?"

"Yep."

"Doing what?"

"Well, Len got promoted to assistant manager at the market, so I took his old job."

Jerry sat his elbows on his knees. "How is it?"

"It's not too bad. You just stock shelves and move around a lot of boxes and crates. Sometimes I help bag groceries and deliver them to old ladies that don't want to come to the store. If I'm extra nice to them, they tip me well. How is it workin' with Bob?"

"Good. I like it."

Stu's eyes drifted back to the boys.

"We should go over and sit with them," Jerry said.

"You can if you want."

"Is something wrong, Stu?"

"Guess I just don't feel much like listening to Danny feed John's ego."

"You don't like Danny, do you?"

"I just don't like how John got star-struck because Danny is a good guitar player and can razzle dazzle a crowd. You would think John would give more credit to those of us that have stuck by him for so long," Stu said, folding his arms.

"I think he gives us credit."

Stu frowned at Jerry. "You do?"

"Well, yeah. He could have dropped us and stayed with Patrick."

Stu moved his hand over his mouth.

"If it makes you feel any better, I understand. It's hard to get John's attention sometimes. I've been waiting for a half hour."

"I don't know how you've been his friend for so long," Stu said.

Jerry shrugged. "I think it's because I accept him for who he is and know that when the chips are down, he is there for me. Maybe you should talk to John about how you feel instead of letting things fester inside you like Patrick did."

"Dinner time," Betty announced.

Everyone got up and moved into the dining room. Jerry wasn't sure if Stu would take his advice, but he knew things would only get worse if he didn't.

67

EVERYONE GATHERED AROUND THE TABLE for dinner, and the food started to be passed around.

"So Danny, did you tell the fellas about the other night"?" Eddie said.

Danny scooped out some potatoes and passed the bowl to John. "No, I didn't get a chance to mention it."

Excited about the opportunity to relive his night of glory riding in Joe's car, Eddie spent the next ten minutes telling his story. "Someday, I'm gonna have a car like that," Eddie said.

"It doesn't sound like a practical car," Bob said.

"Dad, you don't drive it because it's practical, you drive it because you're successful."

"Your father is very successful, Eddie," Martha said.

"Yeah, but he's not in the biz," Eddie said, buttering his roll.

"What difference does that make?" Betty said.

"Because in the entertainment business, it's all about appearances," Eddie said.

"He's right," Stu said. "You don't see Elvis drivin' a Ford pickup."

"Just because those people have a different lifestyle, it doesn't make them more successful than anyone else, it just means they have different priorities," Bob said. "For them, it's all about proving to the world that they are somebody by buying expensive material things and hosting large parties with influential people. But for some of us, success means providing a solid, stable life for our wives and children and helping people that are less fortunate than we are. That is where you will find life's true rewards."

Silence passed through the room as everyone admired Bob for the man he was.

"Gee, Dad, I didn't mean any disrespect," Eddie said.

"I know, son. I realize that you want to pursue that career, and that is your choice, but I want you to think about what kind of man you will become once you obtain your goal."

"Yes, sir."

"My goodness," Mable said. "This is a party. We should all be celebrating."

"I will help clear away the dishes, mama." Betty stood up and started to collect the dishes.

The conversation returned to trivial topics, but Eddie was reserved.

A short while later, Mable came in with plates and silverware. Betty followed behind her, carrying the cake. She sat the cake down in front of Jerry and gave him a pleased smile.

"I feel like we should be singing Happy Birthday," Danny said.

"Or 'For He's a Jolly Good Fellow.'" Bob said.

Everyone raised their voices and sang the song to Jerry.

"Thank you," Jerry said, his face shining.

"You need to cut the cake," Mable said.

"Me? I don't know anything about cuttin' a cake. I wouldn't even know how to start," Jerry said.

"I'll do it," Betty said, sitting next to him.

"Betty made the cake," John said.

"And let John lick the spoon," Danny said.

"I didn't let him—he took it from me," Betty said.

"Sounds about right," Jerry said.

John frowned.

"I think it's time that Jerry opened his present," Danny said.

"A present? For me?" Jerry said.

"But you have to close your eyes," John said.

"I do?"

"Just humor him, Jerry," Danny said.

John stood up. "Here, I will cover them so he can't peek."

"John!" Jerry protested.

John put his hands over Jerry's eyes. "Are you peeking?"

"No," Jerry snapped.

"Okay, Jerry, you can open them now," Danny said.

"I would if John would remove his hands."

John took his hands away, and Jerry opened his eyes to see James with a guitar in his hands.

Jerry blinked his eyes in disbelief.

"We all chipped in to get it for you," Danny said.

"It was just hanging around the store collecting dust," Eddie said.

"It was the Professor's idea to fix it up," John said.

"Really, James?" Jerry said.

James rubbed his neck. "Well, I did string it and tuned it, and Bob refinished it, but yeah, I had the idea."

"It's beautiful," Jerry said, tears in his eyes.

"Once a Hound Dog, always a Hound Dog," John said.

Jerry took it from James and held it gingerly in his hands.

"You think you remember how to play?" Stu said.

"As soon as the dishes are done, we are going to find out," John said.

Jerry smiled and strummed a few chords, the perfect sound filling his heart with joy.

❑■❑■❑■❑■❑■❑■❑■❑■❑■❑■❑■❑

After the dinner cleanup was completed, everyone gathered in the living room, and the boys all sat around playing songs. Everyone clapped and sang along to the songs they knew. Eddie's voice was out of key, but everyone let it slide because Mable was out of tune too.

Betty sat on a footstool and mooned over Jerry from afar.

Bob sat back and watched the boys closely. He noticed that Danny was having an extra good time and more like himself than he had been in weeks.

"Are you likin' the new guitar, Jerry?" Danny asked.

"I love it," he said.

"You say your band is called The Hound Dogs?" Bob asked.

"Yeah, Eds kind of gave us that name," John said.

Eddie puffed his chest out and grinned.

"You fellas sound good," Bob said.

"We're working on it," John said. "We haven't had a chance to practice much lately with Jerry's arm being in a sling and the loss of a rehearsal space, but I am sure we will figure it out somehow."

"Well, you know," Bob said, rubbing his chin. "I may be able to solve that problem for you. There is a space above the record shop currently being used for storage. You would have to clean it out and maybe repair a thing or two, but I think it might work."

"There is only one way I would consider it," John said.

"Okay."

"I insist that we pay you rent. You have done so much for us already. It doesn't seem fair."

"I can appreciate that, but I just sat here and witnessed five boys who are very enthusiastic about their music, and I want to provide the space to do it. That room has been vacant for years collecting junk and cobwebs. I believe in you and what you're doing. When you make it big, then you can worry about paying me back."

Everyone looked at John.

"We will work extra hard not to let you down," John said.

"Nothing like pressure," James said.

"You told me it wouldn't be easy," John said to James.

James chuckled. "That I did."

After the party started to break up, Jerry came over to John.

"Hey, John."

"Hey."

"Can I talk to you for a sec?"

"Sure," they stepped out onto the porch.

"I wanted to apologize for the other day."

"It's nothin'."

"Yes, it is. I know all you have tried to do is help me. I know she's my mom, but I've been hurt so much."

"I know, buddy," John said.

"I want to go see her and try and straighten things out. Do you think I'm okay goin' by myself?"

"You know what I think."

"Will you come with me?"

"Sure, I will."

Jerry smiled at him. "Thanks for the guitar."

"Wha—you kiddin'? You're a member of the group. We wanted to do it for you."

Jerry smiled.

"Now, come on before you get all mushy on me."

Jerry and John went back inside. Danny, Stu, and James were waiting for him.

"You ready to go, John?" James said.

"Yeah," he looked at Danny. "Well, this is it. The next time I see you, you'll be on the edge of stardom."

"I doubt that," Danny said.

"You're going to do great, Danny," James said.

"Thanks, James."

"See ya later, squirt," Stu said, taking Jerry's arm and shaking him.

"See ya, Stu," Jerry said.

Danny made eye contact one last time with John before he left the house. Danny watched them go, a certain sadness in his heart.

PART 3

68

ETTY SAT DISHEARTENED ON THE toilet seat, staring at the picture of a stunning model. She believed the magazine when it declared that if she followed the easily provided instructions, her hair would turn out to look exactly like the pictured model. With a trembling lip, she stood up and looked at her frightening appearance in the mirror. Somewhere she had made a mistake and was left with an unmanageable gnarled mess. Snatching up a comb from the cluttered counter, she attempted to pull a comb through the ratted ends. What made her think she could ever look like a model? Curlers, hairspray, or teasing would never take away her homely appearance.

A loud knock on the door jangled her nerves. "Hey, Betty, you realize you're not the only one who has to get ready to go out tonight?"

"Leave me alone, Eddie," she said, trying to pull the stuck comb out.

"Aw, come on, Betty. You've been there for an hour already."

"You could be in here all day, and you still won't look like Buddy Holly!"

"Ha, ha, you wait. Someday, I am going to make it big in the biz."

"In your dreams."

"What is going on up here?" Mable said, coming up the stairs.

"Betty's locked herself in the bathroom for the last hour, and I need to get in there to get ready too."

Betty flung open the door. The comb was still stuck in her hair, and her eyes were red.

"Go ahead and get ready. I don't care. Because I am not going." She stomped her foot, stormed down the hall, and slammed her bedroom door.

Mable placed her hand on her hip. "What did you do to upset your sister?"

"Me? I didn't do anything. I only wanted my turn in the bathroom."

Mable sighed. "I will talk to her."

"Can I use the bathroom now?"

"Yes," Mable said.

Eddie rushed into the bathroom and closed the door before his mother changed her mind.

Mable walked to Betty's door and knocked. "Betty, can I come in?"

Betty didn't answer, but Mable could hear her crying. "Betty?"

Mable opened the door, and Betty was sitting on her bed with her face buried in her hands. Mable closed the door and sat by Betty on the bed.

"Betty, what is the matter?"

"Nothing," she said, wiping at her eyes.

"Now, that isn't true. You're not going to the show?"

Betty stared at her hands. "That's right."

"Why not?"

"Because look at me, mama! My hair is an absolute mess! I tried to fix it. Honestly, I did, but I failed. Besides, what boy is going to want to dance with me?" she sniffled.

"I think any boy would be lucky to dance with you."

Betty looked at her mother through her blurry eyes. "I'm homely, mama, and awkward."

"That isn't true, Betty."

"Yes, it is."

"You need to dry your eyes," Mable said, handing Betty a tissue. "For heaven's sake, you can't go to the show with red eyes."

"I told you I'm not going," Betty said, crossing her arms.

"Pull yourself together, young lady. I am going to help you get ready."

"You will?"

"Yes, I will, but you must stop crying."

Betty nodded.

"Let's see," Mable said, touching Betty's hair. "What did you do?"

"I tried to tease it as the directions said, but all I did was make a ratted mess."

"That you did. Do you know what dress you want to wear?"

"I don't have any pretty dresses."

"I think your dresses are lovely." Mable opened the closet, and Betty sat on the bed watching her mother evaluate her wardrobe.

"What about his one?" Mable pulled out a dark blue short-sleeved A-line dress.

"That one is so ... plain."

"Well, it just needs the right accessories."

"I don't have any suitable accessories."

"No, but I do. Now, put a smile on that face, and you come with me."

Betty stood up, and her mother put her arm around her shoulders. "I may not be a fairy godmother with a magic wand, but I do know a thing or two about dressing up for a show."

Betty finally smiled and went down the hall with her mother to her parents' bedroom. Betty sat at her mother's large three-mirror dressing table and let her fix the mess she made. It took some time and patience, but when Mable was done, Betty's wavy hair was pulled back by a dainty satin blue headband that pushed her hair away from her face. A light touch of makeup accented her natural beauty, and it shined through in her new confidence.

"Well, what do you think?" Mable asked.

"Oh, Mama, I can't believe it's me!" Betty said, gently touching her curls.

Mable laughed.

"I wish I didn't have to wear my glasses."

"Don't you worry. Your new glasses complement your face perfectly."

"You think someone will want to dance with me?" Betty said.

"I think so," Mable said, giving Betty's shoulders a squeeze. "Let's get you dressed."

With her mother's help, Betty got dressed for the dance, and when she was ready, Betty stood in front of the full-length mirror, smiling at her new reflection.

"Now for the last piece," Mable said, fastening a dainty, lustrous pearl necklace around her daughter's neck. Betty's eyes brightened as she gently touched the elegant strand.

"Mama, these are so beautiful."

"Yes, they are special. They belonged to your grandmother, and she let me wear them the night of my first dance."

Betty turned to Mable with an apprehensive brow. "Are you sure? They are so precious. I would hate for anything to happen to them."

"Nothing will happen, and we want you to wear them."

Betty hugged her mother tightly. "Thank you so much, Mama."

Mable patted her back. "Now you go downstairs—I am sure your brother is going crazy by now."

"Let him wait," Betty said, and Mable laughed.

❏■❏■❏■❏■❏■❏■❏■❏■❏■❏■❏

"Where is she?" Eddie said, looking at the clock above the mantel. "We're going to be late."

"Just relax and sit down, Edward," Bob said. "You are not going to be late."

"I just wanted to get there early before all the good seats are taken."

Bob shook his head at Jerry, who was sitting on the couch.

"Why can't you be more like Jerry? He is very relaxed."

"Because Jerry hasn't put up with my sister for sixteen years."

Jerry scratched his ear and shook his head.

"There you are," Eddie said as Betty walked into the room with her mother behind her.

Bob turned to see his daughter, who had a demure smile.

"Well, well, who is this young lady?" Bob said.

"I don't know," Mable said. "But isn't she lovely?"

"I should say so," Bob said, standing. "I don't know if I should let her go out now. All the young men will be fighting over her."

"Oh, Daddy," Betty said, blushing.

"Doesn't your sister look lovely tonight, Edward?" Bob said.

"Yeah, sure, swell. Can we go now?"

"Never mind your brother," Bob said. "He's afraid he'll be late. Okay, let's go, kids."

Eddie bolted out the door and headed for the car. Bob turned to see Jerry standing mesmerized as he looked at Betty.

"Are you ready to go, Jerry?" Bob asked.

"Huh?" Jerry said.

"Are you ready to go?"

"Oh, yeah, sure," he said, pulling himself out of his trance.

"Maybe you should help her put on her wrap," Bob whispered to Jerry.

Jerry blinked his eyes. "Oh?"

Bob smiled.

"Oh!" Jerry walked over to Betty. "Can I ... uh ... help you put on your ... wrap?" Jerry looked back at Bob for reassurance.

Bob nodded.

"Yes," Betty said with a slight nod.

Mable handed Jerry Betty's shawl, and Jerry put it delicately on her shoulders. She smiled at him.

"Can I walk you to the car?" he said, offering his arm.

"Yes."

"You have a wonderful time," Mable said.

"We will," Jerry said.

Jerry opened the door for Betty, and the two walked outside. Bob smiled at Mable.

"Our little girl is growing up," he said.

"Yes, she is."

"Say, we're going to be alone tonight. That will be different."

"Yes, it will"."

"Maybe we should go to the show."

"Or we could stay here and have our own party," Mable said with a smile.

"That we could."

"Dad!" Eddie yelled from the driveway.

"I better hurry before Edward has a nervous breakdown," Bob said.

"I will go start dinner."

Bob left the house, and Mable watched from the door as Jerry got in the back seat with Betty and Eddie got in the front seat with his father, talking the entire time.

69

THE SATURDAY NIGHT SHOW AT the Beaumont was a total sell-out. The Dice hadn't played a show since Danny joined the group, and expectations were high. Radio interviews with Joe and Will and free ticket contests generated publicity that sent anxious Dice fans into a frenzy.

The energy level behind the curtain was electric. Stagehands were running around, ensuring the lights and mics were working. Danny peeked through the curtains, hoping to catch a glimpse of his friends.

Eddie, Jerry, Betty, Stu, and James were there, but he didn't see John. Disappointed, Danny stepped away from the curtain and headed toward the green room for a glass of water. He spotted Clive in front of him, which meant Joe must have arrived.

"Hey, Clive," Danny said.

"Daniel," Clive said, shaking his hand. "Look at you all dressed up in your finery."

Danny pulled at his collar. "Yeah? I wish it felt more natural."

"I understand that. I can't wait to get home at night and take my suit off."

"Me too."

"So, I was wonderin' if you were still interested in findin' a place to listen to some blues," Clive said.

"Well, heck yeah."

"A friend of mine owns a place down on Quarter Street called The Blue Kat. You come by Thursday night, and we'll give you an education."

"That would be terrific. You mind if I bring a friend?"

"I reckon not."

"Gee, thanks, Clive."

"Don't mention it."

Danny saw Joe come out of the green room with Monica. Stopping, he whispered something in her ear. Monica laughed softly, and Danny's jealousy rose the hair on the back of his neck.

Clive sensed Danny's distraction. "You okay, Dan?"

"Huh? Oh, yeah," Danny chuckled.

"She is mighty pretty, ain't she?" Clive said.

"Who?"

"You best watch yourself. Joe may not act like he cares, but he does. . . a lot."

Danny half smiled.

Monica kissed Joe before walking away. Danny was hoping Joe hadn't noticed him, but he was already walking toward him.

"Well, Danny, I almost didn't recognize you. You look fantastic tonight. Doesn't he, Clive?"

"Yes, sir, he sure does," Clive said.

"You don't have to stay tonight, Clive," Joe said.

"Sir?"

"I know it's your son's birthday."

"Well, yes, sir, it is."

"I know how important those early birthdays are. So, you go on ahead and go home."

Clive smiled. "Thank you, sir."

"Of course. Tell Maribel hello for me."

"Will do. Be seein' you, Danny," Clive said.

"See you, Clive."

Clive tipped his hat and left.

"So, how are you feeling? Good?" Joe said to Danny.

"Yeah, a little nervous."

Joe adjusted Danny's tie as if he was an awkward teenager. "Well, that is to be expected. I'm glad you're here with us tonight."

"Me too."

"Just remember to smile, and the fans will love you."

Danny nodded. "Sure."

"You may want to check on your guitar—make sure it is tuned and ready to go. It sounded a bit off earlier."

"I will."

Joe walked away. Danny's guitar was perfectly tuned, but he figured he would recheck it to have something to do.

70

MARCY SPENT THE ENTIRE DAY with her friends, preparing for the show. It was fun to help fix each other's hair and makeup. Clothes fell where they were tossed, and by the time the girls left Mollie's house, it looked like a tornado had blown through her room. Marcy, Mollie, Doris, and Mae squeezed into Mae's small car. Laughing and talking, they enjoyed the carefree drive to The Beaumont.

Marcy squinted at her reflection in the tiny compact mirror as she fussed with her hair.

"Stop fussing with it, or it will fall," Mae said.

"I know it."

"You act like he's never seen you before."

"I just want to ... you know."

"Turn him on?"

Marcy blushed.

"If he doesn't make a pass at you tonight, he's never going to," Doris said.

"You look perfect, Marcy," Mollie said.

"Thanks, girls."

"How do I look?" Mae said.

Mollie and Doris batted their eyes and flounced their hair in mock imitation. Marcy gave them a warning look.

"You look perfect, as always," Marcy said, opening her purse and searching for more lipstick.

"Teddy Bear" came on the radio, and Mae turned it up. "Now, there is a man I would go for."

"What girl wouldn't?" Marcy said.

"I hope Danny notices me tonight," Mollie said.

"I told you, you should have worn the red dress tonight," Mae said. "He would have noticed you for sure."

"I am not wearing a tight, low-cut dress that shows my boobs! I don't want every horn dog in the place wanting to paw me. Just Danny."

Marcy and Mae laughed, but Doris pulled on her dress and pressed her stomach. Even though she wore an unforgiving girdle, her body would never be perfect like Mae's or her features as charming as Marcy's.

Mollie sat her hand on Doris's leg. "You look lovely tonight."

"You don't have to lie to me, Mollie. I know the truth."

"What are you girls whispering about back there?" Marcy said.

"Doris doesn't think she looks lovely tonight."

"Oh, Doris, you need to quit with all that negative self-talk. You do look lovely," Marcy said.

"Thanks, Mar."

"Look, girls, we are here!" Mae said, pulling up into the valet parking.

"Mae, we can't afford a valet to park the car," Marcy said.

"Oh yeah? Watch this."

The valet came over to the car. "Good evening, ladies."

"Hello," they said with a flirty wave.

"May I park your car for you?" he asked Mae.

"Yes," she said with a seductive smile.

He opened the door, and she got out. His eyes traveled up her long, shapely legs.

"That will be one dollar," he said.

Mae dropped her keys. "Oops. Silly me." She bent over to pick them up, and the valet could see her cleavage. Standing, she stepped in closer to him. "I'm so sorry. I don't have that much money." She felt his tie and bit her lip. "If I have to park in the lot, it will hurt my little feet," she said, sticking her lower lip out. "Can I pay you back later?"

"Yeah, sure," he said, his eyes on her wet red lips. He handed her the claim ticket.

"Thank you so much." She kissed him on his cheek, leaving a red lip print.

"You are so bad," Mollie said to Mae.

"I can't help it if men are so predictable."

She looked back at the valet, who was still looking at her. She gave him a small wave, and they went inside.

71

JAMES WAS TALKING TO STU when Marcy and the girls came in. Any thought or words completely left James as he gazed at Marcy. Her silver dress shimmered in the light, and the thin straps on her dress led to a plunging neckline that exposed a tempting tease of her cleavage. Wispy tresses of hair hung down from the perfect curls on top of her head.

"Wow," Stu said.

She walked over to them. "Hi."

"You look like a movie star," Stu said.

She absently touched the tips of her hair. "You think so?"

"You look gorgeous," James said.

His intense gaze warmed Marcy to her toes. "Thank you."

Stu pulled out a chair. "A seat for the lady."

She casually sat down, and James sat next to her.

"Can I get you kids a drink?" Stu said.

"Something sweet," Marcy said.

"How about you, Romeo?"

"I don't care," James said, setting his hand on the back of Marcy's chair.

Stu walked away.

"It looks like everyone in Madison is here tonight. I bet Danny is so excited," Marcy said.

James continued to stare at her like a dumbstruck schoolboy.

"Are you going to say something?" Marcy said.

"You're beautiful."

She smiled and lowered her eyes.

"I can't wait to be alone with you tonight," he whispered.

"Me neither."

Stu returned with their refreshments.

James grabbed the glass that Stu had brought him and took a hardy drink before even thinking about what it was. Immediately he began to cough.

"You weren't supposed to swallow it whole," Stu said.

"Are you all right?" Marcy said.

James continued to cough, but he nodded his head. "I need to get some water." He got up and left.

Mae leaned over to Marcy. "I think you got his attention."

"Thanks for lending me your dress," Marcy said.

"No problem. It's definitely working."

They giggled.

"Hello, gorgeous," Stu said to Mae.

"Hello," Mae said coolly.

"You mind if I sit here?"

"No."

He sat down. "The color of your dress compliments your eyes."

"Thank you."

"Can I buy you a drink?"

"Okay."

"What are you havin'?"

"I'll take a screwdriver."

"I'll be back," he said, getting up.

John came strolling in at the last minute. He had been flirting with a waitress at the bar before making his way over with a free drink. The only available seat was next to Eddie, so he approached Doris, who was chatting with Betty.

"Hey, beautiful," John said to Doris.

She looked at him, surprised. "Me?"

"Yeah, you. Would you mind if I sit here?"

"Oh, I guess not."

"I sure would appreciate it."

Doris moved to the seat by Eddie, and John sat next to Betty.

"Betty, is that you?" John said.

"Yes," she said softly.

"My, my, but you look lovely."

"Thank you," she said, beaming.

John tapped his finger on the table. "Something is different about you. What is it?"

"I don't know," she said, smoothing out her skirt.

"I may be able to figure it out if I could ever see your face."

Slowly, she met his eyes. He looked closely at her, making her blush.

"She has new glasses," Jerry said in a low tone.

John nodded. "Oh, yeah, that's it. Very nice."

She grinned.

"The smile helps too."

Jerry scowled at John, who didn't notice.

"Hey, Jer, switch with me so I can talk to the Professor," John said.

Jerry was hoping John would move further away from Betty, but he would only be on the other side of her. "Why can't you ever be happy with where you are?"

"Who said I wasn't happy?"

Jerry frowned at him.

"I guess I could pick you up and move you."

"Fine!" Jerry growled, switching places with John.

"Hey, chowder head," John said to James, who was too wrapped up in Marcy to notice him. John knocked on his head.

"Hey, what the . . ." James said, turning to see John. "I should have known it was you."

"He made me switch with him, James," Jerry said.

"So, your woman looks mighty fine tonight," John said to James.

"Keep your eyes to yourself."

"Wooo, you got it bad."

James scowled at him. "I don't need you bothering me tonight."

"Too late."

John looked across the table to see Stu attempting to charm Mae. She turned and made eye contact with John. She ran the tip of her tongue across her lips.

John gave her an indifferent glance and sat back in his chair.

The lights dimmed, and a voice came over the loudspeaker.

"Ladies and Gentlemen, please welcome back to The Beaumont stage, The Dice!"

An explosive cheer rose from the crowd as the curtain came up, and the show started with "Whole Lotta Shakin' Goin' On."

Joe was fully charged and ready to perform. His dynamic persona flooded the stage with a fiery splash of showmanship. Joe and Will stood back-to-back, moving in identical motions and bopping heads. The routine mesmerized the crowd, and their cheers were amplified.

James and John watched Danny execute his unmotivated dance moves in their shadow. Gone was the exuberant young man whose passion for music had rocked Len's party, and a well-rehearsed, unmotivated robot took his place.

After the number was over, Joe took the microphone. "Good evening, guys and dolls! Are you ready to rock the Beaumont?"

A huge cheer echoed through the crowd.

"You all know how special tonight is for us. Not only because we are with you, but we also have a new member," Joe said, stepping over to Danny. "This young man has come a long way since joining us. He has worked hard, and his talent has been a welcome asset. Wouldn't you agree, boys?" Joe looked straight at Will.

Will flashed his alluring white smile while sending daggers with his eyes. "Oh yeah," he said, clapping his hands. Boyd did a quick drum roll for his answer, and the crowd laughed.

"Thank you, Boyd," Joe said. "Everyone, please put your hands together for the newest Dice man, Daniel Bruer!"

Danny stepped forward to be embraced with a loud cheer. James, John, and everyone at the table rose to their feet to clap and hoot for

Danny. He grinned at them, and when he made eye contact with John, his lost spirits were restored.

"Well, it would seem that Danny has his very own cheering section," Joe chuckled. He then stepped away from Danny and reclaimed the spotlight. "We have a wonderful show planned for you tonight, and after the closing number, I have a special announcement for you all, so be sure to stick around for that."

Another loud cheer went up from the crowd.

"Let's 'Shake Rattle-n-Roll'!"

By now, Eric was out on the stage, and the audience was moving. The momentum of the set built and rocked the star-struck crowd. The band was thankful when they could finally take a break.

Danny emerged from backstage and joined his friends.

"Danny!" they yelled, circling him and shaking him. Stu and John remained in their seats.

"Hey, guys!" Danny said.

"How does it feel to be a star?" Eddie said.

"Exhausting."

"Here, have some water," Mollie said, handing Danny a glass.

"Thanks a lot," he said, gulping it down.

Mollie took the empty glass. "You want me to get you another one?"

"If you don't mind."

Eager to please, she held to the glass like it was gold and left with wings on her feet.

James pulled out a chair for him. "Take a load off."

Danny sat down.

"You're killin' it, man!" Eddie said.

"I guess so," he said, wiping his brow. "I can't thank you all enough for comin' tonight."

"We wouldn't miss it. Would we, John?" James said pointedly.

"Of course not," John said.

Mollie returned and handed Danny the cold glass.

"Thank you," he said, dazzling her with his smile.

"You all are going to stay for the after-party? I would love to spend some time with you all," he said, looking at John, who nodded.

"Save the first dance for me, Danny?" Mollie said, batting her eyes at him.

"Of course."

"Me too, Danny," Doris said.

"Yes," he said, emptying his glass and handing it to her.

Mollie's smile was gone, and she glared at Doris, who smiled triumphantly.

"I will see you all later," he said with one last smile as he returned for the closing set.

It was another round of hot rock-n-roll, and when Joe introduced Vanessa, the show reached its climax as they sang "Baby You Got What It Takes."

Danny observed Monica sitting at a nearby table with other close friends of The Dice. Her striking features looked dull as Joe crooned and moved suggestively with his co-singer.

The show closed with "See Ya Later Alligator." Danny had enough of looking like a puppet on the side, and when Eric came over by him, Danny let loose his unique dance moves. It brought the shouting to a deafening crescendo. Danny was sure he would pay hell for it, but he didn't care.

Joe took the mic after the song ended, and the shouting had died down. "I want to thank you all for coming out tonight. It warms our hearts to be back where we belong," Joe said, placing his hand over his heart.

Whistles and claps flowed from the crowd.

"I want to share some news with you all. The Dice will be officially recording our first record this September!"

A resounding cheer came from the crowd.

"I can't tell you how excited we are! So, we invite you to all stay and celebrate with us! Drinks are on the house, and for 'cryin' out loud, get up and dance!"

Music filled the hall, and couples began to move onto the dance floor.

Fans flooded the area in front of the stage, and Danny was caught up in the moment. He was glad when he was finally with his friends and could be himself.

"My gosh, what a night," Danny said.

"Sit down, Danny," Mollie said, offering her seat.

"I'm not going to take the seat of a lady."

"You can have mine, and I'll grab you a beer," Eddie said.

Danny took Eddie's chair that was next to Doris. Doris smiled, satisfied at Mollie.

John stood up. "Come on, let's go dance this one," he said, offering his hand to Betty.

"Me?" she squeaked.

"Come on. I don't do this very often."

She took his hand. Jerry clutched the table as John led Betty onto the dance floor.

"Do you know how to jitter?" John said to Betty.

"Do I!"

"Well, hold on then, little darlin'," he said, whirling her around, causing her dress to come out in a full flare. He brought her back in and moved her around so fast she thought she might lose her balance, but he kept a firm grip on her and didn't let her falter.

The next song was "At the Hop," and Betty was let loose like a vibrant comet. John stepped back with the others to watch her. Her confidence seized the moment, and she twisted like a perfect top. By the song's end, her admirers applauded her.

She hugged John. "Thank you."

Jerry was on his feet, his body tense, and his fingers balled tight.

"Earth Angel" started to play, and Betty held onto John's hands. "Please dance this one with me."

John looked over to see the hurricane that was brewing.

"Of course," he said, pulling Betty tightly in his arms. Her eyes were hazy, making him think she honestly might faint. A few moments later, John felt the tap on his shoulder that he hoped would come. He turned to see a seething Jerry.

"Yes?"

"I want to talk to you," Jerry hissed.

"Okay, can I finish this dance?"

"No, you cannot!"

"It's not polite to leave a lady alone on the dance floor."

Jerry took a firm hold of Betty's hand. "She is finishing this dance with me!"

"Does the lady object?" John said.

"No," she said, smiling fondly at Jerry.

"Fair enough." John bowed to Betty and left the dance floor with a smile.

Jerry turned to Betty and looked at her tranquil face.

"Are you mad at me for cutting in?"

"No."

"You just don't know him like I do."

"I know he's a bad boy."

Jerry rumpled his brow. "What do you know about bad boys?"

"They're dangerous."

"And you like danger?"

She felt his tie. "You're kind of a bad boy, aren't you, Jerry?"

"Maybe," he said, setting his hands on her waist.

She placed her arms around his neck, and they swayed slowly to the music, gazing affectionately into each other's eyes.

72

MOLLIE GROUND HER TEETH WHILE watching Danny conversing with Doris, but his attention was on Monica. She was sitting at the table by herself. He politely excused himself and walked over to her.

"Hi," Danny said.

"Hi," she said with a half-smile.

"Why is a pretty lady like you sitting over here all by herself?"

"Just lucky, I guess."

"Would you dance with me?"

She hesitated a moment and then took his hand.

Danny was a skilled dancer, and Monica was swept away by his flowing moves.

Mollie sat next to Doris, and hope evaporated while they watched the flirtatious dance.

"He's not going to dance with me, is he?" Mollie said.

"It's still early," Doris said.

"How can we compete with her?"

"She is a plastic doll with no heart, and if that is the kind of girl he's into, they deserve each other."

Mollie smiled at Doris. "I'm sorry if I was catty."

"Me too."

"He is so handsome," Mollie sighed.

"Come on, let's freshen up and drink something sinful."

Mollie nodded, and the two left the table.

◻◼◻◼◻◼◻◼◻◼◻◼◻◼◻◼◻◼◻

A slow song started, and Danny held Monica close in his arms.

"You're as talented on the dance floor as you are on guitar," Monica said.

"So are you."

Her eyes flashed. "How do you know I play guitar?"

"Because I saw you."

"When?"

"One day in the studio."

"The last time I was in the studio, I fought with Joe. Did you see that too?"

"Let's not talk about him. Right now, all I want to do is look at you."

She looked into his dark brown eyes that were sprinkled with lust.

"You know I should return to the table before Joe misses me."

"He's not even at the table. If you were mine, you would never be alone."

"Danny, you shouldn't be talking this way."

"Why not?"

"Because."

"Tell me you're happy with him, and I will leave you alone."

"It's not that simple."

"You are the most beautiful woman I have ever seen," he said breathlessly.

"Danny, please . . ."

He lifted her chin. "Just let me kiss you . . . once."

She pushed him away. "In front of all these people? There would be hell to pay if Joe saw."

"He doesn't seem to care about what you see."

"Thanks for the dance." She lowered her eyes and left him alone on the dance floor.

Crestfallen, Danny returned to the table.

"She's not worth it, you know," John said. "You will never have her as long as she is involved with that Liberace wanna-be."

"I don't understand what she sees in him," Danny said, casting his eyes over at Monica, standing next to Joe.

"Money," John said.

"I refuse to believe that."

"It may not be the entire reason, but I'm willing to bet it's at least seventy-five percent of it."

Danny stood up. "I need a drink. You want one?"

"Sure."

73

ORIS AND MOLLIE WERE ENJOYING a drink and conversation in the lounge when Mae found them.

"What are you chickens doing in here?"

"Having a drink. You want to join us?" Doris said.

"Do I," Mae said, sitting next to Mollie. "I didn't think I was going to shake him."

"Who?" Mollie said.

"Stu," Mae said, rolling her eyes.

"I thought you liked him," Doris said.

"Are you kidding? He's so juvenile."

"I think he's rather nice," Mollie said.

"Me too," Doris said.

"I don't want a nice boy," Mae said, sucking on a swizzle stick.

"What's wrong with nice boys?" Mollie asked.

"I don't know. They're so ordinary and boring."

"I don't think Danny is ordinary or boring," Mollie said, sipping her drink.

Mae smiled slyly. "Maybe he isn't the nice boy you think he is."

Danny and John strolled into the lounge.

"Oh, my goodness, there he is," Doris said.

"Who?" Mae said.

"Danny," Doris whispered.

"Where?" Mollie said, looking around.

Doris pointed at him. "Right there."

Mae followed Doris's finger to see John.

"Hey, fellas," Mae called out, waving at them.

"Mae!" Mollie said, grabbing her hand. "What are you doing?"

"Inviting them to join us."

"Why?"

"Why do you think?" Mae said with a wicked smile.

"Hey, ladies, what are you doing in here?" Danny said.

"We wanted to have a quiet drink. Why don't you join us?" Mae made eye contact with John and patted the seat next to hers.

John sat down next to Doris, forcing Danny to sit by Mae. Now no one was smiling.

A cocktail waitress came over to their table.

"What can I get you, gentlemen?"

"Two beers," Danny said.

She smiled and left.

"So, are you ladies having a good time?" Danny said.

"Wonderful," Mae said, running her finger over the lip of her glass.

"I thought you would all be dancing?" Danny said.

"No one has asked us," Mollie said.

"Oh."

John jabbed Danny in the side.

"Ow," Danny said, looking at him. John widened his eyes and nodded his head toward Mollie.

"What?"

"Mollie, would you like to dance with Danny?" John said.

"Yes, I mean, if he wants to."

"Sure, but let me have a drink first."

John closed his eyes, and Mollie's shoulders fell.

The waitress came back with their drinks.

"I propose a crust of toast for Danny," John said, lifting his mug. "To the man of the forgotten hour, may his rise to star doom be swift and immediate. Long live the court jester!"

"Here, here!" they cheered, smiles returning.

Then the cloud of doom returned.

"Hello." Joe stood beside the table with Monica on his arm. "I didn't expect to find my new star in the lounge."

"I was having a drink with my friends," Danny said.

"Oh, how nice of you, and I see your agent is here tonight," Joe said, nodding at John, who politely nodded back.

"Your client fits in well with my group, don't you think?" Joe said.

"Sure."

"Danny, now that you've had a polite drink with your little friends, it's time for you to join me at my table so I can introduce you to interesting, influential people that will boost our career."

Danny met John's eyes. "But I don't want to leave my friends."

"They can join us, there is plenty of room."

"I don't think there is a table big enough for you and your ego," John said, standing.

"John . . ." Danny said.

"I'll see you later, Danny."

Danny wanted to follow John as he left the lounge, but Joe put a heavy hand on his shoulder.

"Ignore him, Danny. He's insignificant. You can't afford to be distracted now that success is right in front of you."

Danny opened his mouth to say something, but his eyes fell on Monica, who turned away.

❏■❏■❏■❏■❏■❏■❏■❏■❏■❏■❏

"Where are you going in such a hurry?"

John turned to see Mae, who had followed him toward the door. "Home."

"Home? It's still early," she stepped in closer to him. "I bet you and I could find some trouble to get into." Mae gazed into John's eyes with unashamed seduction.

"You think so?"

330

She nodded and slipped her arms around him. "My car is parked outside."

"Are you sure you should be driving?"

"Who says we would be driving?" She rubbed up against him and ran her fingertip down the side of his face.

"What about Stu?"

"What about him?"

"I thought you were with him tonight."

"Why would you think that?"

"Because he has been buying you drinks, and you've been teasing him."

"I only did that to make you jealous," she said, bringing her face closer to his.

"It would have only made me jealous if I had wanted you in the first place." John firmly removed her arms from around him.

"What's wrong with you?" she spat at him.

"Excuse me?"

"Most men would kill to have a chance with me."

"I'm sure they would, and most men wouldn't care that you teased and used their friend as long as you left with them."

"You expect me to believe you're some kind of saint?"

"Frankly, I don't care what you believe," John turned, but her words stopped him.

"You're nothing special, you know that? You're nothing but a common, worthless tramp."

"It's nice to know we have something in common."

Mae reached out to slap him, but he grabbed her wrist.

"Now, what do you want to go and do that for? Just when I thought we were becoming friends."

"I hate you," she hissed at him.

"Goodnight, Mae." And with that, John exited The Beaumont.

Fuming, Mae turned to see Stu. She froze for a moment, wondering how much he had seen. Acting cool, she flounced her hair and forced a smile as she approached him.

Stu's expression held a touch of suspicion. "I was wondering where you disappeared to."

"I went to the powder room."

"How did you end up in here?"

"I ran into Doris and Mollie, and they invited me to have a drink with them."

"Why were you with John?"

Mae twisted her hands. "Oh, he wanted me to leave with him, but I turned him down. He wasn't too happy about that."

"I'll just bet he wasn't," Stu said in a low tone.

Mae took Stu's hand and rubbed her thumb over his knuckles. "Why don't we sit down, and you can buy me another drink?"

Falling under the spell of her playful blue eyes, he forgot about his anger and returned to the table with her.

James and Marcy were in their own little world on the dance floor. His arms were tight around her middle, and her hands rested on his shoulders.

"What are you thinking?" Marcy said."

"I'm thinking it's time we got out of here."

She nodded. "I agree."

"Let me tell Stu we are leaving."

"Okay."

James took her hand, and they walked off the dance floor.

Stu and Mae were the only two left at the table. Stu was sitting close to her, and she was staring straight ahead, draining another glass. James walked up and tapped Stu on the shoulder.

"Hey, Stu, I think Marcy and I are going to leave."

"Why is everyone leaving when the party is just starting?" Mae said.

"Mae . . ." Marcy said.

"I haven't even had a chance to dance with James yet," she said, latching onto his hand.

"I'm done dancing," James said, taking his hand back.

"You're all a bunch of party poopers!"

"Mae, calm down, honey," Stu said.

"I don't want to calm down! I want another drink!"

"Don't you think you've had enough to drink?"

"Who are you, my father?"

"Stu's right, Mae. You have had a few too many," Marcy said.

"I am fine," she snapped.

"James, can I talk to you for a moment?" Marcy took James's hand and pulled him aside.

"Darling, I can't leave. Not now."

"You're joking, right?" James scoffed.

"It's Mae. She's drunk, and I can't leave her like this."

James pulled Marcy into his arms. "Mollie or Doris can take care of her. Tonight, you belong to me." He leaned in, and his lips captured hers in a long breathless kiss she couldn't pull away from.

"James," she whispered.

"I want you," he said, nuzzling her neck.

Marcy's head was swimming, and her desire to leave with him was overwhelming, but she would never be able to deal with the guilt of leaving her friend.

Gently, she pushed him away. "I'm sorry. Mae is my friend, and she needs me."

"What she needs is to grow up."

"James, please, I am asking you to understand," Marcy pleaded.

His stance was rigid, and he stepped back. "I understand. I understand you would rather stay here and coddle a spoiled brat than leave with me."

"James, you're being unreasonable."

"Am I? I am your boyfriend, and I should come first."

Marcy blinked at him. "I can't believe you are talking this way."

"You need to make a choice, Marcy. Either you leave with me right now, or I am leaving without you."

Marcy stuck her chin out and folded her arms. "Fine, then I guess you're leaving."

James set his jaw. "If that's how you want it."

"It is," she said, fighting her tears.

"Hey, Marcy," Stu said, walking up beside her. "You need to come and talk to Mae. She's out of control."

James held his stance, and Marcy wiped angrily at a stray tear.

"I'm coming," she turned and walked away.

"What was that about?" Stu said.

James cast his hot glare on Stu before turning away.

"Hey, where are you going?" Stu said.

"I'm leaving."

"Right now? But . . ."

"Goodnight, Stu," James said and left.

Stu looked after James, then back at the table, then back after James. "Damn it!" he said, throwing his arms in the air.

❏■❏■❏■❏■❏■❏■❏■❏■❏■❏

Danny was miserable sitting with Joe and listening to his sickening dialogue with his friends. He occasionally nodded and faked interest, but all he wanted to do was leave. Jerry and Betty came over to talk to him, and he was thankful for the distraction.

"Hey, Danny, me and Betty are going to head home. We want to thank you for the swell time."

"Yes, Danny, we had a lot of fun," Betty said.

"I'm glad. Here, let me give you money for a cab. It's getting late," Danny said, handing Jerry some money.

"Gee Danny, thanks. I will pay you back."

"Don't be ridiculous. You two be careful heading home."

Jerry squeezed Betty's hand. "Don't worry. She's safe with me."

"Hey, Jerry, do you know where the rest of the group is?"

"I'm not sure, but Mae is getting pretty soused."

"Okay, thanks."

Danny smiled as he watched the two of them walk away. Betty held onto Jerry's arm as they left in a dreamy haze. It made him feel better to know something wonderful had begun.

"Hey, Danny, are you ready for that dance yet?" Mollie asked.

"Not just yet. Jerry just told me that Mae is getting drunk. I was going to head back over to the table."

"I will come with you."

74

DORIS WAS BORED AND FEELING neglected. The young man sitting next to her was cracking peanuts, annoying her further. Finally, having had enough, Doris turned to him.

"Do you realize how annoying it is to sit here and listen to you crack peanuts?"

"Nope," he said, tiny bits of peanut crumbs on his mouth as he continued to chew.

"You're disgusting," she said.

"And you're rude."

She turned away from him.

"You want some?"

She turned back to face him. "What?"

"Peanuts?"

Doris frowned at the four pitiful remaining peanuts. "No thanks."

"So, what's your story?" he said, sitting back and crossing his foot over his knee.

"What do you mean?"

"Who are you here with tonight?"

"My friends."

"How come you aren't dancing with one of them?"

Doris shifted in her seat. "Because he chose to dance with someone else."

"I don't dance, so don't ask me."

Doris's face turned red, and she turned her back to him.

"What's your name?" he asked.

"None of your business."

"You're kind of fresh," he said.

"And you're sloppy," Doris said, noticing the bits of peanut shells on his pants. "Look at the mess you made."

He looked at the floor covered in pieces of peanut shells. He shrugged and picked up his drink.

"I would hate to be the one who has to clean up after you," Doris said.

"I live by myself."

"Your house must be a pig sty."

"I like it."

"I bet," Doris grunted.

He looked at her stiff profile. "My name is Boyd."

"You're the drummer?"

"I am."

"My name is Doris."

"I like that name."

"You do?"

"Yeah."

The corners of her mouth lifted slightly.

"Hey, loser," Will said, standing next to Boyd. "I'm bored. What do you say we shoot some pool?"

"I don't know. I was just sitting here talking to Doris."

Will looked her over and snickered. "Come on, Boyd, there is some fine tail in the lounge."

"If Boyd doesn't want to play you, I will," Doris said.

Will laughed.

"You play pool?" Boyd said.

"I do. I have three brothers," Doris said, throwing her shoulders back.

"No kiddin'?"

"Yep."

"You know, I think they have a pool table in the other room. Do you mind if Doris joins us, Will?"

"You got any cash?" Will asked her.

"Will . . ." Boyd said.

"I do."

Will smiled and spread out his arm. "After you."

75

DANNY AND MOLLIE MET STU and Marcy returning to the table.

"Hey, what happened to everyone?" Danny said.

"Long story," Stu said.

"More importantly, where is Mae?" Marcy said.

"Don't tell me she wandered off," Stu said.

"Oh no," Marcy said. "You think she went out to her car?"

"She wouldn't do that, would she?" Stu said.

Marcy groaned.

"What's going on?" Danny said.

"No time to explain. We need to get to the parking lot before Mae drives drunk," Marcy said.

"I'm behind you," Danny said.

The four headed as fast as they could to the parking lot.

□■□■□■□■□■□■□■□■□■□

"What do you mean I have a flat tire?" Mae yelled at the valet.

"I'm sorry, miss."

"You're sorry! Well, you're going to fix it because it's your fault that it's flat!"

"Well, technically, it's not my fault, but I promise we will have someone come out and fix your flat tomorrow."

"Tomorrow? How am I supposed to get home tonight?"

"I'm not sure."

Mae stomped her foot. "I want to see the manager! I want restitution!"

Mae had drawn a small crowd with all her yelling, and the frightened valet had no idea what to do to appease her.

The doorman walked over to them. "What is going on over here?"

"This buffoon refuses to fix my flat tire!" Mae bellowed.

"Miss, you need to calm down."

"I am not going to calm down!"

The doorman took Mae's arm. "Why don't you come inside?"

"I want to see the manager!" Mae said, yanking her arm away and stumbling.

"Okay."

Danny, Stu, Mollie, and Marcy came outside.

"Mae," Marcy said, distressed.

"Oh, Marcy," Mae wailed. "My car has a flat tire, and they won't fix it!"

"That is not true," the valet said. "I explained it would be fixed, but we can't get someone out here until tomorrow."

"How am I supposed to get home!"

"Stu and I can fix it," Danny said.

"We can?" Stu said.

Danny frowned at him. "You do have a spare, right, Mae?"

"What's a spare?"

"Tire," Danny said.

Mae looked at Marcy and then back at Danny. She put the tip of her finger in her mouth. "I don't know."

"Great," Danny said. "Where is the car?"

"I'll show you," the valet said.

Danny walked away with the valet.

"Why don't we go wait inside?" Marcy said, putting her arm around Mae and guiding her inside.

"You coming with us, Stu?" Mollie said.

Stu was looking off in the direction Danny had gone. "Nah, I'm going to see if I can't catch up to James."

"Oh, okay."

He smiled at her and left.

76

BOYD AND WILL WERE LEANING on their cue sticks, watching
Doris sashay around the pool table, pretending to study her
final shot.

"There is no way she can make that shot," Will said to Boyd.

"You said that before the last time she beat you."

Doris bent over, set her cue stick on the table, and examined her
options.

Will and Boyd crouched down to set their eyes on the pocket.
Will rolled his lips as she lined up her cue and teasingly ran it between
her fingers. He glowered at her amusement. Finally, she drew back
her cue stick and shot. They watched dumbstruck as the black ball
traveled on its curved path, hit the bank, traveled across the table, and
sunk into the pocket.

Will closed his eyes tight.

She smiled. "I guess that makes what? Four for me and only two
for you?"

"This isn't fair," Will said.

"What do you mean it isn't fair?"

"The game is rigged somehow."

She laughed. "How can the game be rigged?"

"The table is crooked."

She shook her head. "Maybe I am just a skilled pool player. Have you ever thought of that?" she said, leaning back against the table.

"That's it for me," Will said, handing his money to Doris. "Good luck with the she-devil," Will said to Boyd and left the room.

"I don't think I've ever seen Will lose so many games. You are an excellent shot."

"Thank you," Doris said lazily, playing with the cue ball.

"You want to play another game?" Boyd asked.

"I don't know. I think I should try and find my friends."

"I understand, but I would like a rematch."

"Okay, but maybe we should go to dinner before I win all your money."

He laughed. "You like Italian food?"

"Of course."

"Okay, next Thursday?"

"Okay," she wrote down her number and address on a cocktail napkin and handed it to him.

"I guess I'll see you then."

"I guess you will."

He smiled to himself and put the number in his jacket pocket.

77

DORIS WAS SURPRISED TO FIND her friends sitting in the lobby comforting Mae. Her mascara had run, leaving dark circles under her eyes and her head rested on Marcy's shoulder.

Doris joined them. "Hey guys, what's going on?"

"Mae's car has a flat tire," Mollie said

"Oh no," Doris said.

"Luckily, Danny is fixing it," Marcy said.

"Where is James?" Doris said.

"Don't ask," Mollie said.

Danny came through the door. His sleeves were rolled up, and his hands were black with dirt and grease.

"Did you fix it, Danny?" Marcy said.

"Well, she doesn't have a spare tire, so I patched the flat one the best I could. I think it will hold till she gets home."

"Oh, Danny, you are my hero!" In a burst of renewed energy, Mae jumped up and kissed Danny on the cheek.

Mollie rolled her eyes.

"Where is Stu?" Danny asked.

"He left," Marcy said.

"Oh, okay, I am going to wash up and find Eddie."

"I don't know how to thank you," Mae said.

"Just be careful going home."

"I'm going to drive," Marcy said.

"Cool," Danny said.

"It was a wonderful night, Danny," Doris said.

"We had a great time," Marcy said.

"Look, Marcy, I don't know what happened with you and James, but I am sure it can be worked out," Danny said.

"Maybe," she said. Turning, she took Mae by the arm. "Come on, girls."

"Bye. Danny," Mae said with a flirty wave.

"Hey, Mollie," Danny said, touching her arm lightly. "I'm sorry we didn't get that dance."

"That's all right."

"Next time?"

"Sure."

He leaned over and kissed her on the cheek. "I'll see you soon?"

"Yes," she said.

"Goodnight."

Danny walked away, and Mollie touched her cheek.

78

BETTY SAT CLOSE TO JERRY in the cab, and he held her warm, soft hand the entire way home.

After the cab dropped them off, they strolled up the drive.

"It's a beautiful night out, isn't it?" Betty said.

"Yes."

"I had such a wonderful time. I hate for the evening to end," Betty said, whirling around.

"Me too."

"We could sit on the back porch, drink lemonade, and have cookies," Betty said.

Jerry stopped. "Do you hear that?"

"What?" she said.

He turned to her. "I think I hear music."

"You do?"

"Yes, it's my heart singing."

A shy smile crossed her petite mouth.

Stepping into her, Jerry gently took her face in his hand, and he kissed her tenderly.

When he pulled away, she bit her lip. Then, before he could say anything, she placed her hands on his shoulders and kissed him again.

"You're full of surprises, aren't you?" Jerry said.

"I'm a bad girl."

Jerry laughed, and, putting his arm around her, they finished their walk up to the house.

79

T HE COOL AIR NIPPED AT James's cheeks as he walked to the record store. His footsteps were slow, and his heart was heavy. He hardly slept the night before because the incident with Marcy was constantly tormenting his thoughts. How could he have been so stupid? The alcohol and testosterone had abducted his senses, and he knew he had been out of line.

Eddie was placing new records in their bins when James came in.

"Morning, James," Eddie said.

"Morning, Eddie."

"There's coffee on the counter."

"Great," James poured himself a cup.

"Hey, Professor," Danny said, coming down the stairs as James took his first drink.

James slammed his cup on the counter. "Oh, my Lord, that coffee is . . ."

"Strong?" Danny said.

"It's more than strong," James said.

Eddie walked up to the counter with a crate in his hands. "I made it that way on purpose."

"Are you trying to kill us?" James said.

"No, I just wanted to wake you up."

"I'm awake."

"You ready to get to work, Professor?" Danny said. "Jerry and I started to move the junk."

"Is John here?"

"What do you think?"

James followed Danny up the stairs to the storeroom. Stacks of dust-covered boxes, wooden crates, and outdated magazines blocked the entrance to the room. Sunlight gleaming through the holes in the newspaper-covered windows cast an eerie glow.

"Where is Jerry?" James said.

"I'm here," Jerry said, poking his head up from behind some boxes.

"Look at this mess," James said.

"It's not so bad," Jerry said. "We just need to start moving things around. We can start by putting these magazines and newspapers into these crates and boxes. Some dusting and sweeping, and we will clean this place in no time."

"Grab a box, Professor," Danny said.

The boys went to work, and their spirits began to lift as the clutter cleared away.

"So where is Stu?" Danny asked.

"He had to work," James said.

"He got a job?" Danny said.

"Yeah."

"That's great. Now his mom can't throw him out."

"Hey, isn't this your day off?" James said to Danny.

"Well, yeah."

"So why aren't you home in bed?"

Danny stacked some more boxes. "Because I wanted to help."

"You need your head examined."

"Look at all the busy dogs diggin' for bones."

James turned to see John leaning in the doorway.

"Here's a box—start 'packin'," Danny said, tossing John a box.

"I thought the pack leader didn't have to work," John said.

Jerry threw a balled-up piece of newspaper that hit John in the head.

"Hey, where did that come from?"

"Jerry," Danny said.

"Where?" John said, trying to see above and around the boxes.

Jerry held up his hand.

"Oh, just wait until I get my hands on you," John said.

James took the empty box from John and handed him a full one. "Here, make yourself useful and help me move these boxes in the hall."

John grumbled but started to help James move the boxes.

"So, what happened between you and Marcy last night?" Danny asked James.

"You got in a fight with Marcy?" John said.

James was dusting off some shelves. "Kind of."

"He left without her," Jerry said.

"What? The way you two were ogling each other, I thought for sure it was gonna be a hot night," John said, picking up another box.

"Mae was drunk and obnoxious. So, Marcy decided to stay behind and take care of her instead of leaving with me."

"Mae is a nuisance," John said.

"'I'll say," Danny said. "She almost left alone, but her car got a flat tire."

"Serves her right," John said.

Danny wiped his hand on his pants. "Not only that, but she didn't have a spare tire. I had to patch it myself because Stu wouldn't help me."

"Stu wouldn't help you?" James said.

"Nope, he just took off," Danny said.

"That ain't cool," John said.

"Ain't no big deal," Danny said. "Let's go down and grab the old sofa out of the basement, John."

"Why me?"

"Because you're the pack leader," Danny said with a smile.

Slowly, the years of neglect began to clear away. Old music posters, sheet music, and comic books were scattered among the room's hidden treasures. An out-of-tune piano was buried in the corner like a forgotten castaway. Jerry cleaned the windows while James cleared the cobwebs and swept up the dirt. Danny and John hung the old posters and fixed the broken light. Eddie beat the dust out of an area rug that covered up the scuffed discolored floor.

A couple of hours later, everyone was hanging out in the cleared space. John was lying on the couch reading comic books while Jerry and Eddie set up a record player and other assorted sound equipment. Danny spread out on the floor and enjoyed spending time with his guitar.

James sat down and began to tinker with the out-of-tune piano.

John looked around the edge of his comic. "Hey, Professor, would you mind messing with that some other time?"

"It needs a professional tuner," Eddie said.

"It needs more than that," John said.

"I'm surprised mice aren't living in it," Danny said.

"Maybe they are," Jerry said.

"You know what, fellas? I think I'm going to take off," James said.

"You goin' to see Marcy?" Danny said.

"I'm going to try," James said, putting his hands in his pockets.

"You just need to woo the heart of the fair maiden," John said.

"Yeah, turn on the charm," Danny said.

"I wish that's all it would take. I was pretty dumb."

"She'll get over it, Professor," John said.

"I hope so. I'll see you later."

"Good luck, James," Jerry said.

He gave them a small smile and left the store.

"I wouldn't want to be in his shoes," Danny said. "Girls can be so . . .."

"Unreasonable?" John said.

"Yeah."

Jerry and Eddie eventually left John and Danny alone. John's eyes were closed, and Danny played a melancholy tune.

"I'm sorry about what happened last night, Barnaby," Danny said. "I didn't want you to leave."

"I know it, but it's important that you meet the right people."

Danny looked at John. "But I have met the right people."

John opened his eyes.

"You, the Professor, Jerry, you are the right people. I'm not like those people that Joe hobnobs with. All I did was sit next to him and keep my mouth shut, so I didn't embarrass him. I didn't enjoy fixing Mae's tire, but at least it got me away from them."

"You are in with a group of vipers, that's for sure."

"I would never choose them over my friends."

John smiled. "You're too good for them, Danny boy."

"I just hope this will all pay off someday."

"Just promise me they won't change you."

"They've tried, but I didn't let them," Danny said.

"Is that the incident you won't talk to me about?"

Danny averted his eye and looked at the rug. "Yeah."

John sat up and set his hand on Danny's shoulder.

Danny looked at him, a silence of understanding passing between them.

"I'm so ashamed I still can't bring myself to admit to it."

"We all have those moments in our past, Danny, and we don't need to share them to know someone else has been there."

Danny nodded his head, and John leaned back on the couch.

"So, are you busy Thursday night, Barnaby?"

"I don't know, you tell me."

"I got invited to a blues club."

"How did you do that?"

Danny brought his knee up to his chest. "Joe has a chauffeur named Clive, a super nice guy. He was at the show last night and said I should come down and check it out."

"You know those clubs are in a rough part of the city."

"I know, but I love the blues."

John sighed. "I suppose you won't quit botherin' me till I agree."

"Pretty much."

"Okay." John closed his eyes, hoping to get a few more moments of peace.

"Hey, I got an idea. Let's write a song!" Danny said.

"What?"

"Yeah, we could put our time to good use."

"You're nuts."

"It'll be fun."

John looked at him with a frown. "I don't even have a guitar."

"You can use Jerry's. It's even in tune."

John sighed.

"Let's see, what should we write about?"

John grabbed Jerry's guitar. "Hell, If I know."

"A love song?"

John shook his head.

"Come on, most songs are love songs."

John set Jerry's guitar in his lap. "Love songs are dumb, and they're all the same. She said, he said, he didn't, I couldn't, come back, get the hell out. You know, like that."

"Okay, how did you get the idea to write 'Crawlin' Dog?'"

"I saw one."

"And that inspired you?"

"Yeah, I could relate to him."

"How?"

"Well, it was hot, and I knew he had been hurt and was hungry, but even though he was suffering, he kept fighting and moving forward. Crawling through the dirt and muck, he never gave up."

Danny reflected for a moment. "Do you know what happened to him?"

John sat his foot on top of his knee. "Some good Samaritan may have come along and rescued him."

Danny smiled. "We could write about that old piano."

"What?"

"Come on, let's see. It's old, out of tune, and has yellowish keys. At one time, it was new, and now that it's not, I got the blues!"

John laughed. "You're a goof!"

"Come on, we can do this!"

John saw an enthusiasm in Danny that he hadn't seen since the night of Len's party, and it made him smile. The two laughed and played through the afternoon, which ended with a blues tune about an old, out-of-tune piano.

80

J AMES WALKED OVER TO THE boarding house. His palms were sweaty, and his anxiety was high as he walked up and rang the bell. An answer didn't come immediately, and he rang the bell a second time. Finally, Ms. Moore answered the door.

"Hello, Ms. Moore. Is Marcy in?"

"No, I'm afraid not. I don't think she came home last night."

James's heart sank.

"Are you okay, James? You don't look like you're feeling well."

"I'm fine."

"You want me to fix you some iced tea?"

"No thanks, I think I'll just wait for her out here on the porch."

"Okay."

James sat on the steps for at least an hour before Marcy pulled up in Mollie's mom's car. Her face fell when she saw James sitting on the porch.

"You gonna be okay?" Mollie said.

"Yeah, I guess so."

"Call me later?"

"Yeah."

Marcy got out of the car. She stood at the end of the walk, wishing she could just go inside. James came down to meet her. He could tell by the hard look in her eyes that she was still agitated.

"Hi," he said quietly.

"Hi," she said, walking past him.

"Marcy, I want to talk to you."

She stopped. "Well, I don't want to talk to you." She continued walking.

"Please, Marcy, give me a chance to explain myself," he said, stepping in front of her.

She glared at him.

"I'm sorry. I know I was wrong."

"Yes, you were wrong. I know Mae's behavior was inexcusable, but I couldn't just let her fend for herself. Not while she was in that condition."

James hung his head like a bad puppy. "I know."

"Would you have walked out on Stu if he needed you?"

"No," James said quietly.

Marcy trudged up the walkway.

"Marcy . . ."

She put the key in the lock.

"Please let me make it up to you," James said.

She looked at him.

"Please, I'll do anything."

"I don't know, James."

"What does that mean?"

"It means I don't know."

"Are you . . ." The words were stuck in his throat, and he couldn't say them.

Marcy went inside and locked the door.

81

Wealthy businessman Josiah Burnaby started Chicago's independent record label Burnaby Records. A portly, balding man who loved to gamble and invest in new business ventures, Josiah wasn't interested in starting a record label. Still, his son was interested in the recording business and had no capital to start the studio. Josiah agreed to finance the venture as long as it was profitable. The first couple of years had been a struggle, but with the growing popularity of rock-n-roll music, the label began to show a small profit.

Carlton was worried that Joe would not be satisfied signing with a less established label, but they were the only label that showed any interest in signing The Dice. Carlton told Joe that many new artists signed with smaller labels so that they could have a record to promote to radio stations. Then, once The Dice's popularity grew, they would surely be picked up by a major record label.

To Carlton's relief, Joe accepted this strategy. His only prayer was that he was right.

❑■❑■❑■❑■❑■❑■❑■❑■❑■❑■❑

Joe sat on the seat next to Carlton, watching the uninspired landscape pass by him like a bad movie. Joe acknowledged Carlton when he

357

got in the limo, but since then, he hadn't said a word. Off stage, Joe was not a friendly person. He didn't see the point of conversing with people that didn't interest him. Carlton took comfort in knowing that not very many people did engage him. Carlton was the only manager of The Dice that had lasted more than six months, and he figured it was because he kept their relationship professional and didn't meddle in Joe's affairs. Keeping his distance seemed to be an advantage.

They promptly arrived at the Burnaby offices at ten o'clock for their meeting, but it was a quarter past before the receptionist escorted them into the conference room. Joe hated to be kept waiting, and Carlton hoped it wouldn't sour the deal.

Floyd Brown and Frederick Long were seated at the conference table. Floyd, the younger of the two, had a medium build, with light blue eyes and sandy brown hair combed over to one side. Frederick was a taller, middle-aged man with dark hair and glasses. Both men wore tan ties and white shirts with the sleeves rolled up, which made Carlton feel better about his everyday attire. Of course, Joe was dressed in an expensive steel blue suit with a turquoise-colored tie and gold cuff links. The two men smiled at him and introduced themselves. Joe shook their hands with his usual thin smile. They all sat down at the conference table. There was a pitcher of water and four glasses on a tray in the middle of the table.

Floyd offered some to Carlton and Joe, but Joe refused to touch the dirty glass. Carlton wished the water were vodka.

"So, Mr. Delany," Floyd said.

"Please, it's Joe."

"Joe, we are very impressed with your group. You have a solid, rockin', sound."

Joe crossed his legs. "Thank you. I work hard to be the best."

"You opened last Saturday night to a full house?" Frederick said.

"Most of our shows are sold out. You should see the show. I will make sure to have comp tickets waiting for you at the ticket booth."

"That would be wonderful, thank you," Floyd said.

Floyd opened the folder in front of him. "I am assuming Carlton went over some details with you?"

"Yes."

"Let's get right to it, shall we? By signing this contract, we agree to represent you. We will book the studio time and the production. We will set the release date and distribute the record to local radio stations and record stores. We will ensure to provide Carlton with plenty of copies so that he can work on your distribution and promotion. We are proposing a standard year. After that period, depending on how the first release goes, we renegotiate. We are offering you an 80-20 split."

Joe reflected, and Carlton tapped his fingers on his knee.

"Since we are fronting most of the cost, we get the larger end of the deal."

"Seventy-thirty," Joe said.

Floyd looked at Fredrick with a raised eyebrow.

"I'm worth it, and you know it. You haven't signed a profitable artist in almost a year, and you need a hit. Otherwise, the label faces bankruptcy and a scandal because the owner is a well-known gambler and fraudster."

"Mr. Delany . . .," Fredrick started.

"You agree, or I walk. It's that simple."

Fredrick felt his chin, and Floyd spread open his hands.

"All right, 70-30. Now there is one other detail we are going to need to clarify. We need to know if you have any original material." Fredrick asked.

Joe shifted in his seat. "Well, not yet."

"We were wondering because we think your first release should be an original song. Your group is powerful, and we think you can generate chart toppers. In our opinion, it would be a waste of your talents to do a song that ten other groups have done. Would you agree?"

"Yes," Joe said.

"Now comes the tricky part. One of our songwriters could write a song for your group. However, that will cut your profits. I realize that is not a popular choice, but it might be your only option unless you know someone who can write a song for you. The good news is you'll make your money back if it's a hit." Floyd explained.

Joe contemplated the comment.

"If you need some time to talk this over with Carlton, we understand. Our goal is to have a positive, profitable business relationship."

"I think I do have an original piece in mind that we could use," Joe said, folding his hands across his lap.

"Great."

"It will have to be fine-tuned, of course."

"Of course. Does this tune have a name?" Frederick asked.

"It has a working title that we can work on changing."

"That works," Floyd said.

"It's called 'Crawlin' Dog.'" Joe said.

Carlton's eyes widened, and he opened his mouth.

"You have something to add, Carlton?" Fredrick asked.

Joe gave Carlton a cold, stern glare.

"No, nothing," Carlton chuckled.

"Well, I say we sign these papers so we can move this project forward," Floyd said.

Joe, Carlton, Floyd, and Fredrick signed the papers.

"We just need to have you come back with a demo reel of the new tune, and we will go from there. Sound like a plan?" Floyd said.

"That shouldn't take long," Joe said.

"Excellent. We will wait on the call."

The four men shook hands, and Carlton and Joe left the Burnaby Offices.

"You don't seem pleased with the deal we made," Joe said to Carlton.

"I am just worried about what Danny will say about you using that song."

"You leave him to me," Joe said, putting on his shades. "Shall we have a drink to celebrate?"

"Sure."

"Great, I know just the place. It's been a while since I've been there, but I'm sure they will have no problems finding a table for me."

Carlton's ulcer was bothering him, and his blood pressure was heightened, but a drink or two would quiet the conscience that told him recording that song was a bad idea.

82

JERRY ENJOYED WORKING WITH BOB at the mercantile. Bob was patient and took the extra time needed to train Jerry for the different positions in the store. Bob assured Jerry his hard work and efforts would pay off, and his opportunities were endless. Jerry's confidence and self-esteem grew with every new responsibility he was given, and he was proving to be an asset to the company.

Jerry was organizing the new products, when Bob stepped into the store's back storage room,

"Hey, Jerry."

"Yes, sir."

"There is a woman up front looking for you. She says her name is Nora Smith. Do you know her?"

"Yeah, she works with my mom."

Jerry wondered what Nora could want as he followed Bob up to the front of the store.

"Hey, Nora, what brings you in today?" Jerry asked.

"Hello, Jerry. I was wondering if you've heard from your mom lately. We are worried about her at the diner. She hasn't come in for her last three shifts."

"No, I haven't heard from her. Have you tried to call?"

She nodded. "We can't get any answer."

"Okay, thanks, Nora. I will look into it."

Nora hesitated.

"Is there something else?"

"Well, I don't want to upset you, but she did have a bad shiner the last time she was in."

Jerry sighed.

"I'm sorry, Jerry. If there is anything we can do . . ."

"I will be in touch. Thanks, Nora."

Nora nodded and left the store.

Jerry turned to Bob. "I have to go out to the house."

"Why don't you wait until I can take you?"

"No, I have to go now. She could be hurt." Jerry went into the back and got his jacket.

"Jerry, I don't think this is a good idea. Someone should go with you," Bob said.

"I don't have time for that. I will be back."

"Be careful, son," Bob said.

Jerry nodded and left the store.

Bob picked up the phone and dialed.

"Hello?"

"Mabel, has Danny left yet?"

"No, he is just getting ready," Mable said.

"I need to talk to him—it's urgent."

"Is something wrong?"

"I will tell you later."

Mable called Danny to come to the phone.

"Yeah, Uncle Bob?"

"Danny, I know you're on your way to practice, but something terrible has happened."

"What happened?"

Bob explained the entire story to Danny.

"Oh, no," Danny said.

"I told him to wait until I could take him, but he wouldn't hear of it. I know you are headed to practice, but I'm worried about him."

Danny ran his hand through his hair. Today was more than just a rehearsal. Joe had mentioned that he had some vital information to share with the group regarding the record contract.

"'I'll call Joe and tell him I'm not going to make it today. This is important."

"The keys to the truck are hanging in the kitchen. Take it," Bob said.

"Okay."

"Danny, be careful."

"I will." Danny hung up the phone as Betty walked into the kitchen.

"Danny, what's going on?" Mable asked.

"It's Jerry. He's in trouble." Danny grabbed the keys and hurried outside to the truck when Betty came running behind him and climbed into the passenger seat.

"Betty, what the hell do you think you're doin'?"

"I'm coming with you," Betty said, putting on her seat belt.

"Oh no, you're not! This is a very dangerous situation. I can't risk you gettin' hurt."

"Jerry is in trouble. We can argue about this, or we can go and help him."

Against his better judgment, Danny started up the truck.

83

ERRY'S HEARTBEAT WITH FEAR AS he walked to the house. He was worried about what he might find when he got there. What if Gus locked her in the closet as he had before? He heard John's voice warning him not to go alone, but he didn't have a choice.

Jerry walked up to the front door and knocked, but there was no answer. Turning the knob, he pounded on the door. "Mom?"

Still no answer came.

Jerry walked to the back door, but it was also locked. He grabbed the old dust broom by the door and busted the kitchen window. Gagging on the rotten, moldy smell that greeted him, he covered his nose and crawled through the window. Dozens of flies buzzed around the dirty, crusted dishes stacked in the sink. Various bits of garbage crunched under his feet as he walked into the dimly lit living room.

"Mom?"

The only answer was a sharp whistle of the wind blowing through the cracks around the windows. He swallowed hard as he walked on wobbly legs toward her bedroom.

"Mom? Are you in there?" He didn't hear a sound.

Slowly, he pushed the door open. Horrified, he saw her lying on the bed ... motionless. Her eyes were swollen, and horrible bruises covered her body. In her hand, she clutched a bottle of sleeping pills.

"Mom!" Tears flooded Jerry's eyes as he shook her frail body. She murmured a pitiful moan. He knew he needed to go for help. Turning, he saw Gus standing in the doorway. His face was contorted in a dreadful sneer, and he was holding a baseball bat.

"Well, look what we have here, a little lost boy."

"What did you do to her?" Jerry said in a deep tone.

"Nothin', she didn't deserve."

"She ain't movin'!"

"She's probably playin' possum, thinkin' I won't whip her again."

The room was small, and there was not enough room to maneuver and escape. Jerry desperately tried to think of something he could use as a weapon.

Gus slapped the bat into his open palm. "You shouldn't have come back here. Because when I beat you this time, you ain't gonna get back up."

Jerry narrowed his eyes. "You're the one who isn't gettin' up."

"Woo ... you think you're tough now? Do you, boy?"

Grabbing the glass of water off the nightstand, Jerry threw it in Gus's face. Gus's hands flayed in the air as Jerry slipped out of the room and ran down the hall into the kitchen. Gus cussed loudly and stumbled down the hall. As he rounded the corner, Jerry grabbed a huge knife from the counter.

"What you gonna do with that boy?"

"I'm gonna kill you."

Gus laughed. "You ain't got the balls, you mealy mouth yella pansy!"

Jerry would have run away and hidden in the past, but not this time. This time, he stared straight into Gus's yellow eyes. Clutching the knife tightly, he waited for Gus to make a move ... just one stupid move.

Gus was drunk and clumsy, and when he lifted the bat over his shoulder, it was the break Jerry was looking for. Lifting his leg, he kicked Gus in the stomach as hard as possible, knocking the wind out of him. Grunting, Gus staggered backward and crashed into the table before tumbling to the ground and thumping his head hard on the linoleum. Jerry knelt on Gus's chest and held the knife to his throat.

"Now, listen to me, you worthless bastard. Get your shit and get the hell out of this house! And if you ever come near my mother again, I will personally shove this knife right down your throat!"

Jerry pressed the knife enough to break the skin. A thin trail of blood trickled down Gus's neck. "Do I make myself clear?"

Gus looked up at Jerry's wide-crazed eyes. "Yes."

Jerry slowly stood up and threw the knife aside. He walked out the front door as Danny and Betty pulled up. Betty jumped out and ran into Jerry's arms. "Are you all right?"

He held her trembling body close. "Yes, I'm fine."

"Jerry, what's goin' on?" Danny asked.

"It's my mom. She's hurt, and I need to get her to the hospital."

Running back into the bedroom, Jerry's mom still hadn't moved.

"Can we call an ambulance?" Danny said.

"No, the phone is out."

Danny looked at the frail woman on the bed. "Do you have any idea how many pills she took?"

"No."

"I hate to move her," Danny said.

"We don't have a choice," Jerry said.

Danny carefully picked up Jerry's mom. Betty grabbed a blanket and a pillow before they headed out to the truck. Gus was sitting on the porch, holding his head.

"You better not be here when I get back," Jerry said.

Gus glared at him but said nothing.

84

THE RIDE TO THE HOSPITAL was long and bumpy. Jerry's mother looked more drained with each minute that slipped by. Upon arrival at the hospital, events moved swiftly once Danny carried her into the emergency room. The emergency medical team immediately placed her on a gurney and hooked her up with oxygen as they rolled her away. Betty helped Jerry to fill out the paperwork while Danny called Joe.

Joe's housemaid, Madge, answered the phone. "Hello?"

"Hello, Madge, it's Danny."

"Hello, Danny."

"Can I speak with Joe, please?"

"I will see if he is available."

"Thank you."

Danny waited a while for Joe to pick up the phone.

"Hello?"

"Hello, Joe, it's Danny."

"Where in the hell are you?" Joe snapped.

"I'm at the hospital. I had to help a friend of mine. His mother is in a bad way."

"Why didn't you call me sooner? You know how important" today was."

"I know, but —"

"But what? You thought you could just not show up without a word to me?" Joe said.

"I'm sorry."

"It's a little late for that. How soon can you get here?"

Danny looked over at Betty and Jerry. She had her arm around him, trying to console him.

"I don't think I can make it today."

"What do you mean you can't make it today?"

"I have to stay and help him."

A tense, silent moment passed before Joe answered.

"Well, I guess that is your choice, then. I hope you realize this means that you have forfeited any input on the decisions that need to be made regarding the record."

Danny squeezed the telephone receiver tightly in his hand. He knew this was Joe's way of trying to control him and make him do what he wanted, but helping Jerry was more important than bending to Joe's will.

"I understand," Danny said.

"I will see you tomorrow."

"Yeah."

Joe hung up, and Danny listened to the drone of the dial tone before replacing the receiver on the hook. Sighing, he picked up the phone receiver again and called Mable. He filled her in on what was happening, and she told him they would send prayers and to call if there was any news.

Danny regained his composure and walked over to Jerry and Betty.

"Is everything all right?" Jerry asked.

"Everything is fine," Danny said, sitting next to Betty.

"I wonder how long it will be until we see the doctor," Jerry said.

"Hopefully not too long," Betty said, patting his hand.

Danny picked up a magazine from the waiting room table and settled to wait.

Another hour passed before the doctor finally came out to talk to them. He was a tall man with neatly combed grey hair.

"Mr. Porter?"

Jerry stood.

"Hello, I am Doctor Penrose."

"Hello," Jerry said.

"Your mother is still unconscious and in critical condition. Her body has been badly battered, and there are several bruises. It appears she has several old injuries that have never been addressed. She is dehydrated and has taken a large dose of sleeping pills. We pumped her stomach, but I am unsure how much was already in her system. We took a blood test that should give us more information. Her left eye injury is worse than her right. If she does recover, I don't know if the vision in that eye will ever return. Sadly, the blow she took to her head could cause some brain damage."

"Do you think she'll make it?"

"I'm not sure. We'll have to wait and see. I'll make sure that we inform you of any changes. I'm sorry," the doctor said, setting his hand on his shoulder.

"Can I see her?"

"For a moment."

Doctor Penrose took Jerry to the ICU, where his mother was lying in bed. A large breathing tube was stuck down her throat, and an IV was in her arm. Jerry reached out and held onto her cold hand, tears trickling down his face.

"Mom, I'm so sorry I wasn't there. I wanted to apologize for all the mean things I said to you. I didn't mean them, I swear it." He smoothed down her hair with a trembling hand. A nurse came into the room behind him.

"It's time," she said.

Jerry bent down and gently kissed his mother's cheek. "I love you."

Turning, Jerry left the room with a heavy heart.

Later that night, Jerry was sitting on the back porch steps staring into space. Betty came out and sat beside him.

"Are you going to bed soon?" Betty asked.

"I don't think I can sleep."

She set her hand on his leg.

"There is no reason for you to stay up," he said.

"I'm worried about you."

He took her hand. "This is all my fault."

"How can you say that?"

"I should have never left her alone in the house with that... monster." Jerry buried his face in his hands.

"If you had stayed, he would have continued beating you and maybe even killed you."

Tears were on his cheeks. "The last time I saw her, we argued. John tried to get me to go back and make things right, but I was too stubborn to do it. Now she's in the hospital, and I may never get the chance to tell her how much I do love her."

Betty held him in her arms, and he cried on her shoulder.

"I don't deserve you," he whispered.

"Oh, hush now and stop talking nonsense," she said, rubbing his shoulder. "Why don't we go inside, and I will make you something warm to drink. It will help you sleep. Okay?"

"Okay."

She wiped away his tears and went inside the house.

85

ANNY WASN'T LOOKING FORWARD TO going to practice. He was
sure that Joe would lecture him about missing the meeting, and
he wasn't in the mood for it. He had done what was needed to
help his friend, and that's all that mattered.

Boyd was at the studio when Danny arrived for practice, which
was odd because he almost always was with Will. Boyd was relaxed in
a chair, reading the paper. He looked up to see Danny take his guitar
out of its case.

"Morning," Boyd said, taking a drink of his coffee.

"Morning," Danny said, hooking the guitar up to the amp.

"You want some coffee?"

"No thanks."

Boyd held up a wax paper bag. "You want one of my donuts?"

"No thanks."

Danny sat on a stool and began to fuss with the guitar's tuning.

Boyd took a bite out of a jelly donut. Powdered sugar fell like snow
onto his pants. "So, how come you missed the meeting yesterday?"

"I was at the hospital with a friend of mine."

Boyd continued to chew the red sticky jelly stuck to his lips. "Is
he all right?"

"He's fine. It's his mother that was injured."

Boyd picked up his coffee. "Wow, that stinks."

Danny was hoping the conversation was over, but he was disappointed.

"You should have been here. You missed out on all the news."

Danny ignored the comment and began playing a song to drown out Boyd's annoying voice.

A few minutes later, Will came in. Danny was afraid he might make a rude remark, but he walked over to Boyd instead.

"Did you bring me a coffee?" Will said.

"I did. It might be a bit cold now."

Will took a drink and moaned.

Joe finally wandered in, hiding behind his dark glasses.

"Morning, Joe," Boyd said, his nose buried in the paper.

Joe didn't answer. He set his things down on the piano and looked over at Danny. "How nice of you to join us today."

Danny ignored the comment.

"Now that you're here, I have some important news to share with you," Joe said. "I met with the record executives at Burnaby on Monday, and it was a profitable meeting. The royalty percentage isn't as high as I had hoped, but once we establish ourselves, we will all make more money."

Joe took a few steps forward, rubbing his hands together. "They want us to record an original song instead of covering another artist's tune. They told me one of their songwriters could write the song, but that would cut our profits. So, I told them that we already had an original song we could do. We all agreed yesterday that we would record the song you did at your audition."

Danny stared in disbelief at Joe, his mouth dry. "You can't be serious."

"And why not?"

"Because I didn't write that song. It belongs to someone else."

"Who?"

"A friend of mine."

"What's his name?"

"John Chandler."

"Who's that?" Will said, his nose crumpled.

"He's my best friend, and there is no way in hell I am letting you steal that song from him!"

Joe felt his chin. "Maybe your *friend* would be willing to sell it to me."

Danny narrowed his eyes. "Not a chance."

"You know, money can change a lot of people's minds. I mean, at this point, he is a nobody. Having his song recorded by a famous group could make all the difference to him."

"He has his group, and they will make it famous."

"What group is that?" Will scoffed.

"The Hound Dogs."

"The what?" Boyd said as they all burst out laughing.

Danny glared at them.

"You're joking, right?" Will said.

"The first time I heard the song, that group was playing it," Danny said.

"Where? In the junkyard?" Boyd quipped. Another round of laughter broke out.

Danny stood up. "You can laugh all you want to. I don't care, but that song is off the table, end of discussion."

"You gave up your right to any discussion when you weren't here yesterday," Joe said, his face grave.

"I don't care if I was here or not. It's wrong, and I won't stand for it."

Joe and Danny stared each other down.

"Come on, sit down," Boyd said. "There has to be some solution to this problem, right? Think about it, how many people do you think have heard that song? A dozen, maybe two?"

Joe crossed his arms.

"Maybe we can just change some of the chords, you know, mix it up. Write a few new words, give it a different name, and voila! We have a new original tune." Will said, waving his hand in the air.

"Problem solved," Joe said.

"He's gonna know that it is a direct rip-off of his song," Danny said.

"I don't care if he notices it or not. The song will change enough that no one is going to care what the hell he wrote. Everyone will believe it's original to The Dice. Are we clear?"

Danny's rage pulsated through his veins. "I can't in all good conscious condone this."

"You need to think long and hard about what you say right now," Joe said. "You are in a group that is about to make a record. We are going to be big and make lots of money. You will be able to have anything in this world that you could possibly want, or you can get a job with your *friend* scraping trash up out of the gutters. Now, I suggest you respect my decision and let's get to work."

Danny stood motionless unable to respect or accept anything. Unstrapping the guitar, he laid it gently in its case. Joe turned to see him close and lock the case.

"What are you doing?"

"What does it look like?" Danny picked up his coat and put it on.

"If you walk out that door, you're finished! Do you hear me? Your career will be over!"

Danny met Joe's hateful glare and walked to the door. "Goodbye Joe. I quit."

Danny walked out the door and before it could close behind him, he heard a glass smash up against the wall shattering into a million pieces.

◻■◻■◻■◻■◻■◻■◻■◻■◻■◻

Danny walked to the bus feeling better than he had in months. His entire spirit was souring. He was free! Free to wear his clothes, free to play his guitar, free to dance, free to sing, and most of all, he was free to be himself!

Laughing, he ran down the road, his heart full of joy, knowing he would never have to put up with Will or Boyd's stupidity and Joe's constant rules and complaints. Maybe he had walked out on stardom, and maybe he would be poor, but he would be happy, and he would be free.

86

ANOTHER WEEKEND WAS APPROACHING, AND the thought of spending another Saturday night at home without Marcy was torturing James. He went to the coffee shop twice to talk to her, and she avoided him. Final exams for the term were coming, and the last thing he needed was to be upset and distracted. James was sitting on the grass in the park when he saw John coming toward him.

"Hey," James said.

John plopped his books down and sat next to him. "You studyin'?"

"Yeah"

"Me too."

"But now you're not?"

"I was falling asleep trying to study the same boring rules I have been studying for months. So, I thought I would take a break and get a cup of coffee," John said.

"I didn't know you drink coffee."

John stretched his legs out in front of him. "I don't, but I am willing to try anything at this point. So where is the coffee shop, anyway?"

"Across the street," James said, pulling a pencil out of his bag.

"You want to come with me?"

James looked at him. "Oh, I get it. You're trying to get me to go over there and talk to Marcy. Well, you can just forget it. I have tried that already. Twice, actually."

"She still givin' you a hard time?"

"Yeah."

John pulled his legs up. "You don't have to play the game, you know."

James shook his head. "I'm afraid to push her. I don't want to lose her, John."

"I understand that, but just because you made a mistake doesn't mean you have to suffer forever. Just be firm with her. Tell her you want to talk to her, and don't take no for an answer."

"And how do you propose I do that?"

"You wait for her to come home or whatever, and when she gets there, you take her firmly by the hand and tell her that you want to talk to her, and she will listen."

"I don't know," James said, rolling his pencil between his fingers.

"If she thinks she can push you around, she will. Believe me. Be firm and make it clear you're done with the games."

James sighed.

"You want to resolve this, don't you?"

"Yes."

"You can do it. Now, onto the reason why I wanted to talk to you. We need to have a group meeting. Now that we have the space, we need to get busy," John stood. "I'll see you Friday night at seven."

James opened his mouth.

"And don't go sayin' you can't make it. Remember when we talked about hard work? You got Saturday off to study your brain out." John walked away.

James looked across the street at the coffee shop. John was right. Enough was enough. He was tired of playing games. He would go over to the boarding house and face her. The issue needed a final resolution even if it meant losing her.

87

MARCY LOCKED THE COFFEE SHOP door and headed home. It had been a long hard day on her feet, and all she wanted to do was relax in a hot tub, and go to bed. So far, she had been thankful for the busy days because she didn't think about James often. She knew she was being stubborn and unreasonable. He had come into the shop several times attempting to talk to her, and she ignored him. She wanted to believe that he was just another man and she didn't need him, but the ache in her heart told her otherwise.

James was waiting for her on the stoop when she arrived at the house. She stopped abruptly, and he slowly rose to his feet. Her desire to continue the fight was dissolving.

They walked toward each other and stopped a few feet apart.

"Marcy," he said.

"James."

"I want to talk to you."

"Not tonight. I'm tired," she said, walking past him, but he stepped in front of her.

"I don't care. You and I are having this out. I am not going through another sleepless night being upset over this."

"How do you think I feel?"

"I don't know because you won't talk to me. For all I know, you broke up with me, and for what? Because I wanted you to spend the night in my arms?"

"I wasn't upset about that, and you know it. I was upset because you wanted me to choose between being with you and helping my friend."

"It's not that I didn't want you to help Mae, I just wanted you to choose me. I know I was selfish and stupid, but I wanted to be with you so badly. Can you blame me for that?"

"No," she said softly.

"I know I was wrong, and I'm sorry. I don't want to be without you anymore, Marcy. I love you and—"

"What did you just say?"

"I said I'm sorry."

"No, the other part?"

He gazed into her alluring brown eyes that were searching his.

"I love you," he said.

"I love you, too, James."

Wrapping her up in his arms, he kissed her. She held onto him tightly as their passion spilled over. It began to rain, but they didn't care, they were in each other's arms.

"We're soaking wet," she said as she pulled back from him.

"I don't care."

She laughed. "Let's go inside and get dried off."

"Okay."

They went inside.

"I'll go upstairs and grab some towels," she said, running upstairs and into the hall bathroom. When she came back out with the towels, James was standing outside her bedroom door.

"You want to use the bathroom?" Marcy said.

He shook his head and went into her room. She bit her bottom lip and followed him.

Tonight, there would be no more fighting, obstacles, or misery as the rain poured outside. Long lingering kisses, exploring gentle hands, layers of wet clothes fall to the floor in a crumpled heap. The enchanting night would be spent in each other's arms, celebrating the love they had waited so long to share.

88

JOE SPENT THE REMAINDER OF Wednesday at the Starlight with Will. There wasn't enough liquor or snow to appease his rage. He showed up at Carlton's office the following day without an appointment. Claire tried to call and warn Carlton, but she was too late.

Carlton climbed the stairs to his office whistling. He was in an exceptionally good mood and he wasn't going to let anything spoil it.

"Morning, Claire," Carlton chimed when he came through the door. "Are there any messages?"

"No, but you do have a visitor."

"Oh?"

She pointed.

Carlton turned to see Joe seated in the waiting area. His eyes were two black spheres as he glared at Carlton like some hound from hell. "Joe? Did we have an appointment?"

"We need to talk now!" Joe got up and stormed into Carlton's office.

"Cancel any morning appointments, and get me an antacid," Carlton said as he went inside his office and shut the door.

Joe sat in the seat across from Carlton's desk flexing his fingers.

"What's going on, Joe? You look infuriated."

"That's because I am."

"Why?"

"That little gutless runt Danny quit the group yesterday."

"Oh, no," Carlton said, sinking into his chair.

"Oh, yes. Well, he doesn't get to quit that easily. He signed a year-long contract and hasn't even done three months. I have invested too much time in him for him just to walk away!"

"I am assuming he quit because of the song."

Joe didn't answer, but his foot was swinging.

"I told you that was a bad idea. You are asking him to sell out his friend."

"How do I know this *friend* is real?"

"What is his name?"

"John Chandler. He's the leader of some ridiculous band named the Hound Dogs," Joe said, waving his hand in the air.

Carlton wrote down the name. "If this person is real, depending on who he is, he could cause us real trouble. We have to be smart about this. Let me do some digging and see what I can find out. Okay?"

"I don't care how many damn rocks you have to dig under. I want this Chandler found!"

"I understand."

"Once we find him, we can tighten the screws on him and Daniel! You better have some results for me by tomorrow. I can't afford this project to stall any longer than necessary. Am I clear?"

"Yes, Joe."

"Don't disappoint me," Joe left his office, slamming the door.

Claire came in shortly after Joe left with a glass of the fizzy antacid. Carlton gulped it back without gagging.

"What was that all about?" Claire said.

"Danny Bruer quit the band yesterday."

"That nice young man that was in here awhile back?"

"Yeah. This is all I need. Just as everything was coming together. Hold my calls, will you?"

"Sure," she left the room.

Carlton picked up the phone and dialed.

"Hello, Lou? Yeah, it's me, Carlton. I have a job for you."

89

THE BLUE KAT WAS HARD to find if someone didn't know where to look for it. It was a small building that was tucked between two abandoned buildings. A neon sign hung in the window with various blue letters burned out. The blue cat wore a pink tie, and its tail looked like it was moving up and down, even though sometimes the light was shorted out. Inside, old unmatched tables and chairs filled the main room with a primitive bar at the north end. Pictures of cats, Muddy Waters, Howlin' Wolf, and other Blues artists covered the walls. It was a strange combo, but it added to the hodge-podge atmosphere.

"This place is a lot different than The Beaumont, huh Barnaby?" Danny said.

"I'll say. I like it," John said.

"Me too, I don't feel so tense."

"Hey, fellas," the waitress said with a dazzling smile. She was slim, with shoulder-length brown hair that flipped out at the ends. Her checkered capris and yellow crop top were set off by a quirky purple hat that set crooked on her head. "What can I get you?"

"We'll take a couple of beers," Danny said.

"Okay," her green eyes drifted over to John. His chin rested on his hand, and he smiled at her. She smiled back and walked away.

"She's cute, huh?" Danny said.

John watched her take another customer's order.

"Barnaby?"

"Huh?

"I said she's cute, huh?"

"Cute? Cute? Come on, Danny, cute went out with grade school."

"Whadda, you want me to say? She has a nice ... hat?"

"That's better," John said, leaning back in his chair.

More people started to come in. Some were people of color, which may have been a cause of alarm in the suburbs, but the beatniks and other social outcasts didn't even notice. They were there for the music.

The waitress brought their drinks. "You need anything else?"

"Not right now," Danny said. "What time does the band go on?"

"About a half hour."

"Great."

"I'll be back to check on you later," she said, glancing at John before walking away.

"Bo Diddley" began to play on the old jukebox that made an odd grinding noise. Danny started to drum his fingers on the table and bob his head.

John crossed his legs. "I haven't seen you this relaxed in a long time."

Danny picked up his glass. "It's been a long time since I enjoyed a night out."

"You made it, huh, Dan?"

Danny looked up to see Clive. "Hey, Clive!"

"Did you have any trouble findin' the place?"

"No, but you're right. It's well hidden."

Clive set his hands on the back of a chair. "This your friend?"

"Yeah, Clive, this is John."

"Nice to meet you," Clive said, shaking John's hand.

"Likewise," John said.

"You like the blues, John?"

"Yup, I sing, um, almost every day."

"You do?"

"Yep. Woke up this mornin' rolled out of bed, hit my head, stumbled down the stairs, Duchess kicked me out the door, and went to school achin' and sore."

Clive laughed. "Yup, I know that feelin'."

"You wanna join us, Clive?" Danny asked.

"Later. Right now, I'm needed on stage."

"You didn't tell me you played?"

"Bass."

"Nice."

"I'll see you cats later," he said, walking away.

It was standing room only when the show began. "Hoochie Coochie Man" was the opening number, and people danced where they stood. Danny was happy to join them, and when the waitress brought them another round, she danced beside him. John shook his head and enjoyed his drink.

During the break, Clive joined them. "Well, what do you think, Dan?"

"You have to ask him?" John said. "I don't think he stopped movin' once."

Clive laughed. "The blues was made for shakin'."

"Yes, sir!" Danny said, raising his glass.

"I gotta take a break," John said, standing.

"You gonna make a pass at the waitress?" Danny said.

"No, you knucklehead," John said playfully, punching Danny's arm as he passed by.

"He doesn't know, does he?" Clive asked.

Danny looked blankly at Clive.

"I heard about it yesterday. Joe was powerful mad."

"You know why I had to quit, don't you?"

Clive rested his arms on the table. "I heard it was because you were jealous of Joe's talents and refused to follow his direction."

Danny laughed. "Really?"

"Now, I didn't say I believe it."

"It was because they wanted to steal John's song."

"What song is that?"

"It's called 'Crawlin' Dog.'"

Clive felt his jaw. "I gotta an idea if you're up for it."
"Are you kiddin'? I'll do anything."
'Then here's what we're gonna do."

90

THE CROWD WAS STILL FIRED up when the second set started, and more people were dancing.

The waitress stopped by John and Danny's table.

"How come you're not dancin'?" she asked John.

"Because I would rather appreciate the music."

"Or maybe you just haven't found the right partner yet," she said, winking at him.

He looked her over. "Maybe I haven't."

Danny came back to the table.

"Hey," Danny said.

"Hey," the waitress said.

"It's lonely out there without you."

"I have drinks I need to serve."

"So, when are you going to tell us your name?" Danny asked.

"I guess when you ask."

"Okay, what's your name?"

The waitress tilted her head. "What's yours?"

"Danny."

"I'm Margo."

"Nice to meet you, Margo."

"Nice to meet you, Danny."

Margo turned to John. "So, are you going to tell me your name?"

Danny hid a smile.

"What do you think my name is?" John said, casually leaning on the back of the chair.

"Trouble?"

He chuckled and she walked away.

The crowd was excited when the band started their second set. Danny stayed at the table, but he was sitting on the edge of his seat. After the opening song, Clive took the mic in his hand.

"You all look mighty good out there, shakin' what you got."

"Woo hoo," the crowd yelled.

"You know, we got ourselves a live celebrity in the house tonight," Clive announced. "And we would like to invite him to come up on stage with us and play a number or two. Please put your hands together for Daniel Bruer!" Danny got up and walked on stage with a large grin.

"You know folks, the first night I met this young man, I was takin' him to a party. Now you gotta understand I have been drivin' for a lotta years, and I've hauled many asses all over the town."

The audience laughed.

"Now, hardly any of um said but three words to me, let alone thanked me for the ride, but not Daniel here, he introduced himself right away, and when I found out that he liked the blues, well, hell, I knew he was different."

Danny grinned at Clive.

"Someone hand this boy a guitar," Clive said. One of the other band members handed Danny a guitar.

"You know 'Dust My Broom'?" Clive asked.

That was all Danny had to hear to start the song. He was fully pumped, and his pent-up energy was released. His body melded with the guitar, and his skilled fingers gave the song the extra sharp twang it needed.

The group didn't pause when the song ended as they slid right into 'Maybelline.' Danny didn't need any special prompting or notice. He was right in step as if he belonged with the group.

Margo joined the crowd that was dancing up front by the stage. Kicking her feet to the beat, her jazz hands fluttered in front of her. She didn't care that she was out of step with everyone else; she was having fun dancing to the beat of her own drummer. Glancing up, she made eye contact with Danny, and he mimicked a similar move. She covered her face with her hands and laughed.

The song ended, and Danny bowed for the enthusiastic applause. Turning his head, he looked back at where Margo had been standing and she was gone. He then turned his attention to Clive, who nodded.

Danny walked up to the microphone.

"Thank you so much for the warm reception. It feels good to be among good people who love to hear the blues as much as I do. I talked with Clive earlier, and he agreed we could play an original piece with another celebrity in the audience tonight."

"He wouldn't dare," John said under his breath.

"Not many people have heard of him or the band that he has started, but that is only a matter of time, believe me. Please welcome the leader of The Hound Dogs, John Chandler."

Everyone was clapping. Danny could tell by the glare on John's face that he wasn't happy, but he was willing to risk his wrath.

The cheering and clapping continued until John rose reluctantly to his feet and walked onto the stage.

"I am gonna kill you," he said to Danny.

"You just worry about singing. We'll take care of the rest." Danny went back to the mic. "This is a tune that John wrote. The name of the song is 'Crawlin' Dog.'" Danny turned and handed the mic to John, who wasn't smiling.

John looked out at the crowd. "I don't have the stage presence that Danny has, so this could be a bit rocky, but like I always say, when things get rocky, Let's Crawl the Dog!"

Danny started the song, and because the band was experienced, they could improvise the rest. The sound of "Crawlin' Dog" being played by a full band sent chills down John's spine, and he felt confident letting his stage persona shine through.

The song's reception was strong, and it appeased John's anger.

"Thanks, man," Danny said, shaking Clive's hand. "I owe you big time."

"He didn't look pleased gettin' called to the stage."

"Trust me. It was for his own good. Do you think this is gonna be enough?"

"Well, I am gonna say a lotta people who never heard that song heard it now. We are gonna get the word out there, brother."

"Can you come over and sit with us for a bit?"

"Yeah, but you can't hide from him forever."

"I know."

John had gone back to the table and sat down. Several people came over and told him how much they liked his song.

Margo brought John a beer and sat down by him.

"Look at you pretendin' to be so shy, and inside you're a rock star."

John shook his head. "Not even close."

"You're very talented."

"Danny's talented."

"You don't accept compliments, do you?"

He didn't say anything.

"You know what else?"

"What?"

"You're cute too."

John rumpled his lip. "There's that word again."

Margo walked away, passing Danny and Clive. They walked to the table and sat down with John.

"That's a little rockin' tune you got there," Clive said to John.

"Thanks."

"You got it written down somewhere?"

"It's in my head. That is the only place it needs to be."

Clive looked at Danny, making John more suspicious.

"You thought about layin' it down on wax?" Clive said.

"Maybe someday, but I'm still tryin' to get my band together."

"Oh?"

"The thing we need the most is a drummer."

"Drummers are hard to find. Everyone wants to play the geetar."

John laughed.

A Black, wiry man with a limp walked up to their table. "Evenin' gents. Is this old man here hasslin' you?"

"I don't hassle anyone except the ladies," Clive said.

They laughed.

"Boys, this here is the owner of this rat hole, Kat Price," Clive said.

"I wanted to tell you, boys, I like your style," Kat said.

"Thanks," Danny said.

"I was thinkin' the Hound Dogs should come in here and play a set."

"We accept," Danny said.

"Danny!" John snapped.

Clive set his hand on John's arm. "Danny's a bit exuberant. The group is having' a few growin' pains right now, but it ain't 'nothin' they can't overcome. I think they could open a set here on a Thursday night. Whadda, you say to that, Kat?"

Kat looked at John. "What does the top cat say?"

Danny and Clive looked at him.

"Free beer and a bit of jingle jangle for your jeans," Kat said.

Clive nodded at John.

"All right. I accept."

"Wonderful. We'll iron out the details," Clive said to Kat.

"You do that. Now, you all have a wonderful night." Kat nodded at them and walked away.

"Now don't you worry about a thing, John," Clive said. "The people that come here on Thursday nights are easy goin', and it'll get you used to bein' up in front of a crowd. I wouldn't steer you wrong."

"I appreciate the vote of confidence," John said.

"You'll get there, it just takes time," Clive said.

Danny and Clive made small talk about various blues artists. John was half listening to them. He was watching Margo cleaning the tables. His eyes followed her to the bar, where a man in a cheap suit was looking at him. John made eye contact with him and he looked away nervously. John thought he belonged in a cheap cocktail lounge, not a blues club.

"Hey, Margo," John said, signaling Margo to come over.

"You need another one?" she said.

"You see the guy at the bar in the suit that looks like an old couch?"

"Yeah."

"Do you know him?"

"No. Why?"

"I think he's watchin' me."

"Maybe we should give him a show," Margo said, bending over and kissing John.

"You're a bad girl, aren't you?" John said.

"Why don't you come and find out," she said, taking his hand. He looked at Danny, who was standing with Clive by the stage. So, he followed Margo into the woman's washroom, where she locked the door. They began to make out hot and heavy in the cramped space. A loud thump in the hallway made them stop.

"What's that?" John said.

Margo pressed her finger to his lips. "Shhh . . ."

Arms around each other, they waited for the next sound.

"I'm gonna look out the door," Margo said.

"What if a woman is standin' out there?"

"I'll just tell her I'm busy."

"But they'll see me leave."

"So? You never been caught neckin' before?"

"Not in a woman's washroom."

Margo slowly turned the lock on the door and peeked outside, then closed the door quickly.

"What?" John said.

"It's that guy," Margo whispered.

"The guy at the bar?"

She nodded. "Are you in some kind of trouble?"

"Not that I know of."

"Why don't you wait in here until he leaves?"

"I'm not hangin' out in here!"

"Be sensible! I'll be right back." Margo slipped out the door before John could protest. She pulled the door tight and then, turning, saw Danny.

"Hey, I've been lookin' for you," Danny said.

"Oh?" Margo said, straightening her shirt.

"Yeah, have you seen John?"

"Uh ... well ... I thought he was at the table?"

"No."

"Have you checked the men's washroom?"

"Not yet."

The bathroom door began to open behind Margo. She pulled it closed and kept her hand on the latch.

Danny raised his eyebrow. "Is someone in there?"

"Huh? Oh no," she said with a giggle. "The door sticks sometimes."

The door began to open again, nearly dragging Margo inside.

"Dumb door, stay closed!" Margo said, slamming the door closed.

Danny's lip was twisted, lifting his cheek.

Margo laughed but kept her hand on the door latch.

Danny disappeared down the hallway.

"The coast is clear," Margo said.

John opened the door. "Boy, I thought the writing on the men's room wall was bad, but this takes the cake."

"Hurry. Let's get back up front before Danny comes out of the men's room."

"You think he knows I was in there?"

"I don't know, but let's not wait to find out."

John was lounging at the table coolly when Danny came back. "Hey."

"Where have you been?" Danny said.

"Right here," John said, smiling innocently.

Danny shook his head.

"Are you ready to go?" John said.

"Yeah, it's late."

Danny laid some money on the table. John followed Danny to the door. Catching Margo's eye, she blew him a kiss, and he winked at her.

91

THE RIDE BACK TO TOWN was quiet. John was relaxed with his eyes closed.

"You wanna spend the night at the house?" Danny asked.

"Don't you have to work tomorrow?"

"Uh, yeah, but not till later."

"Okay."

They rode in silence for a while longer.

"Are you mad at me?" Danny finally asked.

John didn't open his eyes or say anything.

"You're makin' me feel like I'm waitin' for my father to come home or somethin'."

"Good," John said.

Danny sighed.

They got to the house and went up to Danny's room.

John laid on his bed, puttin' his hands up behind his head.

"I am not gonna let you sleep until you tell me if you're mad at me," Danny said, sitting on the floor.

"I'm not happy," John said.

"I only did what I thought was right."

John turned on his side and rested his head on his hand. "There is somethin' you're not tellin' me."

"I was hoping not to have to tell you tonight."

"You're scarin' me, Dan."

"I quit The Dice yesterday."

"You what?"

"I quit The Dice."

"And you were afraid I'd get upset about that?"

"No, it's the reason why I quit."

By now, John's brow was rumpled.

Danny took a deep breath. "Joe was told by the record company that he needed to develop an original song for their first record. Joe told them the first Dice record would be 'Crawlin' Dog.' He wanted me to agree to it, but there is no way in hell I would do that to you. So, I quit."

Danny could see the veil of darkness come over his friend's face. It was almost like watching Jekyll and Hyde.

"Can you understand why I pushed for the crowd to hear 'Crawlin' Dog' tonight? Now there is proof that it's your song, and tomorrow, we are gonna write it down."

John's look was scaring Danny. "Barney, please say something?"

"I am gonna crush his skull like a walnut."

"Look, he doesn't even remember what the song sounds like. He may be able to remember some of it, but there is no way he can remember all of it. This isn't over."

"You better believe this ain't over. He is sorely mistaken if he thinks I will stand by and let him take that song from me."

"Try and calm down. We'll figure this out. There is nothing we can't do together."

John half-smiled at him, then laid back on his hands and closed his eyes. Danny let his breath out, said a prayer, and turned out the light.

92

DANNY AND JOHN CAME DOWNSTAIRS the following morning shortly before breakfast was ready.

"I hope you don't mind. I stayed here last night," John said to Mabel.

"Of course I don't mind. You're welcome anytime."

John kissed her on the cheek and stole a piece of bacon.

She shook her finger at him, but she was smiling.

Jerry was at the table with Betty and Bob.

"Morning, boys," Bob said.

"Morning," Danny said.

"Mornin', Mr. Bruer," John said.

"You can call me Bob, John," Bob said.

John smiled at him and sat next to Danny. "How are things goin', Jerry?"

"All right, considerin'."

"Considerin' what?"

"My mom, she's in the hospital."

"What?"

"Yeah, she took too many sleeping pills. I barely got there in time."

"Oh, no. How did you know she was in trouble?"

"A coworker of hers came out to the mercantile and told me."

"He went out there all by himself, too," Danny said, piling pancakes on his plate.

"You did? Was Gus there?"

"He was," Jerry said coolly.

"And?"

"And Jerry kicked his ass," Danny said.

Bob raised an eyebrow.

"Oh, sorry," Danny said.

"You did?" John said.

"Well, no, he was drunk, and all it took was one good shove to push him over."

John laughed. "Good for you, Jerry. I'm proud of you."

Bob cleared his throat and scowled at John.

"Not that I condone violence or anything," John added.

"Well, I am proud of you too, Jerry," Mable said.

"Mable!" Bob said.

"It's about time someone stood up to Gus Palmer. It's not right that he terrorizes Jerry and his mother."

"I know it took great courage to stand up to Gus, and you did what you had to. I am proud of you, too," Bob said.

Jerry smiled and sat up taller in his chair.

"So, how is she now?" John said.

"I guess she's fadin' in and out of consciousness. Doctor Penrose wants to talk to me this mornin'."

"You need me to come with you?" John said.

"Bob's takin' me."

"I can take him, Uncle Bob," Danny said. "That way, you won't be late to the store."

"That would be a great help, Danny. Thanks," Bob said.

"If we can take the truck, I can drop him off at the store later."

"All right."

"I am thinkin' about gettin' my own wheels," Danny said.

Bob exchanged a concerned glance with Mable.

"I have been savin' my money. I can afford somethin' used. Besides, it will help me when I get a new job."

"I thought you would finish school," Bob said.

Danny was lifting his fork to his mouth and stopped. He looked at Mable, who was buttering her pancakes. He then looked at John, who took a drink of coffee.

"Well, I don't know about that," Danny said, wanting to move away from the topic.

"It was agreed that you would be finishing your education before you came to stay with us."

Danny chuckled. "I know, but now I've proven I can be a productive member of society without it."

Bob's look was somber. "We will finish this discussion later."

"Betty, you best hurry, or you'll miss the bus," Mabel said.

"I'm not going to school today, Mom. I am going with Jerry to the hospital."

"You are going to school, young lady," Bob said.

"But Daddy!" she protested.

"Your father is right, Betty," Jerry said. "You shouldn't miss school."

"But this is important."

"I can fill you in later."

She pouted her lip out and stormed out of the room.

"Excuse me," Jerry said, going into the kitchen.

Betty grabbed her books and sweater.

"Honey," Jerry said.

She ignored him and went out the back door.

Jerry followed her outside. "Come on, Betty, don't be mad."

She turned to him. "I'm not a baby, you know. I shouldn't have to go to school when being there to support you is way more important."

Jerry felt her face. "I know you care, and I appreciate it. I will tell you everything tonight, okay?"

Betty pouted and looked at her feet.

Jerry lifted her chin. "I'll take you out for ice cream."

Betty fought a smile, and her face puckered.

Jerry pinched her cheek, and she laughed.

The bus pulled up.

"Have a good day," Jerry said.

Betty kissed him and ran down the walkway to the bus.

93

THE ROBIN'S SONG FILLED THE early morning air with joy as the sun stretched its limbs against the clear sky. Joe enjoyed a cup of coffee under the colorful umbrella that shaded the black wrought-iron table on the back patio. Reading the morning paper was the only time Joe could relax and enjoy some solitude. Monica came out of the house in a pink silk robe and house slippers with a tuft of pink feathers on the top.

"So, you did decide to get out of bed?" Joe said, taking a drink of coffee.

Monica sat down across from him and crossed her legs. "It's not that late," she said, pouring herself a cup of coffee. "I hate it when the muffins are cold."

Joe turned a page.

"Did you use all the butter?"

"No."

"You always use all the butter, Joe. It's a wonder you aren't fat," Monica said, scooping out a generous helping of sugar for her coffee.

"Look who's talking," Joe said.

"I exercise."

Joe laughed. "Shopping and going to the beauty parlor is not exercise."

"You spend more time fretting over your wardrobe than I do," Monica said, demurely, taking a sip.

"That's because I am a showman. I have an obligation to my fans to always look my best."

Monica rolled her eyes.

Joe poured himself another cup of coffee.

"So, did you find a replacement for tonight?" Monica asked.

"I don't know. I put in a call to Kyle."

"Kyle? You think he would play for you after you fired him?"

"What the hell else am I supposed to do?"

Monica looked at her fingernails. "You could call Danny and tell him that you're not going to steal his friend's song, and maybe he will come back."

"I am not stealing his friend's song!"

"What would you call it, then?"

"I am willing to pay him for it if I can find the fool!"

"Why don't you just ask Danny to introduce you to him?"

"It's not that simple."

"Why not?"

"It just isn't."

"Excuse me, sir," Madge said, coming out onto the patio. "There is a phone call for you."

"Who is it?"

"Mr. Gates."

"Thank you, Madge," he picked up the phone. "This better be good, Carlton."

"I found him," Carlton said.

"Chandler?"

"Yes, he was at a club last night with Daniel."

"Is Lou still tailing them?"

"Yes, they spent the night at Daniel's house. He is going to trail them today and get back to me later. What do you want me to do now?"

"Wait until you hear back from Lou. Then once we get more information on this Chandler, I can meet with him and settle this once and for all."

"Have you found a replacement for the show tonight?"

"Not yet," Joe said through his teeth.

"Do you think I should cancel the show?"

"No, I don't want you to cancel the show," Joe snapped.

"Whatever you say, Joe."

Joe sighed.

Monica lifted her cup to her mouth to hide a smile.

"I expect to hear from you later with an update," Joe said.

"Will do," Carlton said.

Joe hung up the phone and rubbed his temples.

"You know, if Kyle can't play with you tonight, I could fill in," Monica said, swinging her foot.

Joe looked up at her. "You?"

"Yes, me."

"Don't be ridiculous."

"Why is it ridiculous? I know the material and have seen the show a hundred times."

"Yes, but you don't know the routine."

"You mean this routine?" Monica stood up and pretended that she had a guitar in her hand. Smiling broadly, she moved from side to side, then stepped forward and back.

He frowned as he watched her. "All right, you can stop now."

"Are you sure? I think there is one part where maybe I turn around." She turned around in a circle, moving her hips with the same strained smile on her lips.

Joe took another drink of coffee.

Monica sat down and stared at him.

"I suppose it isn't a horrible idea."

Monica clapped her hands.

"Now, don't go thinking it will be some kind of permanent arrangement. It's only for the weekend. Understand?"

"Of course," she said with a satisfied smile.

94

JERRY DRUMMED HIS THUMBS ON the arms of the wooden chair while he waited for Doctor Penrose. He hoped the news about his mother wouldn't be as bad as he imagined. He was worried about what would happen to her if she was released. No one had seen Gus since the day his mother was admitted to the hospital, but Jerry knew he was out there somewhere, and his blood ran cold.

"Good morning, Mr. Price," Doctor Penrose said, stepping into his office.

Jerry stood up. "Good morning, Doctor, and please call me Jerry."

"All right, Jerry, please have a seat."

Jerry sat down, and Doctor Penrose sat behind his oak desk.

"I can't tell you how sorry I am to burden you with these important decisions, but we can't locate your mother's husband."

"Did you check his job?"

"Yes, apparently, he hasn't reported for work since Tuesday. Do you have any other ideas where we might be able to contact him?"

"I assume you checked the house?"

"Yes. Have you been to the house since your mother has been in the hospital?"

"No. The only other place I know to find him is at the bar on Gabel Road."

The doctor nodded and made some notes. "I am sorry that the diagnosis for your mother is not more positive. I am sure it is no surprise that she is in feeble health. She has malnutrition and losing bone density, which, left untreated, could lead to osteoporosis. She suffered quite a beating. The amount of brain damage she has will take some time to determine. She has been drifting in and out of consciousness, and in the moments when she is conscious, she is confused and fretful. She has asked for Mathew on more than one occasion. Do you know who he is?"

"He's my father," Jerry said.

The doctor nodded and made another note. "She will need to use a wheelchair until she can regain strength. I am going to recommend her to be transferred to Bethany."

"The asylum?"

"It's not an asylum. It's a long-term care facility where she can receive the care and treatment she needs."

"How long?"

"I am not sure yet."

Jerry looked at his hands.

"I'm sorry."

"Can I see her?"

"Yes, but I must warn you, if she is conscious, she may not recognize you. Do you think you can handle it?"

"Yes."

"I would recommend not staying long."

"Understood."

A nurse escorted Jerry down a long, colorless and sterile hallway to a small cheerless room.

She was asleep when he walked in. The oxygen tube was gone, but the IV was still in her arm. The bruises on her face were a dark purple, and she looked older than her age. Jerry stood by her bedside and took her frail hand. It was cold, and he gently rubbed it. Her right eye fluttered open, but the left was still swollen shut.

"Hey, Mom," Jerry said softly.

She looked up at him through a haze. "Mathew?"

Jerry felt a pang in his heart.

"Have you come to take me home?"

"You're not strong enough yet."

"I want to go home. The baby will be here soon."

Jerry swallowed hard, tears threatening to flow from his eyes.

"What shall we name him?"

"I don't know."

She looked at the ceiling, then back at him. "I think we need to paint this room. The paint is peeling again. I want it to be blue this time. The baby will like blue."

Jerry smiled and patted her hand.

A nurse came into the room. "I'm sorry, Mr. Price, your mother needs her rest."

"I need to go, Martha, but I will be back to see you soon, okay?" Jerry said.

"Do you love me, Mathew?"

"You know I do." Jerry bent over and kissed her cheek.

Martha smiled widely at him as he stroked her hair. "You be good for the nurses, okay?"

"Okay."

"If you behave, I'll bring you some strawberries."

"They are my favorite."

"I know. Now get some sleep."

She nodded and closed her eyes.

95

AFTER DANNY AND JOHN DROPPED Jerry off at the mercantile, Danny wanted to look for a car.

John wasn't convinced that was a good idea, but Danny insisted that his uncle would be all right with the purchase if he didn't spend all his money.

There was only one car dealership in Madison. It mainly sold used cars, but a few new vehicles were parked in front of the building to attract customers. After looking at all the mediocre cars that filled the lot, the turquoise 57 Chevy stood out like a pearl among empty oysters.

"So, what do you think of this one?" Danny asked John.

"I think it's expensive," John said.

Danny gently ran his fingers over the chrome. "But look at how the chrome shines in the sun."

"Yeah and look at the price tag."

"I love the fins and color. Imagine the fun we could have in this beauty."

"And after you buy it, you won't have a dime in your savings."

"You're starting to sound like my uncle."

"Bob is a smart man."

A man in a dark suit with a sly smile and slicked-back hair approached them. "Afternoon, boys."

"Hello," Danny said.

"Name's Pearson," he said, offering his hand to Danny.

"Danny," Danny said, shaking his hand.

"And your name?" he said to John.

"Theodorus," John said.

"Exotic name. So, you lookin' to buy a car, young fella?" Pearson said to Danny.

"I am."

"We have a lot of fine used cars on the back lot. They need some work, but you're young and can poke around under the hood."

"Actually, I was interested in this one."

Pearson put his hands on his hips. "Ah yes, she is the gem on our lot."

Danny crouched next to the car to check the rims.

"Be careful now, and don't touch it. I don't want to have to scrub off any grimy fingerprints."

"She's the most beautiful car I have ever seen," Danny said.

"Yes, sir, she has many admirers. I expect it won't be long before someone comes along and snaps her up," Pearson said, snapping his fingers.

"Can I see the inside?" Danny said, trying to look in the window.

"Oh, I don't think that would be possible."

"He's not wanting you to touch it with your grimy fingers," John said, wiggling his fingers.

Pearson chuckled. "Well, you understand that I can only let serious buyers view the merchandise inside."

"I'm a serious buyer," Danny said.

Pearson looked him over. "Well now, son, your father might be a serious buyer, but you?"

"Come on, Danny, we don't need to be taking up any more of this gentleman's precious time," John said. "He has more important matters to tend to."

"Well . . ." Pearson said.

"Obviously, he needs to take time to pull his head out of his ass."

Pearson's jaw dropped down.

"That's a shame. I was gonna pay cash, too," Danny said, pulling a large wad of cash out of his pocket.

Pearson blinked at him.

"You all have a nice day now," John said.

Danny winked at Pearson as he left the lot with John.

◻◼◻◼◻◼◻◼◻◼◻◼◻◼◻◼◻◼◻

John and Danny walked down the block, laughing.

"You know, Dan, you shouldn't walk around with that much cash in your pocket."

"Nah, it ain't no big deal. It's a bunch of singles, actually. I keep my real money in my sock."

John laughed.

"Whadda, you say we grab a couple of hotdogs and eat in the park?" Danny said.

"Sold."

After picking up their lunch, the two sat in the tranquil park under a large elm tree.

"I really love that car, Barnaby."

"Who wouldn't? But maybe you should think about gettin' somethin' a little less expensive."

"I will find another job."

"Sounded like Bob wanted you to go back to school this morning."

Danny ignored John and took a bite of his hotdog.

"He said something about an agreement you made before you came out here?"

Danny set his elbow on his knee and cast his gaze across the park.

"You don't want to talk about it?" John said.

"Bingo," Danny said.

"What was the last grade you completed?"

Danny hesitated. "I was almost through my junior year."

"Okay."

"Well, more like half."

"Oh boy."

"I'm too old to go back to high school," Danny said.

"How old are you?" John asked.

"Eighteen."

John squinted his eyes. "Seventeen."

"I'm gonna be eighteen real soon."

John shook his head.

"I would still be older than everyone else."

John took a drink of his soda. "I don't think you would go back to high school. I think you could go for your GED at the Community College.""

"It's still school," Danny groused.

John leaned back on his hands. "I don't think it would be as bad as you think."

Danny shrugged. "Maybe I could stomach going to college. I'll have to think about it."

John twitched his feet. "The break is comin' up soon. I can't wait for that."

"Maybe we could get some work together."

John frowned at him. "Are you kiddin'?"

"No, think about it. We're gonna need to be getting us some electric guitars here soon. It's the direction of things now. Plus, think about how much better we'll sound."

John raised his eyebrow. "We? Whadda, you mean by we?"

"You know, the group."

"What group?"

"The Hound Dogs," Danny chuckled.

"How do you know I want you to be a group member?"

"Well, I just assumed."

"You assumed I would want to take you just like that?" John snapped his fingers.

"Well … yeah."

"Hmmm, I dunno. Maybe you'll have to do an audition, and then, of course, there would be a vote."

"A vote?"

"Everyone's opinion matters in the group. Unless I don't like it, then we do things my way," John said, munching a chip.

Danny thought about John's words for a moment, before he smiled. "You're joking."

"Am I?"

Danny's face fell.

Letting his gaze wander, John noticed a man across the park standing under a tree. He slowly leaned forward and squinted his eyes. "Hey Danny, you see that guy over there?"

"Yeah."

"He was at the club last night."

"Oh, yeah?"

"Yeah, I think he's following me."

Danny looked over at him. "Are you sure it was him?"

"I would recognize that suit anywhere. I'm gonna go talk to him."

Danny followed behind John, but when the man saw them, he turned and ran.

"Oh hell," John said as he and Danny began to chase after him.

96

L OU MILLS WAS A MIDDLE-AGED man with a reddish crooked toupee. He wore out-of-style suits that he bought off bargain racks, and his belt strained to hold his pants up. He knew it wouldn't take the two young men long to catch up to him. He ducked down an alley, hoping to lose them, but a large fence was at the end of the path. He heard them coming and looked around for a quick escape. He tried to jump up and grab onto the fire escape, but it was too high. Losing his footing, he landed on his behind just as John and Danny closed in. Lou pulled himself up to his feet and began to back up.

"Afternoon," Lou said, trying to regain some of his dignity.

John's rough exterior and the scowl on his face made Lou nervous.

"Who the hell are you, and why are you followin' me?" John asked.

"What makes you think I'm followin' you?"

"Because I saw you last night at The Blue Kat."

"Oh," Lou said, wiping his brow. "I was hired to find you."

John placed his hands on his hips. "Who the hell hired you?"

"Carlton Gates."

"Who is that?"

"The manager of The Dice," Danny said.

"He wanted proof that you were a real person."

John glared. "Well, here I am."

"That you are. Then I will just be on my way," Lou said, walking forward, but John stepped in front of him.

"Not so fast. We are gonna make a little phone call first."

"Oh?"

"Yes, come on, and don't try and make another break for it," John warned.

Lou nodded and blinked with a grin.

The trio walked back down the alley and then to a nearby telephone booth.

"You call your boss. I wanna talk to him," John said.

Lou nodded and began to search his pockets. "Uh...uh...hold on a minute."

John frowned at him.

"I'm sure I got one somewhere," Lou said.

John looked at Danny, who shrugged.

"Uh, do you have a dime?" Lou said.

"Uh," John said, reaching into his pocket.

"I have one," Danny said, handing a dime to Lou.

"Thank you," Lou said, looking at the booth.

"Now what?" John said.

"Well, you see, the problem is . . ."

"What?" John said, losing his patience.

"I don't think I can fit in the booth to make the call."

John sighed. "Give me the dime."

Lou handed it to him.

"What's the number?"

Lou told John the number as he dialed. When the line started to ring, John handed the receiver to Lou.

"Hello?"

"Hey Carlton, I found John Chandler," Lou said.

"Great, where is he?"

"Right here."

"What?"

John took the phone from Lou. "Carlton?"

"Who is this?"

"The man you think doesn't exist."

"Mr. Chandler?"

"You better start explainin' why this man in a vaudeville suit is followin' me."

"There seems to be some kind of misunderstanding. I merely wanted to set up a meeting with you to come into my office and discuss some business with my client and me."

"Who is your client?"

"Joe Delaney."

"What a coincidence. I want to talk to him too."

"You do?"

"Yes."

"Wonderful. When are you available?"

"Right now."

Carlton chuckled. "Oh well, I'm afraid today won't be possible."

"I disagree. Either I get a phone call from Dalamey in the next five minutes, or your friend here is gonna start missin' some teeth."

Lou's eyes grew wide.

"You're joking, of course," Carlton said.

"Am I laughing? The number is 62456."

"But . . ."

"Five minutes."

"Mr. Chandler . . ."

John hung up the receiver. "That should get his attention."

Sweat poured off Lou's brow. "Please, please don't hurt me! I'll give you anything you want! I don't have very many teeth left."

"Relax, I'm not gonna hurt you," John said. "I had to say somethin' to get that dimwit's attention."

Lou let his breath out.

❑■❑■❑■❑■❑■❑■❑■❑■❑

Carlton called Joe, praying he would answer.

"Hello, Delaney residence."

"This is Carlton Gates. I need to talk to Joe right now. It's an emergency."

"I'm sorry, Mr. Gates, he isn't in."

"Did he say where he was going?"

"I think he was headed down to the club. Can I take a message?"

"No. Thanks," Carlton hung up. He picked up the phone and called The Beaumont.

"Front desk, how may I help you?"

"Hello, this is Carlton Gates. I am Joe Delaney's manager. Do you know if he is there or not?"

"I can check."

"Please hurry. It's important!"

The girl put Carlton on hold. Carlton opened a desk drawer and rummaged through the various remedies for his ailments.

❑■❑■❑■❑■❑■❑■❑■❑■❑■❑■❑

"So, Lou," John said. "You sure you don't know what they want with me?"

"Yes."

"It has to be about the song," Danny said.

"I'm sure it is," John said, leaning up against the phone booth. "You think he'll call, Danny?"

"I dunno."

"It looks like Dalamey doesn't care about your teeth, Lou," John said.

Lou rocked back on his feet.

"Hey Lou, if they call back, what do you say we have some fun?"

Lou smiled.

❑■❑■❑■❑■❑■❑■❑■❑■❑■❑■❑

The girl at the Beaumont finally came back on the line. "I'm sorry, Mr. Gates. He hasn't arrived yet."

Carlton sighed. "Can you please tell him to call me as soon as he gets in?"

"Of course."

"Thank you." Carlton hung up and called the number back.

"Hello?"

"Mr. Chandler?"

"I told you I wanted to talk to Dalamey."

"He wasn't available right now."

"Oh, that's too bad," John nodded at Lou, who started to yell.

"Help! Help!"

Carlton gripped the phone receiver tight. "Good Lord, man! What are you doing to him?"

"I am a man of my word, Mr. Gates," John said.

Lou screamed, then smiled.

"Look, this has to stop. You are torturing an innocent man!"

"I told you my terms."

"And I told you, he's not available. Let's make a meeting, and we can settle this like men, not barbarians!"

John was quiet for a minute, and Lou screamed a couple of times. Clearly, he was enjoying himself.

"Ten o'clock in your office tomorrow morning," John said.

"It's Saturday . . ."

"Ten o'clock," and John hung up.

Danny smiled at John. "You're makin' Joe come into the office the morning after a performance? He is gonna be pissed."

"He's gonna be even more pissed when I lay his ass out."

"We're gonna have to work on your diplomacy," Danny said.

"All right, Lou, you're free to go," John said.

"Thank you."

"By the way, seein' how you're some secret agent and all, you might want to consider gettin' a new suit. Somethin' that makes you blend into the crowd."

"Thank you, I'll do that."

John smiled at him, and he walked away.

"Poor guy," Danny said.

"Oh, I dunno, I think he rather enjoyed havin' his teeth knocked out."

Danny grinned, and they walked back to the park.

97

WILL AND BOYD WERE LOUNGING backstage, enjoying a few drinks before the show. Will was in a sour mood and stretched out on the couch. The top two buttons on his shirt were undone, and his uncuffed shirt sleeves hung open around his wrists. Boyd was seated in the easy chair, browsing a magazine.

"I wonder whom Joe got to fill in tonight," Boyd said.

"I don't even want to think about it," Will said, draining his glass.

"I think he was going to ask Kyle."

Will chuckled. "Oh, yeah, there's a great idea."

"I can't imagine he would agree."

"I would hope not." Will held out his empty glass. "Pour me another drink, would you?"

"Another wild night?"

"Something like that."

Boyd took his glass. "Was she pretty?"

Will put his arm up over his eyes. "Yeah, but she talked too much. I hate it when they think you care about their interests, who their friends are, and all that junk."

Boyd handed Will the refilled glass. "Beautiful women are high maintenance."

"That's why I never go out with one for very long."

"An attentive, charming, sweet, loving woman is way better in my book," Boyd said, returning to his chair.

Will opened an eye. He was too self-centered even to notice the change in Boyd, but now it was apparent. Boyd wasn't the unkempt mess that he usually was. His suit was pressed, his shirt had no hint of a stain, and his shoes were polished. Even his hair was neatly combed, and there was no hint of stubble on his face.

Will sat up. "Who is she?"

"Who's who?"

"The woman you're dating?"

Boyd took a drink. "What makes you think I'm dating someone?"

"Because you look sharp, and you've only had one drink."

Boyd shrugged. "Maybe I just decided to improve my image."

"It's not that chubby stiff-haired shrew, is it?" Will said, turning his glass in a circle.

Boyd's lips were in a tight line. "She's not a shrew."

"You're kidding, Boyd. Her?" Will said, sneering at Boyd.

"She's charming and a great cook."

"I can't believe you."

"Well, believe it, and now that you have expressed your opinion, I won't tolerate you disrespecting her anymore. Now, let's move on to another subject," Boyd said, picking lint off his pants.

Will was dumbstruck and at a loss for words.

The door opened, and Joe walked in with Monica on his arm. Unwelcome memories flooded Will's mind, and his grasp on the glass tightened.

"Hey, Joe ... and Monica," Boyd said.

"Boyd," Joe said.

"Can I fix you both a drink?" Boyd said.

"No," Joe said. "I can see you two are already hitting the booze."

"I only had one, Joe," Boyd said.

"And I haven't had enough, Joe," Will said.

"You better not mess up the show tonight, Will," Joe said.

"Or what? You'll ground me?"

"Maybe I'll fire you."

Will laughed. "You haven't got the balls."

"So, did Kyle agree to fill in for Daniel tonight?" Boyd said.

"No, but I found someone better."

"Like who?" Will said.

"Monica will be taking his spot."

"Is that some kind of joke?" Will said.

"No. She knows the songs and the moves. She will be fine."

Monica met Will's hateful eyes.

"Excuse me, I'm going to get ready," Monica said. Kissing Joe on the cheek, she smiled at Will and left the room.

"Are you outta your mind letting her fill in?" Will said, setting his glass down.

"What the hell was I supposed to do? Cancel the damn show that has been sold out for weeks when I have the perfect replacement?"

"You may not have to fire me. I may quit."

"Go ahead, you big baby. All you do is complain, complain, complain. If it weren't for me, you would still be at home being mommy's little darling."

Will stood up, his hand clenched in a fist.

"Guys, guys," Boyd said, stepping between the two. "Calm down. Everyone is feeling the stress tonight, but that's no reason to be at each other's throats. Will, we need Monica tonight until we get a replacement, and Joe's right, you've been hitting it a little hard tonight."

Will sneered at Boyd. "Who the hell do you think you are? You think you can judge me just because you got a plump little tart?"

Boyd lifted his chin, his jaw set.

"You're right, Boyd, we need to all cool down," Joe said, setting his hand on Boyd's rigid arm.

Boyd pulled his arm away from Joe's grasp. Picking up his jacket, he left the room.

"You better go for a walk, drink coffee, or take a cold shower. I don't care which, but you better be dressed and sober enough to perform tonight. Understand?" Joe hissed.

Will sized him up, then, muttering something under his breath, he left the room.

Joe sat down in a chair, his head in his hand.

"Excuse me, Mr. Delaney," a front desk clerk said, coming into the room. "I have a phone message for you from Mr. Gates."

Joe took the message. "Thanks."

She curtseyed and left.

"What the hell does he want?" Joe said, picking up the phone and dialing.

"Hello?"

"Carlton."

"Hey, Joe. I wanted you to know I talked to Mr. Chandler on the phone earlier today."

"And?"

"He agreed to meet with us tomorrow morning at ten."

"Tomorrow morning? Tomorrow is Saturday," Joe said.

"I know it. It was the only time he had available."

"Did you talk to Danny?"

"No."

"That little shit isn't worth the trouble he's causing me."

"I'm sorry, Joe."

"Yeah." Joe hung up the phone with a thud.

98

MONICA SAT IN FRONT OF the sizeable lighted mirror in Joe's dressing room. She hummed to herself as she applied her eyeliner. Satisfied, she began to work on securing her fake eyelashes. Joe entered the room and noticed her perfectly V-shaped back in a short cream-colored slip.

He walked over to the couch and took off his jacket. "You should put some damn clothes on."

Picking up her hairbrush, she looked at him through the mirror.

"Did you hear me?"

"I'm not ready to put my dress on yet. I don't want to smudge my makeup on it."

He took a small bag out of his jacket pocket and sat on the couch.

"Didn't you just get done telling Will not to get high before the performance?" Monica said, concentrating on her image.

"You want some?" Joe said, laying out a line.

"No thanks. I want to do a good job tonight."

A few minutes later, Joe got up and walked to the clothes rack. Monica watched him put on his jacket and check himself in the mirror. Pulling on his sleeves, Joe searched for the right set of cufflinks. Out of the corner of his eye, he watched Monica walk over to the clothes rack and pull a shimmering royal blue dress off the hanger. She slipped it on and walked over to Joe.

"Can you zip me up?" she said, turning her back and lifting her hair. Joe slowly zipped the dress up. Pausing, they stood in front of the full-length mirror, looking at the reflection of an artificial illusion of perfection.

"You look lovely tonight," Joe said.

"Thank you." Monica walked over to the couch and sat down to put her shoes on. Joe watched as she fumbled with the tiny buckles on her silver shoes. Once the buckles were secure, she walked back over to the dressing table to put on her lipstick.

Joe walked up behind her. "Did you bring your sapphire necklace?"

"No."

"Do you remember when I gave it to you?"

"Of course."

He ran his hand down her left arm. Reaching her hand, he held it out. "Your finger is barren too."

"Joe. . . ."

He slipped his right arm around her middle. "I don't know why we fight. When harmony is so much more enjoyable."

He nuzzled her neck, causing tiny hairs on her skin to prickle. She wanted to walk away from him and deny her desire, but instead, she leaned back into him.

"Joe, the show is going to start soon," she whispered.

"I don't care," he said in her ear.

"You can't be serious?"

"Can't I?"

"You've never started a show late."

"Well, my dear, there is a first time for everything." And he locked the door.

99

J OHN REGRETTED HIS DECISION TO make the meeting for early Saturday morning. He had stayed up with Danny goofing off on their guitars till the wee hours of the morning. The walking and waiting for the bus to take them to Carlton's office didn't help their moods. The hot bus rattled along the bumpy county road leading to the main thoroughfare. Small animals scurried as the large, lumbering machine left a cloud of murky dust behind it.

"I can't wait to get my car. I am gettin' tired of buses," Danny said.

John was reclined in the seat next to him with his sunglasses on.

"Are you sleepin'?" Danny said to him.

"I wish," John mumbled.

The bus dropped them off two blocks away from Carlton's office. They walked along the bustling street in the warm sun. The closer they got to the building, the heavier the burden weighed on their minds.

"Are we ready for this?" Danny said.

"I'm never gonna be ready to see that jackass," John said, opening the door.

Joe was already seated in Carlton's office when they arrived. Danny thought he was ready to deal with the situation, but his confidence left him when he saw Joe's cold, vengeful glare.

"Good morning, gentlemen," Carlton said. "Come in and have a seat."

John and Danny sat down.

"Where is he?" Joe hissed at Danny.

"Who?" Danny said.

"Chandler."

"Right here," Danny said.

"*Him!* You expect me to believe that *he* wrote that song! You must take me for some kind of fool!"

"We already know you're a fool," John said.

Joe was on his feet, his face red.

"Joe," Carlton said.

"I should have known you were behind this. You worthless, ignorant degenerate!"

John stood up.

Carlton stood up. "Everyone sit down, and let's talk about this like civilized gentlemen."

John held Joe's stare tensely before they both sat down. Carlton released the breath he was holding and sat down.

"Mr. Chandler," Carlton began. "I am assuming that Daniel told you that The Dice have expressed interest in recording your song. Is that correct?"

"I heard The Dice was interested in stealing my song, yes."

"I didn't say I wanted to steal it. I merely suggested that we record it," Joe said.

"Without my permission, of course."

"Your permission, indeed!"

"Mr. Chandler," Carlton interjected, "what Mr. Delaney is trying to say is he is willing to make you an offer for the song."

"Well, you can tell Mr. Dalamey not only no, but hell no," John said.

Joe's eyes were narrowed slits. "I am willing to offer you more money than you could see in ten years."

"I would rather die than sell my song to a filthy fraud like you."

"If you insult me one more time . . ."

"You'll cry?"

Joe jumped out of his chair and stepped toward John before Danny stood up and blocked him.

"Joe, you better sit down and cool off," Danny said.

"You better listen to Danny, Dalamey. Unless you want to take this outside, and we can finish this right now."

Joe looked at John's hardened eyes before sinking into the chair. John sat back in his chair and folded his hand across his stomach.

"All right, the song is off the table," Carlton said.

"I want somethin' in writin' sayin' this charlatan isn't gonna try and steal it," John said.

"Why you . . ."

"Now, Dalamey, you're not playin' nice."

Carlton's head was in his hand. "I will have the paper drawn up."

"Start drawin', 'cause I ain't leavin' here without it."

"I can't type," Carlton said.

"Guess you're writin' it, then."

"Just write the damn thing, Carlton!" Joe said.

Carlton took a pen and paper out of his desk and began to write. When he finished, both Joe and John signed it.

John stuck the paper in his pocket. "You ready to go, Dan?"

"Not so fast," Joe said. "I'm not done with him yet."

"I have nothin' further to say," Danny said.

"Well, I have plenty to say. Have you forgotten that you signed a contract with me? It says that I own your ass for one year."

Danny looked at Carlton, who nodded.

"You can't make me stay in a band I don't want to be a part of!"

"No, but I can sue you for breach of contract."

Danny swallowed hard.

"Whadda you want from him?" John said.

"I want to recoup my damages."

"What damages?"

"Where do I begin?" Joe said, tapping his finger on his chin.

"You know I don't have anything," Danny said.

"Well, you should have thought about that before you screwed me."

"All right, you bastard," John said, standing. "If I give you my song, will you let Danny out of his contract?"

Danny stood. "John! No! I won't let you do it!"

Joe sat back in his chair. "Well, well, maybe you're not the imbecile I thought you were."

"No," Danny said, shaking his head.

"Will that satisfy your sick, narcissist ego?" John said.

"Joe, please don't do this. I will give you whatever you want," Danny said.

"Let me take my client to the other room for a moment," John said, taking Danny into the waiting room.

"Danny . . . .."

"I don't care, John. I'm not gonna let you do it!"

"Calm down and listen to me."

"No, no, no," Danny said, walking around the room and running his hand through his hair. "This is all my fault! I'm nothing but trouble! I'm an idiot!"

"Come on, Danny."

"It's true," Danny said, tears in his eyes. "All my life, I have been nothing but a loser. My parents sent me away because my father couldn't bear the shame of having a juvenile delinquent for a son. You're my first true friend, and I will be damned if I let him take this from you!"

"Danny," John said, taking his shoulders. "It's not the end of the world. Now stop it! That bloodthirsty vulture in there isn't going to stop causing you pain and suffering until he has finished you. Now let me do this for you."

"I'm a failure, John."

"So am I." John turned and went into Carlton's office. He stood in front of Joe, ripped up the piece of paper, and threw it in Joe's face.

"There, it's finished. Are you happy now?"

"Just like that, you rip up a piece of paper, and this all goes away?" Joe said.

"That's right—you got what you wanted."

Joe chuckled. "I'm afraid it's not that simple. I invested a lot of time and money into Daniel to just let him walk away."

"He invested time and effort in your lousy lounge act."

"If it weren't for my coaching and expertise, he wouldn't be who he is today."

"You think you're responsible for Danny's talent?" John laughed. "Let me tell you something. Danny was born with his talent. The music he plays comes from his soul, not from your ego. He has more talent in his little finger than your entire diseased body."

Joe rose to his feet. "Want to bet?"

John looked Joe squarely in the eye. "Name it."

A crooked grin split Joe's mouth. "In one week, we each play a song at The Beaumont. If Danny wins, I rip up the contract, and you can keep your song, but if I win, I get the song, and Danny will satisfy whatever damages I see fit."

"The Beaumont? You want Danny to meet your challenge at a venue full of all of your fans? Not a chance."

"Venues are expensive," Carlton said.

"The community center isn't expensive," Danny said.

"The community center? Are you out of your mind? There is no way in hell I am taking my expensive equipment into a den of thieves," Joe said.

"So, bring your basic gear," Danny said.

"No, no way. Not going to happen!"

"Are you afraid you might be judged on the music if people see you on a smaller stage without all the lights and flash?" John said.

"This is ridiculous. That place doesn't even have a proper stage."

"Some boards and nails are all that is needed," Danny said.

"It's not a bad idea, Joe," Carlton said.

"Now, where will we find an impartial person to judge this fiasco?" John said.

"I'm confident that Carlton will find someone."

"Me?" Carlton squeaked.

"You think we're going to accept a judge your manager picked out?" John said.

"Well, I will not accept someone *you* picked out."

"That's because we know decent people."

"I have an idea," Carlton said. "What we need is an audience. Each of you will play a couple of tunes, and then we will let them decide who the winner is?"

"If we're going to have an audience, why not give them a show?" Joe said, stretching his arms out.

"A show?" John said.

"Why not? You have a band, don't you?"

"Well yeah, sort of."

"Deal, but only if you agree to face us under a different name," Danny said. "That way, we know the audience isn't rigged."

Joe puffed his cheeks out and tapped his foot.

"Joe?" Carlton said, afraid Joe might explode.

"Fine," Joe said, waving his hand in the air.

"We're going to need more than a week," Carlton said.

"Two," Joe said.

"Three," John said.

"Agreed," Carlton said.

Joe scowled at him.

"We need the time as well, trust me."

"Three, final offer," Joe conceded.

John looked at Danny, who nodded.

"No hype, no fancy promotions, no frill suits," John said. "Just two bands playin' a barebones rock-n-roll show. Agreed?"

"Agreed." Joe offered his hand to John, and against his will, John shook it.

"Three weeks," Joe said, leaning up against the desk. "Oh, I win by forfeit if you don't show."

"And if I catch you pullin' some funny business . . ." John started.

"We'll be there," Danny said, pulling John out the door.

John and Danny left Carlton's office, and even though it was hot outside, it felt good to be moving away from the building.

"I guess you know we just made a bet with the devil," John said.

"Yeah, but isn't that what rock-n-roll is all about?"

John laughed, and Danny joined him.

100

J AMES STOPPED BY STU'S HOUSE so they could walk together to
practice. Stu had cut his hair, which he combed neatly to one
side, and was wearing his glasses. It had been difficult for Stu
to wear them when he was younger because the other kids picked on
him, so he spent many years hiding them in his desk and squinting at
the chalkboard.

"Wow, you look ... different," James said to him as they walked
down the street.

"Yeah, I figured I need to clean up my image now that I'm a
working man. Besides, the glasses make me look smarter."

"So, you like working at the market?"

"Yeah, it's not too bad. They hired a new clerk last week."

"Oh, yeah?"

"Yeah, she's a cashier, but she's been helpin' with inventory when
times are slow. Len was training her, but she spent the last few days
with me."

"Ah."

"She is petite and can't do much heavy lifting, so I manage the
boxes for her."

"Good thing she has you to help her."

Stu rolled back his shoulders. "Yeah."

James hid his smile.

"Have you had a chance to work things out with Marcy?" Stu asked.

"Yeah, we um … talked things over and made up."

"That's good. She's a great girl."

"The best."

"I'm thinkin' it won't be long until you two are married."

James cleared his throat. "I don't know about that. I have to graduate first. I will not marry her until I can provide for us."

"You are definitely on the right road to make that happen."

"So are you, now that you have a job."

Stu shook his head. "I ain't gonna get married."

"You're not?"

"Nah, I got too much livin' to do. That's one of the perks of bein' a rock-n-roll star, you know? The chicks."

James laughed.

"I don't wanna be tied down."

"Now, you sound like John."

"We have a lot in common."

"I don't know. You're more relatable and easier to talk to. He's so obstinate and closed off."

Stu smiled. "Gee, thanks, James."

"I mean it, Stu. You're a good guy."

"So are you, even if you are a little square."

James frowned, and Stu laughed.

101

JOHN AND JERRY WERE UPSTAIRS when Stu and James arrived at the shop. It would be the first time Stu had seen the rehearsal space, and he was awestruck as he looked around the room.

"Wow, this place is fab," Stu said.

"Told you so," James said.

"Stu, is that you?" Jerry said.

"Yes."

"I didn't recognize you with the specks."

Stu adjusted his glasses. "Yeah, I don't wear them very often."

"You cut your hair too?"

"I did," Stu said, sitting next to Jerry on the floor.

"He's improving his image," James said, setting his guitar down.

"Is that right?" John said.

"Yeah, I make better tips that way."

"Oh, I figured you were chasin' a skirt."

"Hey, Professor. Hey, Stewy," Danny said, coming into the room.

Stu looked up at him with squinted eyes. "What are you doin' here?"

"Yeah, don't you have a show tonight?" James said, sitting next to John on the couch.

Danny sat on a stool. "No, I quit The Dice."

"No foolin'?" James said.

"Yep."

"Why?"

Danny looked at John.

"Go ahead," John said.

"They wanted to steal 'Crawlin' Dog' from John," Danny said.

"Can they do that?" Jerry said.

"They were going to try, but Danny blocked their move," John said.

"So, they backed down?" James said.

"Not exactly," Danny said.

"What does that mean?" Stu said.

"We've been hit with a challenge, boys," John said.

"A challenge?" Jerry said.

"Well, you see, Danny signed a contract."

"Oh no," James said.

"And Dalamey refuses to let him out of it. So, after some back and forth, we bet that Danny has more talent than he does."

"Yeah, we all know that," James said.

"But how are you going to prove it?" Jerry said.

"In three weeks, we will meet The Dice at the community center. Each group will play a couple of songs, and whomever the audience thinks is best wins the contest," John said.

"And Danny is released from his contract?" James said.

"Yep, and I get to keep my song."

"Wow," James said.

Jerry scratched his head.

"They're gonna cream us," Stu said.

"Stu," Jerry said.

"The way I see it, we have a decent chance," Danny said. "John and I have been spending a great deal of time together, and his playing has improved greatly."

"I wouldn't go that far," John said

"Give yourself some credit."

John shrugged.

"We have three weeks to practice and polish our sound," Danny said.

"Yeah, but you're forgettin' somethin'," Stu said. "We don't have a drummer."

"Well, it's time we address that," John said.

"Good drummers are hard to find," Stu said.

"What about that one guy?" Jerry said.

"What one guy?" John said.

"You know, the one who quit that band a couple of months back? Remember, we went and saw them at the Dock Side."

"Nope," John said.

"He has his own kit."

"Don't care. We need someone decent, not someone who beats on them like a toddler."

"We could post a flyer downstairs in the store. People are always comin' in here lookin' for groups to join and such," Danny said.

"Good idea, Daniel," John said.

"I could post one in the coffee shop," James said.

"I'm sure we can post one in the mercantile," Jerry said.

"What about the market, Stu?" Danny said.

"Yeah," Stu mumbled.

"Suppose it wouldn't hurt to put up a few around the campus," John said. "You put the flyer together, Daniel?"

"I will talk to Eddie," Danny said.

"We got some hard work ahead of us," John said. "But they are meeting us on our turf, without their name, so we have some advantage."

"Without their name?" James said.

"It was one of the stipulations," Danny said. "We are trying to make this as fair as possible."

"Good luck," Stu said under his breath.

"Well, boys, I think that concludes the business," John said. "Unless someone else has business they want to bring to the floor?"

"Aren't you forgetting something?" James said.

John rubbed his chin, then shook his head. "No, I can't think of anything."

"What about Danny?" James said.

"What about him?"

James sighed. "Don't you think it's time that he became an official member of this group?"

"Oh, yeah, he expressed interest to me a few days ago. I guess I must have forgotten."

James shook his head.

"Does anyone object to Daniel joining the group?" John asked.

"No," James said.

"No," Jerry said.

Everyone looked at Stu, who was picking mud off his shoes.

"Stu?" Jerry said, nudging him.

Stu looked up at the blank faces around him.

"Is there a problem?" John said.

"No problem," Stu finally answered.

John looked at Danny's grinning face and crossed his arms. "I haven't decided yet."

"Don't listen to him, Danny," James said. "You've been one of us ever since that night you jumped on stage beside us."

"Damn right," Jerry said.

Danny smiled.

John walked over to Danny. "Stand up."

Danny stood.

"Raise your left hand and put your right hand over your stomach," John said.

Danny complied.

"Do you, Daniel Bruer, plea by unreasonable insanity to pledge allegiance to the Hound Dogs and do hereby swear to disrespect any other members except the Pack Leader and to dismiss any law or regulations put behind me here out?"

"I do."

"Do you promise to howl at the moon, chase after girls, be a bad, disobedient pup, and pee on any hydrant you see, or at the pleasure of your liege till death do you fall apart?"

"I do."

"By the powers thrust upon me by the laws of the state of Hullyabalabooby, I now pronounce you Daniel Bruer, a member in misunderstanding of the Hound Dogs. May Elvis Presley have mercy on your misguided shoe soles."

Danny smiled at John, who began to howl, and they all joined in, but Stu.

"Are we keeping with tradition?" James said. "Doesn't Danny have to buy us all a beer?"

"Ah ... that he does," John said.

"I don't mind," Danny said.

"You're coming with us, aren't you, Jerry?" James said.

"I dunno."

"You have to, Jerry. We're brothers now," Danny said.

"Come on, Jerry, we promise not to get you in trouble with the little lady," John said.

"It'll be our secret," Danny said.

"Okay," Jerry said with a smile.

"Then let's go, boys!" John said.

Danny, John, and Jerry went down the stairs, talking and laughing. James turned to Stu, who was still sitting on the floor.

"Hey, Stu, aren't you coming?" James asked.

"I don't think so," Stu said, standing up.

"What?"

"I have to open tomorrow."

"It's only one drink."

"I know it."

"You're passing up a chance to have a drink and flirt with girls?"

Stu picked up his guitar. "I guess I am."

James frowned. "What's the matter?"

"Nothing."

"You're lying."

"I'm just tired, all right?"

"You know, I don't have to go with them. I could spend the evening with you like old times, remember?"

"Thanks, buddy, but I think I just want to be alone."

"Are you serious?"

"Yup."

"All right," James finally relented. He knew something was bothering Stu because he had been acting funny since Danny had entered the room. Danny? James thought back and realized that Stu had never accepted Danny like the rest. Was he jealous? That seemed so ridiculous, but it made sense somehow. Hopefully, no one else noticed when Stu didn't howl with the rest of them. He would need to convince Stu to open up to him before someone else noticed something was wrong.

"What took you so long?" John said when Stu and James walked out of the store. "We almost left without you."

"I was just trying to convince Stu to join us," James said.

"You're not coming with us?" Jerry said.

"No, I gotta work tomorrow." Stu was hoping that John would object to him leaving, but he was too wrapped up in Danny to notice.

"I'll see you soon, Stu?" James said.

"Yeah, of course."

"Good night, Stu," Jerry said.

He gave him a half-smile and walked away.

"Well, what are we waitin' for?" John said, leading them down the street. "We got beer to drink and girls to chase. Except for Jerry, of course."

"And the Professor," Danny said.

"Ah, yes, I meant to ask you how it went?" John asked.

"Can we talk about this later?" James said.

"How what went?" Jerry said.

"Yeah, we want to know, too," Danny said, moving to James's right side.

"Well, you see, Marcy has been givin' him the business since the night at The Beaumont," John said, talking over James.

"Oh, yeah," Danny said.

"And I told him he didn't need to be takin' any more grief off of her, and he needed to set her straight."

"And so, did you?" Danny said.

James nodded. "We talked."

"And?" John said, moving closer to James.

"And what?"

"Did you two kiss and make up?" Danny said, moving closer too.

James's eyes darted from Danny to John. How could he answer the question and not give himself away?

"Well...yeah," James said, averting his eyes.

"I think he's blushing," Danny said.

"I am not," James snapped.

"Oh, he is!" John said.

John's teasing only made James blush more.

"Oh! Oh! My little Professor is all grown up now, is he?" John said.

"John, stop," James said.

"Why, you sly hound dog," John said, placing his arm around James's shoulders.

"Congratulations, Professor," Danny said.

James stuck his hands in his pockets.

"What happened?" Jerry said.

Danny whispered in Jerry's ear.

"Oh? Oh!" Jerry said. "Congratulations."

"Now we have even more reason to celebrate!" John said. "Come on, boys, I feel like singin'."

"What shall we sing?" Danny said.

"'O Danny Boy'?" Jerry said.

They all laughed and began to sing as they continued their walk toward the 2 Shot.

102

STU WALKED THE LONELY DARK road toward his house. He didn't want to be angry or jealous or anything else. Danny deserved to become a member of The Hound Dogs. He was vibrant and talented and didn't have to struggle to play the guitar like he did. Stu could practice in his basement for another year, and Danny would always be able to play circles around him without even trying. Danny would have the relationship Stu wanted with John. Danny would be the success that Stu would never be.

Standing at a crossroads, Stu paused, a lonely breeze passing by him. Turning left, he walked down a less traveled road to a house where laughter, music, and conversation filled the hollow rift in the night air. Stu reached out and rang the doorbell, and the door opened.

"Stu?"

"Yeah."

"Hey, buddy! I was beginning to think you weren't coming."

"Am I too late?"

"Are you kidding? Come on in, and let's get you a drink."

Stu stepped inside the house, and Patrick shut the door.

ABOUT THE AUTHOR

Rebecca Hendricks is a writer, and author of the new novel *Hound Dogged.*

Rebecca has made a career doing accounting and Judicial Assistant work, but her passion has always been writing and creating colorful and exciting stories. Starting at a young age, Rebecca could be found in her room, spending countless hours writing stories in long hand or typing her work with one finger on her father's antique typewriter.

Rebecca is a Colorado native where she lives with her husband, dog and two  cats. She enjoys urban exploration and camping with her husband and their Golden Retriever, Haley. In her limited free time, she enjoys restoring and giving new life to old dolls.

Sign up for Rebecca Hendrick's Newsletter
And receive and exclusive short origin story
Hound Dogged Beginnings for FREE!

at

subscribepage.io/hounddoggedsign-up